Testimonials I

Before I submitted the final draft of my [   ]t copies to a number of friends and business associates – past and present (30 in all). I asked for suggestions and overall impressions. I then requested a favor – if they liked it, and only if they liked it, and/or found it helpful – would they compose a couple of sentences that I might be able to use in this section of the book. I did tell all of them that what they were receiving was far from the final draft (a "little white lie") with the hope that this will make them want to purchase WHAT A CROCK!.

This first message is from my son and, frankly, has nothing to do with this book. I asked him if he would write something for me and offered a few suggestions. He totally disregarded them – and I'm glad he did. I suspect that anyone who is a parent or grandparent will understand why I've put this at the top of my list.

"Philip Barnett is more than just an author; he is my father. That 'relationship' began shortly after my 1st birthday, when he unselfishly decided to adopt me. Without his guidance, wisdom, and yes, at times, necessary strictness, I would never have attained my current status. He taught me to be passionate about the things that are important to me, to be honest and fair, and to put myself in a position to like what I see in the mirror. When almost everyone else around me doubted my potential, my father always believed in me. Thank you Dad".
Justin Barnett
Vail, CO

"Philip and I were roommates shortly after we graduated from college, and we have remained friends ever since. It's easy to describe him in one sentence. Philip gets it, in a world where most people struggle to find out what 'it' is."
David Krebs
CEO, Krebs Communications

"As an administrator of a large organization I valued Mr. Barnett's advice for three reasons: I find him to be smart, experienced and creative. For those same reasons WHAT A CROCK! is sure to be a valuable reference book."
David C. Berliner
Regents' Professor and Dean Emeritus
College of Education
Arizona State University

"Philip is, to say the least, a unique individual. During the busiest time of my life he was able to get to know me, when most people never could get past my outer office. When I had to say no (because I was inundated with requests) to most of the non-profits that asked me to sit on one of their Boards, and/or do a PSA (Public Service Announcement) for them, Philip figured out a way to get me to change my mind (I noticed that all three of these occurrences are mentioned in his book). While is certainly almost always true that success is '10% inspiration and 90% perspiration,' Philip manages to come up with great ideas, even when sweating heavily."
Jerry Colangelo
Past Owner, Phoenix Suns & Arizona Diamondbacks

"Who Moved My Cheese?"

WHAT A CROCK!

CHEESE IS FOR MACARONI AND PHOTOGRAPHERS

VOLUME I

By

Philip Barnett

"Who Moved My Cheese?" WHAT A CROCK!

Copyright © 2012 - Marketing 101, LLC

ISBN: 1463636164
ISBN 13: 9781463636166

Here's the Thing

Before saying anything else I will repeat the words of one of my most severe critics, who constantly asks me, "Philip, why do you feel you have to show off or brag so much?"

Of course I don't "have to" do this. And whether or not I'm showing off, or bragging, should make absolutely no difference to you – unless, when you finish this book, you can honestly say that you did not learn some very valuable lessons.

As Dizzy Dean once said, "It ain't braggin' if you can do it." Now, "Diz" won 150 games in his career – but he also lost 83. I think you'll discover that I offer about the same ratio. And Dizzy "learned from losing." In his entire career he only lost two games in a row three times. Again, I'm pretty sure I approximate that. If nothing else, I'm a quick study.

In many ways this is the equivalent of a mini-autobiography. There are only a few chapters (they are followed by **) that don't contain something you will (hopefully) find useful and appropriate to where ever it is you are now and where you see yourself going. While this is directed at adults, I believe you will find a good part of it to be of great value, especially for high school and college students.

That being said, I suspect it will not take very long before you'll want to point out that, that if I keep patting myself on my back so often, I will eventually dislocate both my shoulders.

What's My Purpose?

Over the past few months I have conducted a "mini survey" (36 participants). The qualifications were that the participants be at least 35 years old and have a college diploma.

How many of you are aware of the book title "Who Moved My Cheese? 29

How many of you have read the book? 19

How many of you own the book? 6 (this number dropped to 2 when 4 people wrote back saying that they couldn't find their copy).

How many of you can summarize the book using at least two sentences? 0

How many of you feel that the book has had an impact on your life? 1

The reason these retention numbers are so unimpressive is because that book asks people to do some things that most readers can't. Specifically it requires a change in several aspects of ones personality, especially as it relates to being more of an extrovert and far more proactive.

Consider the ages of most of the people who have read "Who Moved My Cheese?" At that point in one's life, most things that relate to your personality have been pretty close to having been written in ink. You may be able to make some changes but, after a short period of time, you will return to who you have been. If you go back to where you were, which most people do, it is very difficult, if not impossible, to remember where you "had been", for a relatively short period of time.

This explains why most golf lessons end up being relatively unproductive. You make some changes in your swing but, within a few rounds, you go back to where you were. These lessons are really most helpful to people who were really good in the first place, and who just require some "tweaking."

The only way you can change "muscle amnesia" to "muscle memory," is to have the teaching pro accompany you for several rounds, correcting you as you go along, and requiring that you hit another ball every time you make a mistake. Aside from the fact that the golfers behind you would become irate, unless your "teaching partner" stayed with you for a month or two (which would be prohibitively expensive), and you played every day, you are going to revert to where you were before your lessons started.

Dr. Johnson is not going to spend that much, if any, time with you whereas this book, this reference book, need not ever be outside your reach.

Consider the previous paragraphs and, you will understand why, when it comes right down to it, "Who Moved My Cheese?" provides temporary relief at best and why so many people cannot remember anything about it a few months after reading it.

The day that "Who Moved My Cheese?" (WMMC) reached 7M in sales I decided that it was time to stop procrastinating and do something—write this book. The only thing I admire about WMMC is that the publisher was able to sell it for $19.95, which is incredible when you think about it - people were willing to pay almost $7 a word. After all, the entire treatise could just as easily be written in one sentence: "Don't sit still." This may be the first time in literary history where the title on the cover is longer than the book that lies beneath. But Dr. Spencer Johnson and Putnam Books would have had a heck of a time trying to sell a philosophy that can be written on one line of an index card.

To demonstrate what I'm talking about consider a hypothetical symposium called "So You're Thinking About Building a House." I believe that if you put Dr. Johnson on a stage with Tony Robbins, Stephen Covey, and Zig Ziglar, they would all tell you that building a house is a great idea, that you needn't feel guilty about wanting to build a house, that you shouldn't worry if your first house falls down, that you should ignore people who complain that your house will not look like theirs, and that you should approach the task with enthusiasm and without trepidation.

When the lecture was over, you would be chomping at the bit and would run out of the auditorium ready to get started (pretty much where you were before you paid $20 or $200 or $2,000). When you got to the parking lot, you would come to a screeching halt, turn to the other members of the audience, and say, "How? How can I find an architect? Who is the best source for the materials will I need? Where is the best place to build? How do I find out what permits will be required? How can I tell if a contractor is a crook?"

And, by the way, does anyone really care "who" moved the cheese? If you're hungry the questions you should be asking are:

- **"Where Did My Cheese Go?"**

- **"How Can I Find My Cheese?"**

- **"When Will I Get My Cheese Back?"**

- **"Where can I buy More Cheese?"**

- **"What Happened To My Cheese?"**

- **Why would anyone care about "WHO?"**

How to ....

"Who Moved My Cheese?" WHAT A CROCK! is not meant to be a "WHAT" book. You probably already know "what" you want to do, and I have no interest in trying to get you to change your mind. In contrast to that approach (the world inhabited by the "motivators"), this is a "HOW" book. Simply stated, you know what you want to do and I'm going to help by telling you how to do it. Here are a few examples, in no particular order of importance.

- **How to get a job.**

- **How to get into college or graduate school.**

- **How to reach an unreachable person.**

- **How to get a raise.**

- **How to write a resume.**

- **How to write a grant application.**

- **How to get a grant.**

- **How to create a customer with a lifetime value.**

- **How to evaluate advertising.**

- **How to get prizes for a charity's auction.**

- **How to get more business.**

- **How to get new clients.**

- **How to retain existing clients.**

- **How (and why) to fail on purpose.**

- How to keep more customers.

- How to make a 1st (and 2nd) impression.

- How to write press releases (maybe).

- How to set a selling price for a product or service.

- How to set a selling price for you.

- How to provide the highest level of customer service.

- How (and when) to give away your product or service.

- How to create a proper marketing budget.

- How to hire the best person.

- How to inspire the troops.

- How to get free ideas (good ones).

- How to "seed" a mailing list.

- How to get from here to there.

- How to get from there to here.

- How to deal with "no."

- How to get to go out with that "special" girl (guy).

- And lots, lots more.

I Think an Explanation is Probably Necessary

In the previous drafts of this book I began with my autobiography. However, since I've done so many things, and probably think far too highly of myself, it rambled on and on, until one might have begun to wonder when the book was going (if ever) to begin. So, it now can be found near the end of the book, under the heading "Who I Am, Where I've Been, What I've Done and What Makes Me Tick and Tock."

This was followed by an introduction that was so long that it suggested an overture that lasted longer than the entire musical. Most of that also can be found near the rear exit, under the title "Prequel" (I'm shocked to learn that's now considered a real word. I guess George Lucas's influence is greater that I thought, since it's not in my dictionary).

There was also an "Author's Plea" asking you to tell all your friends, contacts, neighbors, co-workers, etc. to buy the book, and to do so by every means possible, including e-mails, phone calls, and via texting, Facebook, Twitter, etc. (Until very recently I did not know how to employ the last three methods). This is now where it belonged in the first place because, if you are like me, you won't recommend something sight unseen (or "ears unheard," "mouth untasted" and "nose unsmelled").

"The journey of a thousand miles begins with but a single step" – and you are now approaching the starting line, albeit it at a very slow and easy pace.

Introduction to the Table of Contents

Several times I repeat myself, other times I'm repetitive and I have even known to be redundant. The best way to demonstrate this is the previous sentence which I hope, at the very least, made you smile. The fact is that some of my "plagiarizing of self" has me reiterating a point, albeit using slightly different words. This occurs because I think that some things are important enough to warrant mentioning more than once.

The fact is, this is not "War," not "Peace" and certainly not "War and Peace." Depending on your reading speed, you should not need more than an hour or two to finish it. Actually, there's another way to figure this out—it should be about eight times longer than it took you to read "Who Moved My Cheese?" My first reading was finished, while waiting on hold, to talk with my bank. I devoured it (the pun is very intentional as I do love cheese) in less than fifteen minutes (I know, I know – no one can ever get to speak to a live person at a bank within 15 minutes). Given the time I was actually on hold I could have read Dr. Johnson's "shorter than a term paper" book 2 ½ times.

Throughout the book you will find **"NUGGETS."** Sometimes these will be a sentence or two, and other times they will exceed the length of many chapters. These "pieces of gold" are those things I feel to be a bit more important than the stuff I think is really important.

They are easily identified because they are called **"NUGGETS."** This word is always in a larger type face, in all caps and bold print. The **NUGGET** itself is always in **bold print.**

Sometimes these appear at the end of a chapter and sometimes in the middle. In a few places they come one right after another (and even after another another). And, occasionally, they have no connection, whatsoever, to where they are found. As I will point out, these are the ones that suddenly came to mind but, since I couldn't figure out an appropriate resting place, I just let the idea immediately go directly from my mind to my keyboard.

There are also "*Notes.*" These are always in parenthesis and italic type. Sometimes they refer to something I've just written and, in keeping with the spirit of my tendency to be discombobulated, they may be related to another part of the book or, on occasion, have no connection to anything at all. One of my proofreading friends told me that **"Who Moved My Cheese?" What a Crock!** is like going on a scavenger hunt, where you search for the clues by going in any direction you wish but still end up with whole "pot of gold."

Table of Contents

(Note: In keeping with my unorthodox way of writing, this "table" rests under enough "food"- for thought - to feed a small army, as it is longer than almost all of the chapters it names. But don't despair – the 146 chapters fit onto 410 pages which means that the average chapter is less than three pages long).

* Probably the most important chapter in the book.

** These are the only chapters that do not include
at least one "teachable moment."

Mea Culpa, My Fault, I'm Sorry

(Note: This chapter, although appearing at the front of the book, was not written until I had finished authoring it).

I tried to write this in the third person, by creating a fictitious mentor (I've actually had at least a dozen). However I found that confusing. Then I tried a mixture of "He did" and "I said." Halfway through that attempt I got so lost that I had to take a couple of days off, then start over again. The result of all of this is that my book is in the first person, meaning that it contains an almost overwhelming number of the words "I," "I'd," "my" "me" and "I've.

However I don't feel particularly guilty about this because almost every story I tell, or example I provide, comes from things I have experienced, in one way or another (what a surprise – the letter "I" appears four times in the previous sentence. Don't say I didn't warn you).

Nonetheless, this is not intended to be looked at as an autobiography, even those it is chock full of autobiographical information,

Finally (and never trust me when I use this word), no matter how hard I tried you will still discover variations of the title of this chapter strewn throughout this book.

(Note: I have frequently – actually three times – been asked why a few of my chapters are so long. The explanation is that many of them contain more than one pertinent fact or suggestion. What I expect is that you, the reader, will extrapolate the parts of them that are appropriate to your situation. From where I sit, multiplicity is far better than empty shells. And besides, as you will discover in the chapter entitled "Telling Them Who You Really Are," I can be terse and pithy, to the point that there are several sentences consisting of no more than three or four words.

Before I Get to Where We're Going

I have never written a book before (something you will probably figure out in a page or two). This would much easier if I were attempting a novel. In that case I could create the outline of a plot, and then start to fill in the pieces.

There are those who say that non-fiction should be even easier, as it requires far less creativity. And, more often than not, time is literally on your side, as timelines are used as chapter headings. These can be "ages" (as in "Iron"), centuries, decades, years, months, weeks and even days (I'd probably call that one "24," unless, of course, someone has beaten me to it).

My book covers four subjects – in no particular order of importance. In fact, you will find the sequencing to be much closer to chaos than order.

Customer Service

Sales and Marketing

Applying for a job or to a college/acquiring new clients and/or business

Other (and there's lots of "other")

When I tried to separate the chapters into those categories I realized that there was so much overlapping, co-habitation if you will, that I was about to enter what is known as "The Futility Zone." The longer you stay there the harder it is to get out - so I moved quickly.

Perhaps some of you are familiar with the suggestion that the best way to give a speech is to begin by telling the audience what you are going to talk about, followed by talking about it and finishing by repeating what you just said. The goal is to "pound in" your message.

While I understand that thought process, it runs the risk of having the audience start to tune out, before you get to your summary. My preference is to send an e-mail, with an outline of my speech. It contains enough "teaser" copy to make the reader want to be there when I speak. Then a few days after my presentation, I send another e-mail, containing the highlights of what they heard.

Someone suggested that I arrange my chapters by the subject matter (i.e. "Your best customer is your customer"). Aside from being incredibly hard to do, I decided that spreading out these chapters out was preferable as this will, hopefully, make the reader think that the subject matter must be really important since it's mentioned several times throughout the book. If the chapters were contiguous, those multiple references might be viewed as one single point, which would detract from my "think about this more than once" intent.

The price that you, the reader, pays is that you are going to find that I rarely go from Point A to Point B. There will be times I jump to Point R, number 23 or even to train platforms.

But here's the good news. This book is short enough that this shouldn't matter. When you've finished you should find yourself saying, "Aha, I get the point. In fact, I get lots of points." You might even want to go back and tear out the half dozen pages that address your situation most directly.

Perhaps you should to look at this as a collection of "mini books" (I am attempting to be the James Patterson of non-fiction) kind of like "sliders" for the brain. You may be hungry when you start reading but by the time you finish that hunger should be sated. Let's face it – if you took a platter full of sliders and moved them all around, would you be any less full when you completed your meal?

The really good thing (for me) about this "tear out the pages" suggestion is that when you tell your friends that this is a "must read," and they ask to borrow your copy, you can explain what happened and tell them to go to www.whatacrock.info, click on "Buy Now," and, within minutes, they'll have their own copy, on its way.

A former employer of mine once asked, "Philip, do you ever stop selling?" My answer was the absolute shortest response in the history of me. "No!"

Preface

Over the past several years, an industry has been created around such phrases as self-help, motivational speakers, and inspirational books.

Here are my suggestions.

If you need self-help, don't read a book. Talk to your mirror and tap into all your own strengths.

If you need motivation, don't read a book. File for bankruptcy.

If you need inspiration, don't read a book. Volunteer for Special Olympics.

Let's face it; "The One Minute Manager" has about ten second's worth of good advice. Besides, you know that trying to solve any business problem in one minute is like taking an aspirin for a concussion.

And "Chicken Soup for the Soul" is nothing more than a regurgitation of the lives of others. It doesn't help you learn how to get a job, sell your product, or pay your bills.

Finally, "Who Moved My Cheese?" is almost an insult to the intelligence. By now most of you know that reading about a bunch of mice, trying to find something they lost, does you very little good. Theory may be necessary but, if that's all you get, it explains why so many high school graduates don't know how to balance a checkbook. This book is designed to teach the necessary reality, as opposed to being a philosophical treatise about where algebra and calculus might lead you.

Telling you that you are hungry belabors the obvious and does you little good. Without ingredients, recipes, utensils, and baking pans, along with some helpful hints, your stomach will still be growling.

Think of most self-help/motivational stuff as *modern art* - designed to confuse, impress, and provoke. This book represents *commercial art* - designed to help you get the job done, whether that is getting hired, finding more clients, increasing the size of your business, or receiving an acceptance letter from a school.

Introduction

"An ounce of practice is worth tons of preaching."

—Mahatma Gandhi

I had read Dr. Johnson's book. In fact, I have read it four times—in a total of less that one hour. The actual story is fifty-one pages long. If you subtract the illustrations of wedges of cheese, this number drops to thirty-six. There are ten half pages, which brings the final total down to thirty-one. The margins are wide, the type is large, and the amount of space above and below the words on each page is generous (industry standards state the average number of words-per-page is 350- 400. Dr. Johnson barely manages to come up with 200). So, when it comes right to it, the story of "Who Moved My Cheese?" runs about twenty pages, which works out to a selling price of about $1 per page. Furthermore, the words *cheese* and *cheeseless* (which, although used, is not a real word) appear 172 times, almost five times per page.

Dr. Johnson is also the author of "The One Minute Manager," "The One Minute Sales Person," "The One Minute Father/Mother," and "The One Minute Teacher." In less time than it took me to write, edit, rewrite and re-edit this paragraph I could have become a better manager, father, salesperson, or teacher. It's surprising that he didn't combine his titles and call the book I'm talking about here "How to Find Your Cheese In One Minute Or Less."

Here are a few of Dr. Johnson's "observations."

- **Mice appear to be a lot smarter than men – I guess that Tom and Jerry would be perfect contestants on "Jeopardy."**

- **"If you don't change you will become extinct." Well, I guess that takes care of "If it ain't broke don't fix it." I suggest that Dr. Johnson take a good hard look at "Playboy." They were a hugely successful magazine, but, every time they "changed" (i.e. books, movies, clubs), their bottom line got worse and worse. The polar opposite is ESPN. Every expansion they've made, over the past 30 years, has been related to sports.**

- **Dr. Johnson tells you that if you imagine new cheese, even before you find it, you will be led to it. He seems to equate imagination with hard work, perseverance and creativity – none of which he mentions. If imagination led to success, the entire country would be occupying the space at the top of the mountain. He must have had it really easy getting to where he is now because most of us know that the formula for success is 10% inspiration and 90% perspiration, and he seems to believe that it's the other way around.**

If this is beginning to sound like I am opinionated, I congratulate you on your perceptivity. I am a typical ex-New Yorker, never afraid to speak up, often louder than I probably should. The major difference between me and the author, who seems hung up on mice, is that I will not attempt to be cute (as in "littlepeople" – another of the good doctor's invented words) or obtuse. And I will not force you to read between the lines, so you won't find yourself thinking, "I wonder what he meant by that" or "OK, but what do I do right now and how do I do it?"

You will find no allegories, theories, or fairy tales. That's why my basic speech, given hundreds of times, is called "Practical Magic." Of course, it's not really magic at all as I reveal how I've done all my "tricks." Those presentations, and this book, are designed to give listeners or readers idea after idea that they can't wait to steal. My advice? Go ahead! Nothing would flatter me more.

If you want theories, I am the last person in the world to listen to. However, if you are looking for "telling it like it is/ like it should be," pull up a chair but only if, up until now, you have been standing.

Don't expect pure logic, at least when it comes to sequencing. I quickly figured out that if I made putting my thoughts in crystal-clear order a critical requirement, this might be one of those books that never gets published. Rather than making sure that every *i* is dotted and every *t* crossed, I have taken everything I've learned and thrown it against the wall. I suppose this does, in one sense, put me into the noncommercial art business, a la Jackson Pollock. However, hopefully, what you're about to peruse will not require any kind of interpretation.

Sometimes you will read of events from last year and others will be from 50 years ago. Most good ideas are timeless. But you will find a recurring theme: if you want to be exactly like everybody else and do what everyone else does, you will end up as unappealing as the white line that runs down the middle of the road. "Dare to be different" (innovative, creative) should not, at least as far as I am concerned, be a theory related to "cheeseology" or "cheesism" (I guess I can make up cheese-related words as well). Rather, it's just the first step, followed by a myriad of suggestions as to several possible courses of action. I know a lot of people, ages eight-eighty, who can tell me, "Don't be afraid to try something different." However, if I asked, "How should I proceed?" most would be dumbfounded, which is apparently what happened to Dr. Johnson, his mice, and his *fromage* (other than "oui" and "crème brulee" this is only word of French I know).

Dr. Johnson's book might more aptly be described as "I Love the King's Attire" in that it resembles the fairy tale, "The Emperor's New Clothes," in which the subjects were so intimidated that they refused to point out that their monarch was walking the streets as naked as the day he was born. I've read enough books about cheese, and other analogies, and have attended enough seminars and lectures given by Harvard MBAs to realize that it's about time for someone to tell these people to get dressed. The theories they offer are almost always bare of substance. They are the sizzle, without the steak.

This reaffirms the difference between me and "Mr. Cheese." Moralizing can usually be reduced to a sentence or two. When the intent is to educate (which is what I hope I'm doing here) instead of inspire, more words are needed, and you'll need more than a minute to absorb them. This is easily demonstrated by the number of people who will tell you that they get all the inspiration they need from just 46 words – the condensed version of the "Ten Commandments." To condense these even more I will not be the least bit surprised if Dr. Johnson comes out with a book called, "The 10 Commandments – In Less Than One Minute."

The practical solutions I offer will, I believe, provide you a diverse and compelling wardrobe. Not everything will fit you perfectly, and there will be times where there will be clashes of pattern or color, but that shouldn't matter because you will also find several "perfect fits" in appropriate hues, so that by the time you finish this book, you will be far better dressed (equipped) to move forward toward your goal - finding a job, getting more business, acquiring new clients, or receiving an acceptance letter.

Goals are always worth repeating because, as the saying goes, "If you don't know where you're going, any train will get you there." The choice is yours, but if you're going into battle (remember, in many cases you will be fighting off people who want to accomplish the same things you do), wouldn't you feel more secure carrying ammunition that has been tested under combat conditions rather than ideas provided to justify a speaker's desire to collect fees from a couple of hundred conference attendees or royalties related to the sale of a book?

(Note: I bet you thought I would never get here. If you did you would have lost because here it is, the first chapter).

Here's What I'm Talking About

(Note: Although you've already read the next two paragraphs they are being repeated because they serve to clearly define my approach (practical) to the one employed by individuals who seem to be allergic to the word "how").

Consider this hypothetical symposium, called "So You're Thinking About Building a House." I believe that if you put Dr. Johnson on a stage with Tony Robbins, Stephen Covey, and Zig Ziglar, they would all tell you that building a house is a great idea, that you needn't feel guilty about wanting to build a house, that you shouldn't worry if your first house falls down, that you should ignore people who complain that your house will not look like theirs, and that you should approach the task with enthusiasm and without trepidation.

When the lecture was over, you would be chomping at the bit and would run out of the auditorium ready to get started (pretty much where you were before you paid $20 or $200 or $2,000). When you got to the parking lot, you would come to a screeching halt, turn to the other members of the audience, and say, "How? How can I find an architect? Who is the best source for the materials will I need? Where is the best place to build? How do I find out what permits will be required? How can I tell if a contractor is a crook?"

In other words, as I've said, you would leave as you came in—with a desire. And nothing would have changed, other than what you hoped to do would have been confirmed as a valid goal. Actually, you would probably be worse off because the money you had spent to be "encouraged" would require that you eliminate the extra flat-screen TV in your new house.

To see things in a slightly different light, consider this analogy (OK, you caught me. I guess I told a small lie when I said "no analogies"). You're hungry, and a helpful baker (motivator) tells you that your intention, to bake a loaf of bread, is a worthwhile pursuit. He or she may even provide (or sell) you the flour, water, baking powder, and yeast.

Do you recognize this loaf of bread story? (I would have said "parable" but that would suggest that there are some moral or religious lessons involved and that would really be stretching things). Isn't it the same as most of those self-help gurus telling you that your personal hunger, a result of stagnation, failure, etc., can be eliminated if you use their "ingredients?"

That may be all well and good but you still need a recipe. So, the end result is that you are no closer to making that loaf of bread than you were before.

I assume that if you have attended a "So You're Thinking About Building a House" motivational lecture, it indicates that building a house was at the top of your agenda. My role is to provide you with a plan, the tools, and the materials so that your structure can move from being a dream to a residence ready for occupancy, using methods that have been time-tested. You can be rest assured that what you are going to read will almost always work, whether you're trying to do something as simple as help your child sell magazine subscriptions or help yourself land a multimillion-dollar contract. In fact, since I decided that so much of this represents the basics, I named my company Marketing 101.

Mario Cuomo pointed out, "We campaign in poetry, but we govern in prose." Theoreticians speak in whimsy and paint with the broadest of strokes. They never get to the point of providing real action plans, ones that won't take five years to implement. Poetry may get the girl to go on the date, but prose provides the money to pay for the meal. Once again, a comparison relating to fine art versus commercial art is appropriate. Having skill in the former might get your painting on a wall in the museum, but the latter will make a sale more likely.

You are probably aware of the phrase passive–aggressive. Well, it would take a whole lot of passive people to balance me off. But please don't think I'm bragging about my cut-to-the-chase and don't-mince-words approach. That's who I am, but it doesn't always work - for me or anyone else. I'm not suggesting a personality transplant. But take whoever it is that you are and blend that in with specific goals and the best ways to attain them. What I really represent is a kind of tour guide.

At this point, or shortly hereafter, you may come to the conclusion that I am angry. You would be correct but not for the reason you probably think. My anger is directed at myself – for not writing this book several years ago. As far as the "snake oil" books and speeches are concerned, I am almost bemused by the fact that so much money has been spent for so little product.

Brain Surgery it's Not

This book contains examples of perspectives that you can use in both your business and personal life. And you will be able to do things almost immediately instead of saying to yourself, "I think I understand what he or she (the motivator) wrote or said, but what do I do now?" There will be no need for wondering. In fact, you should be able to start implementing before you are halfway through this book.

You'll find that everything in this book boils down to a few basic marketing premises.

I present some generalizations, but please don't think of them as theory. Instead, picture them as pragmatic umbrellas with the spokes being the chapters. A perfect example of this is the word marketing. A majority of people believes this to be synonymous with advertising—but it's not. Marketing is the umbrella and advertising is but one spoke. Among the others are sales, graphics, publicity, branding, and public relations.

Getting My Feet Wet (in the Agency Waters)

(Note: Since I have already warned you about the back-and-forth nature of my sequencing, it seemed appropriate to start just where you would expect me to – in the middle. This story happened at almost the exact mid-point between the time I got my first job and the time I'm writing this sentence).

Here's a bad news/great news example, something that happened just after I joined an advertising/marketing agency, where my title was VP, Corporate Development. Before anyone gets too impressed, if it could have fit on a business card it would have read, "The guy whose job it is to find new clients."

I dove right in, but it wasn't too long before the CEO, of the company I was trying to add to our roster of clients, told me to back off, that my continual messages were not getting me anywhere, insofar as having them sign on the dotted line. I asked him to consider how aggressive we would be, on behalf of his company, if we were hired. He thought that was self-serving and, for all intents and purposes, told me to get lost.

Suffice it to say, my boss (our CEO) was not particularly pleased with my initial efforts. He suggested I consider trying a gentler approach, after which he left for an extended (two-month) European vacation. The week before he returned, the Board of Directors of the company I was in the courting, fired their CEO. It seemed that they were losing market share to more aggressive competitors. I suppose my reaction could have been "I told you so," but that would have been a waste of time. And, besides, who would have cared enough to listen?

So I took my smugness (and trust me, smugness doesn't pay your mortgage) and turned it into something positive. I was able to get in to meet the new CEO and brought along the same aggressive marketing proposal I intended to present two months earlier. I think he must have been a reformed hippie or a frustrated jazz musician because he said, "I'm picking up what you're laying down." The company became a client, and I haven't looked back since. The new message from my boss was a variation on the song title, "I Love You Just The Way You Are."

Look Beyond What is Found Between Your Two Ears

When you come up with what you believe is a brilliant idea, plan, or strategy, you probably think that it will move sliced bread to second place on the latest-and-greatest list. However at that point, it's only your ego that is running the show.

To temper that "me, myself, and I" mentality, ask a few people for their opinion. Eliminate anyone who patronizes you by telling you what you want to hear. Don't ask the advice of close relatives; they probably already think you are brighter than you are, and you're not looking for flattery. Finally, do not seek the counsel of anyone who is afraid of offending you.

Put together a group of four to six people who don't know each other. Give each a one-page executive summary of your idea, and ask for an overall impression (it might be wise to require that they sign a non-disclosure form).

In their responses look for words that should serve as a warning, words such as offensive, insensitive, insulting. If that's the feedback you're getting, start again from scratch.

However, if you're receiving comments such as "ridiculous," "no market for it," or "you're wasting your time," don't take them to heart, at least not yet.

Before you consider bringing your efforts to a halt, get input from people who you consider part of your target market (see earlier comment about non-disclosure forms). If they don't express some interest in your idea, it should be, once again, back to the drawing board.

You'll find it easy to get this input because we all love to give our opinions; we all think ourselves as insightful. But, one of the most important principles to remember is to leave your "I'm so smart" attitude behind. Don't start a request with, "Wouldn't you agree that—?"

With all this being said, don't necessarily give up, at not until you've gotten feedback from a handful of people considered experts, in the arena where you hope to compete. I can tell you that the best idea I ever had came when I was 23 years old. If I hadn't listened to only one person I thought to be an expert, I would have made so much money that I would be able to give this book away – and not even charge for shipping and handling.

He Didn't Know as Much as I Thought He Did

I have made enough bad business decisions to fill a number of pages in a book entitled "Here's What Not to Do." In this case my mistake was to give up after getting only one opinion.

It was in 1965 when my family was having dinner at the home of my mother's brother (my uncle). One of the other guests was Milton Gross who, at the time, was the leading sports columnist for the New York Post. Given the milieu in which he operated, I thought he would be a perfect person to ask for an opinion.

My premise was that most sports' fans were interested in more than one sport, but their ability to buy same-day tickets was severely limited – purchase them at the box-office.

My idea was to increase the number of venues, specifically by putting "offsite box-offices" at locations where other sports were played – cross pollination if you will. My family had season tickets for the New York Giants football team and, on all but one Sunday when they were playing at home, the New York Rangers' hockey team had an evening game at Madison Square Garden.

I'm sure, at least a couple of times a year, I would have been able to convince my Dad to purchase Ranger tickets during halftime of the Giants game, The football games ended about 4:30 PM and the hockey games started at 7:00 PM, so we could easily travel to midtown Manhattan, and still have time for a leisurely dinner.

After giving Mr. Gross a brief description of my plan, he responded with just five words – "It will never work kid."

At that point I decided not to pursue it and, three years later Ticketron was born. In 1990 they were sold to

Ticketmaster a company that, 12 years later, had annual revenues of $747M.

If I had written this book back in 1965 (which would have been impossible since the only things I knew a lot about were Machiavelli, the Beatles and Roni Katz, the first love-of-my-life), and then read it, I probably would have avoided the two humongous mistakes I made.

1. I only asked one person for an opinion.

2. Of far greater importance I asked the wrong person. My idea was related to business, not sports per se. As is the case with most sportswriters, Mr. Gross knew as much about business as I did about the structure of the Peruvian government.

As I said, I've tripped over my own feet several times, but this was the one that sent me sprawling. Lots of us can easily start a sentence with the words "If I only had," as in "If I only had invented the cell phone (or thought up the Internet, before Al Gore did). At least, for me, these have no connection with reality (I have a hard enough time figuring out how my phone works). However, I still occasionally, 46 years later, kick myself in the back as I whisper, into my own ear, those words, "If only I had....."

Your Best Customer is Your Customer

A few years ago, I ran across an acquaintance I hadn't seen in a year or so. When I inquired about his business, he told me, "I guess I'm treading water. Each month I've got a dozen people walking out the back door and an equal number of new ones coming in the front door." I responded, in keeping with his aquatic theme, that he was drowning. The people leaving were his customers, while those entering for the first time might only be window shopping or, even worse, may have stopped in to ask for directions or to use the restroom. I suggested that he stop spending money on things designed to get more people to come in (advertising) and instead budget for programs that would "nail the back door shut," to keep them inside or returning more often (marketing).

A friend of mine, in Connecticut, owned a boutique. He went so far as to create a separate entrance for existing customers. Among the benefits for those using "Door # 2" was the offer of an adult beverage of their choice, and an assortment of "finger-food," as soon as they walked in. It ended up costing him about $3.00 per customer. This simple act registered $109 on the "While I'm in here I think I'll buy something for my wife/girl friend/daughter/ mistress" Richter cash register scale. The average amount of money spent by a first-time customer was $48.

If you need more of a reason, consider this. It is said that it costs seven times as much to acquire a customer as it does to retain one. The gap is actually much greater than that, as the acquired customer may be a one-time-only buyer, whereas a retained individual can have a lifetime value of major significance.

Your Second Best Customer is a Clone of Your Best Customer

This is a relatively simple subject. Find out as much as you can about your current customers. This should include more than basic demographics. You want to know things like their age and sex, what kind of car they drive, what magazines they subscribe to, what their political affiliation is (if they will tell you), if they are married, how many children they have, etc.?

Once you accumulate this data start to look for patterns. For example, if you have customers living in 10 different zip codes, but 70% of them reside in only four of those, make note of that fact.

The more "conditions" you employ in the pruning process the more likely it is that you will find another "Dolly" (that was the name of the cloned sheep). At this point a direct mail campaign may be well worth your while, since you will have a truly targeted market. And, if it's very successful, you can make your rules a bit less restrictive.

Similar information and comparisons can come about from interaction between you and your customers, whether you a restaurant, movie theatre, hotel, dry cleaner, etc., etc.

Where Does Your Dough Go?

Stop and think. Consider how valuable you are to businesses you pay daily, weekly, monthly, or annually. People who smoke often don't consider cigarettes that expensive when they purchase one pack every day. In New York City that pack costs $14, a price not looked at as being outrageous – after all, that's only $.70 per cigarette.

But someone who smokes one pack a day will spend $5,150 dollars over the next year. Add to that $5 a day at Starbucks, and that's another $1,825. People able to kick both habits would save more than $6,900 every year. If you want to pay for a child's college education, and have these two addictions, go "cold turkey" on the day your son or daughter is born. By the time they reach the age of 17 you'll have more than $115,000 (not including interest) in a college savings account. And then there's the icing on the cake. Marlboro and Starbucks won't give you tax deductions.

Of course, this is not all a bed of roses as there would be two vendors seeing the disappearance of one of their best lifetime customers (surveys show that most people patronize the same establishments when making these type of purchases).

Consider the next set of figures (they come from someone who has never made more than $60,000 a year – the remuneration one gets, from running a non-profit, will never bust one's piggy bank).

I have lived in Arizona since August of 1991, exactly twenty years ago, as of this writing. Since I have retired, I have had to keep a watchful eye on my budget, so in most of the cases the numbers I'm about to cite, although rounded off, do not represent guesswork or rough approximations.

Groceries (not including prescriptions)	$ 97 per week	$100,880 in 20 years
Cable/phone/internet	$150 per month	$ 36,000 in 20 years
Insurance -medical, automobile, home	$400 per month	$ 96,000 in 20 years
Entertainment, six rounds of golf per month	$300 per month	$ 72,000 in 20 years*

This does not include food and beverages. The profit margin on beer and soft drinks is the highest a facility realizes.

I could easily keep going—car (maintenance, gas, tires), magazine and newspaper subscriptions, cell phone, dry cleaning, clothing, repairs, on and on, but I think I've made my point. Actually, I'm making two points.

NUGGET

Look at these figures from two different perspectives, that of both a buyer and a seller. When you spend the amounts of money I've mentioned, you should have real power and leverage because, if they are smart (and not all of them are, as evidenced by my subsequent story about tires), providers of products or services don't want to lose you. Here's but one small example.

A standard subscription to the New York Times costs about $60 per month. The publisher is always offering special deals, at half that price. But they are only good for new customers, and last only twelve weeks.

I called the paper and told the person I was connected to that I wanted this $30-per-month offer. When he ascertained that I was already a customer, he told me that it was restricted to new subscribers. After mentioning that I thought it was ridiculous that someone who may stay with them for only twelve weeks was getting a better deal than a long-time customer, I asked that he please cancel my subscription (it can never hurt to say please rather than make a demand). The person at the other end of the conversation then told me that he could give me that offer again, but only for one additional twelve-week period.

When that period of time was up, I called again and made the same request. The person I spoke with looked up my record and discovered that I was not new to the fold. Therefore I was told that what I was asking for was impossible.

I asked to speak to a supervisor. I gave him a summary of what had happened to date and again said that I wanted to stop receiving the paper. I went on to add that, between my parents and me, we had been subscribers for well over 80 years, so I would be sad to see this relationship end.

He asked me to hold for a minute. When he came back on the line, he said he was pleased to tell me that the half-price rate would be mine for as long as I wished.

This was a smart man, and our exchange demonstrates both sides of the shopping aisle. At the reduced rate, I will be a $7,200 customer over the next 20 years, during which he would have no acquisition costs to worry about. Knowing that, there was no reason to let me go. So, the NY Times gets $30 of my money every month, and I save $30 every month.

The phrase *win–win* gets bandied about a lot but is rarely true. In most cases it's the person telling you that you win who ends up as the only one winning. However, in this case, the result was two happy campers. I was saving money, and he was retaining me as a subscriber. In fact, he asked that when that the current 80-year figure reaches 100 (as the saying goes, "From his mouth to God's ears") would I contact the paper, as they would like to turn it into an event—and reduce my monthly bill to $0.00.

And this is not an isolated incident. A few months ago I called USA Today to see if I could extend my subscription, for another six months, at a cost of $.50 per copy (the newsstand price is $1.00). I spoke with someone, in their customer service department, to make this request. When the person at the other end of the phone said this could not be done, since it's for new customers only, I asked him to please cancel my subscription. No sooner did those words come out of my mouth he said "Let me switch you to our subscription sales area." When I repeated my previous conversation the salesman told me that he would be very happy to give me that special price for another six months.

Stop for a minute and think about this in terms of choreography – a series of movements that have been designed to maximize income. Their strategy was to initially say no, that this offer was for new subscribers only. At that point a full 90% would say something akin to "Well, I just thought I'd ask." The other 10% are the "mini-me's" (or I am the "mini-them"). Now do the math. They will now have nine people paying $1.00 per issue and one paying $.50. So they collect a total of $9.50, for an average of $.95 per issue.

Since Gannett (their corporate parent) probably has some pretty smart people working for them I'm sure they "crunched" lots of numbers, beginning with the fact that if everyone replicated my action, and they offered the same deal they did me, they would end up receiving $.50 per issue They know what price they wish to average, and that $.50 per issue is far to low. What they should have done was test the reaction to a price of $.75 per issue. I, for one, would have had no problem with that.

Now, this extra $.25 may not sound like a lot, until you learn that their average daily circulation is 1.8M. If that extra quarter is obtained from only 5% of that number, they would be receiving it from 90,000 people. Multiply that by $.25 and you end up with an extra $22,500 – per day. Since they don't publish on weekends, I get my paper 250 times a year.

The annual results of their "pricing choreography?" $5.625M would go to their bottom line.

NUGGET

It never hurts to ask, and to do so with great frequency. If you indicate that you are prepared to stop a subscription, you will be surprised by what might happen. And, by the way, this includes requests for interest rate adjustments on your credit cards and reductions on your cable TV bill.

In fact, there are times you can act without even bothering to "negotiate." When my former wife and I adopted our son he was living in California. Since we were in Connecticut, it required the permission of courts in both states. I obtained all the necessary documents and, to be on the safe side before submitting them, I asked a local attorney to look over everything. He called me, later that day, to tell me that he wouldn't change a word.

A week later I received an invoice from him – for $5,000. I wrote a letter that said, "Larry, I'm sure this was not done on purpose but your secretary obviously put the decimal point in the wrong place. So, in this regard, please find enclosed my check in the amount of Five Hundred Dollars ($500.00) representing payment in full for your services rendered." He cashed the check and I never heard from him again.

Getting "Tired" – a/k/a Capture and Use Customer Data

I know three things about my car: where the ignition key goes, how to put gas in it, and the phone number for the AAA. When something goes wrong, the last person in the world I turn to is me. I want a professional who knows what he's doing (based on my experience "he's" correct since I've never met a female mechanic, although, if

Marisa Tomei, from "My Cousin Vinnie," were ever to go into this business, I would be her first customer). This saves me time, money, and an enormous amount of frustration.

A number of years ago, when I needed new tires, I went to my local Discount Tire store. An employee sold me four, each of which came with a 40,000-mile warrantee. As part of the transaction, they captured my name and address so that (as it was explained to me) they could get in touch if there ever was a product recall.

I was surprised that the facility did not ask me for my e-mail address, but what shocked me was that they didn't inquire as to how many miles I drove each year. If they had, I would have told them 20,000, which meant that I would probably need new tires in two years, and **they would be the only one with that information.** What an incredibly powerful piece of data to have! In twenty to twenty-two months, they would have been positioned to remind me, with a postcard (or e-mail), that I should stop in and have my tires checked. Would I have done that? You bet. I would have appreciated the fact that they kept track of my potential need and informed me of it. And I would have been pleased with how they had made my life a bit easier.

Although I suggested this type of customer-retention program to their corporate office, and personally handed my business card to their CEO (and asked for his in return), I never got a response. The next time I needed tires, I didn't return to that tire store (a competitor, with comparable prices, had opened about ¼ of a mile closer to my house), and I haven't been back since. Because the store didn't bother to stay in touch, it lost thousands of dollars of revenue from me, and my son, over the last two decades.

There are other examples. How many businesses categories regularly say something to this effect: "Because you have been with us for X years, and we value your business, here's what we are going to do for you"? In my experience, the answer is two - hotel chains and airlines. Yes, you will find little loyalty programs here and there – i.e. ten car washes gets you one free one – but not enough to fully demonstrate the concept of "customer equity" (to be discussed in a future chapter).

No wonder so many businesses are in trouble. Since moving to Arizona, I have played golf at least three times every two weeks. That's seventy – eighty times a year. After all those rounds, only one general manager, at a course I rarely played, seized the opportunity and got my contact information so that he could write/e-mail to say, "Thank you for your patronage, and because of it, here's a special offer, one that is good for your golfing buddies as well." What was the result of his offer?

A friend and I played this course once a year. Between greens fees, cart and a couple of beers, we probably spent $120. When I got a personal e-mail, telling us that there was such a thing as a free lunch, four of us played the following month. We spent $300. It seems that the more of you there are, the more beers you drink There are more bets to be won/lost – and beer is one of the most profitable items at almost any facility that sells it. Just look at what you pay for a six-pack in a supermarket and compare that dollar amount to what appears on a golf course's menu (or, for that matter, that of any dining facility that sells beer, wine and/or soft drinks).

Before we left he gave us each a certificate for a free round, including lunch, the fourth time we visited. This was a very smart GM. His offer got us to come back twice more, in order to get the free round. By the time we were done for the year we had spent well over $1000, which was at least $800 more than we originally had intended.

This GM never let any grass grow under his feet (a good quality to have if you're in charge of a golf course). He asked for permission to send of each of us an e-mail that could be forwarded to all our golfing friends, one that would include a slightly different special offer. I never did find out how this played out but I am pretty sure he picked up at least 20 new "clients," and probably a lot more. His cost to do all this? About as close to nothing as one can get.

Remember - out of every 100 hundred dissatisfied customers, only three will take the time to tell the provider of the product or service why they are unhappy. However, 10 dissatisfied customers will each tell 20 other people, and it's unlikely that any of those people will subsequently buy what that provider is selling. But it is not all bad news - the same percentages apply to customers who are pleased.

NUGGET

But remember this. While it is a nice gesture to recommend things such as golf courses, restaurants, books and movies, if you have young children, never ever share the name and phone number of a really good babysitter.

NUGGET

To retain customers, you need to communicate with them, and to do that, you must know who they are. Once you've got that information, you must use it. A number of examples of employing information are given throughout this book.

NUGGET

You can turn your customers into unpaid ambassadors for your business, or you can watch them dig your grave. Communicate with them regularly, but you can do that only by knowing who they are.

You Never Get a 2nd Chance to Make a 1st Impression – or a 2nd one

If you hear this a thousand times it is not nearly enough (that's why you will find these 11 words sprinkled throughout these pages). Your receptionist can be your most important employee. Your waiting area can determine if a new client returns. The cleanliness of your restrooms can impact a customer's feelings about you and your business more than your prices. Don't kid yourself; right or wrong, people do judge books by their covers all the time. If they do turn to the first page, consider this.

NUGGET

When you get a new job or account, put as much effort as is humanly possible into your first assignment. As I just said, you never get a second chance to make a first impression. As well known as this adage has become, no one ever speaks of the addendum: <u>you never get a second chance to make a second impression</u>. As discussed later, a retained customer is far more important than a new one. The latter may just be trying you out, but the former has come back because you passed that second-impression test.

The first impression landed you that client or customer, but please, please, please don't rest on your laurels (or

35

wherever it is that you go to relax). Flag that account, and make sure that the first order or job assignment is handled as perfectly as something can be. This second impression will be highly instrumental in getting a second order, which is, by far, the most critical one because, when that happens, you may well have a customer for life (more about "Lifetime Value of a Customer" can be found elsewhere). That will happen because you passed the try-out, or test. It is those responsible for impression number two that should get the most thanks.

As Harry Truman noted, "It's amazing what you can accomplish if no one cares about who gets the credit." Your client doesn't know who used the right packaging material, or who applied the final coat of paint. All they care about is the prompt delivery of the product they bought, with the price and quality they expected.

You'll Be the Only One There

(NOTE: IF YOU TAKE ONE THING AWAY FROM THIS BOOK LET IT BE THIS NEXT CHAPTER – SPECIFICALLY THE FIRST FIVE PARAGRAPHS (the rest of it will allow you to say to yourself, "Boy, am I glad that wasn't me").

People tend to do to business with people and companies that make them feel special. This next example is a case where I got a piece of advice that has brought millions of dollars in additional revenues to the businesses that have taken it to heart.

At one point in my career, I had been doing business with a Japanese company for a couple of years. All my dealings had been with Mr. Takito, the company's American representative - a Tokyo native living in NYC. One day he called me to let me know that his boss, CEO Mr. Mazaki, was going to visit and that he would like to meet me. When we got together over lunch, he and I immediately hit it off. Fortunately, I remembered the adage that we have been given two ears and one mouth, and they should be used in that proportion.

I learned that many years earlier he had started a business that provided packaging material. For a while he was literally a one-man show, doing everything from bookkeeping to sales calls. Business grew quickly and thirty years later, his company's annual sales were approaching $500M. His two sons now ran the operation, but there was one job he refused to relinquish.

From his first day of operating, he made a note of the date that he made his initial sale to a customer. A year later he showed up at the customer's office with a small anniversary gift to recognize their relationship and friendship. It was never anything expensive but was always appreciated. Mr. Mazaki then explained his reasoning to me.

"Philip, in Japan, as in most countries, when the holidays come around, businesses are deluged with gifts from their suppliers. It has reached the point that if you ask their executives, a week later, who gave them what, they are unable to answer with any degree of accuracy. However, when I show up on February 3rd, May 27th, or whatever the specific day is, **I am the only one there,** and I am always remembered. I never spend a great deal of money on the gifts, but this truly is a case where it has been the thought that counts. In fact, a couple of my customers now periodically celebrate my visits. Every fifth year, when I arrive, they have a small party for their very good friend. Me."

There is one other part to this story that has nothing to do with anything I've just related. Let me take that back, as it certainly helps explain why I was much quieter than usual.

The three of us went to a very exclusive Japanese restaurant. They asked me if I liked sushi. When I told them that I had never had it before, they explained what it was. After hearing their description I said, "Sure, I am pretty much willing to try anything once." Besides, after they virtually recommended the dish it would have been in very bad taste (barring allergies) to ignore what they said. So, Mr. Mazaki ordered three individual sushi platters.

Immediately after they were put on the table the trouble began. I had already told them, as I am telling you now, that I have never mastered the art of chopsticks, to the point that, if I attempted to use them, I might starve to death. Had I tried to use them, and failed, the disaster might not have occurred. Unfortunately, I picked up my fork.

I can remember what I was thinking, word for word, even though it was more than thirty-five years ago. "How strange," I thought. "This is a Japanese restaurant and I am looking at a traditional Japanese meal. So why is there a dollop of guacamole in the center of the platter?" Oh, if only I had stopped with that thought.

But no. The next words running through my brain were, "I love guacamole. And, since it's a relatively small amount, I can fit all of it on my fork."

For those of you who know what wasabi is you can probably figure out what happened next. My skin first turned pink, then red, and then purple. Perspiration started pouring off my face. Talking was out of the question. I drank all three glasses of water and all three beers - there are a few times when one has to give up any thought of being politically correct. When my pulse

38

had finally gone down to about 100, and they had given up trying not to laugh, they explained that wasabi is known as Japanese horseradish and is about fifty times stronger than any American version. And it is at least ten times hotter than the hottest jalapeño pepper.

This explains, in part, why I was such a good listener.

NUGGET

Telling someone that he or she is not part of a crowd but a remembered and valued client/customer is incredibly powerful. I have used this technique several times, and it has never failed to impress. Its application is limited only by your imagination. When I worked in the nonprofit world, where it is said that you can never say thank you too many times, I learned that a handwritten card, marking the anniversary of a gift, brings another gift far more often than any other type of correspondence or solicitation.

The "Isms" – Optimism and Pragmatism

My guess is that we have all shared the experience of wanting to make a connection with someone well known – a powerful person who might help us advance in whatever our career might be at the time. The problem, of course, is that these people never seem to be available. They are protected by secretaries or administrative assistants and your attempts to write to them always seem to get form letter responses, if any at all.

I suggest approaching this from several different perspectives. All are based on the same belief. There are a lot of ways to get into a house so why try to fight

39

your way through the front door, where people are lined up. Instead, case out the house and pick a side door, a window or even the equivalent of a chimney.

Now before getting to "things that have worked," let me toss in a bit of my own two-bit philosophy (although given the price of books these days "two-bits" seems more than a bit understated).

I have always been a true optimist who has never attempted anything without believing that I was going to succeed. If I buy a Powerball ticket, and they announce numbers that differ from the ones I have, I consider calling the lottery commission and respectfully suggest that they recheck the results, as it appears obvious that those that were announced were in error. If you don't believe you will, or even might, succeed, why bother? Far too often I've heard people say, "I don't know why I'm doing this."

If you ever find yourself thinking, "there's no way I can get this contract or job," don't bother trying (with one exception that you will discover, a bit farther down my literary road). If you have that attitude you will invariably not give it your best shot, which makes the likelihood of failure even greater. Don't waste another minute. Signal that your "pursuit-of-new-business car" is making a turn.

However, with all my unbridled optimism I have enough left-brain pragmatism in me to be a realist, who understands the importance of words like "odds" and "likelihood." What this means is that my chances of success are probably not very good, if I am competing with a number of other competent individuals, agencies, etc. But that is only true if we are competing on a level playing field.

That being said, I don't think I have ever allowed the playing field to be level – and yes, I can almost always tilt it in my favor. The last thing I want is to fit in with the crowd and look or behave like everyone else. I'm not talking about doing anything in bad taste but I am talking about "discernable differentiation." I will occasionally crash and burn but I believe that the adage that says "No risk, no reward" should always be considered.

NUGGET

If I had a list called "The Important Things to Remember," this would make the top six. When Erasmus said, "In the land of the blind the one-eyed man is king" he did not mean that you had to be screaming at the top of your lungs.

Just think of a chandelier with a dozen 60-watt bulbs in it. In order for you to stand out you don't have to be a 500-watt variety (which would be a distraction). All you need is one 75-watt bulb, or be blue instead of white.

One + One = Three   One + One + One = Seven

This chapter deals with the fact that, if more than one person is involved, there are dynamics you might not have considered. As an example I will use a family, but please understand that this is just as applicable in the workplace.

Let's start with Mom (M) and Dad (D). In this case one + one = three, because there are three separate entities. There's M, there's D and then there's MD. This is important because every study I've ever read states that people who change who they are, in order to compromise, quickly become someone else. Consider how often you've heard someone say, "She's (he's)

41

not the person I married." Just think of a vertical line connected, at its end, to a horizontal line. While both lines bring a lot to the party (at the point they meet), the fact is, each line, in and of itself, is still there.

M wants to see movie #1 and D wants to see #2. To avoid an argument, many couples will, as a compromise, agree on #3 with both of them saying "#3 is OK with me."

Think of how silly this is. In order to not have controversy neither person gets to do what they want. The solution is really very simple. On the first trip to the movies go see #1 followed, a few days later by #2. And, there's nothing wrong with going to a multiplex where they can both get to see their first choice. It will certainly make for conversation when you meet for coffee or a drink afterwards. But no gloating is allowed. It's not a good idea to say, "Boy, did you make a mistake because the movie I saw was great."

Now, let's move onto the fact that one + one + one = seven. How does this work in the business world? See if you recognize a scenario that resembles this.

Your office looks out on employees X, Y, and Z. You can meet with each one individually, in pairs (XY, XZ and YZ), or all at the same time XYZ. There are so many times that these combinations are applicable. For the sake of brevity (please stop laughing) I'll just offer a few possibilities. Employee X has not been pulling his or her weight. Rather than confront him or her directly, you might ask Y and Z if they are aware if anything might be wrong with X (there may be a very good explanation that X doesn't want to share with their boss, such as the fact that their girl/boyfriend is moving to another city). And, of course, there are all those times when one or more person is on vacation, or out sick.

NUGGET

Compromise is overrated. While it may be necessary to get legislation past (although not lately), it is rarely appropriate in the business world. If you go to see a client to present an idea, and they don't like it, preferring their own (surprise, surprise), finding a middle ground will almost never work. Instead tell them that you'd like to look at a different approach. When you do try to incorporate a little bit of what they said. If you start out your second presentation with the words, "Part of this is based on the fact that we loved your suggestion that we ....," you will put the audience on your side.

You have more assets (and more danger of conflict) than you probably thought existed. Take advantage of those assets, manage the conflict, and you'll be in good shape.

The Limb You Crawl Out On May Be Stronger than the Tree

I'm going to discuss my viewpoint about resumes at length, a bit later on but, for the moment, picture a Human Resources Director who has 100 job applications on his or her desk, yours among them (the same holds true if you are trying to land a new account or client and see 100 company/agency representatives knocking on their door). Half of them are highly qualified, with yours being one of them. If you read the same "How to Write a Resume" book that everyone else did, yours will look like everyone else's and your chances of getting the job will be one in fifty. Now, if you are going to fail, 49 times out of 50, I suggest that it's time to break a few rules or, as the cliché says, "push the corner of the envelope" (I'm using this phrase although I don't know exactly what it means).

Here is a case of "pushing."

Many years ago I was responsible for designing a booth at a trade show. I had been to several of these before and surmised that, from 50 feet away, it was hard to differentiate one from another. Each year they seemed to get more ornate (and expensive) but not more distinguishable.

My answer was an exercise in simplicity. I did our entire booth in black and white. Amidst a sea of color it stood out incredibly well (and cost far less to produce). I told people that it wasn't even necessary for them to know my booth number. I let them know what floor it was on and that it would be as easy to find - as if it were written in, you guessed it, black and white. You would have thought I had put a giant magnet in there, the crowds were so great.

NUGGET

If you are ever responsible for assembling one of these booths, find out if the event is in a state where the workers are unionized. If it is, bring your own tools. I was in the old New York Coliseum on a Sunday, preparing for a show that was opening the next day. I had a nail that needed to be hammered in. There was a guy walking by, wearing a big tool belt. I stopped him and asked if he would mind lending a hand (actually a hammer). "No problem" he said – and five seconds later the task was completed.

Two weeks later I got a bill from the show management company – for $75. After I caught my breath I called them, convinced they had made a mistake. Not at all,

I was told. The rate for a carpenter was $37.50 per hour, with a minimum billing of one hour. And, since it was a Sunday, all work was considered overtime and thus was billed at twice the standard rate.

There is one other caution here. In situations like this you are not allowed to do a job like this yourself. Nonetheless bring a hammer. Just be sure the coast is clear before you go tap, tap, tap. And do it quietly.

Now, where was I (I find myself saying that a lot)? Oh yes................

Go West, Not So Young Man

I moved to Phoenix in 1991. It only took a couple of weeks of reading the newspapers, and watching television for me to realize that Jerry Colangelo was the number one mover and shaker in this market. He owned the Phoenix Suns basketball team and seemed to be chairing every important committee in town. I tried writing, and calling, with the results one might expect. Time for plan B.

I noticed that Mr. Colangelo was scheduled to give a number of speeches to civic and business groups and that these were open to the public. For the next four weeks I appeared at every one of the five presentations he made. I made sure to get there very early so that I could get a seat in the first row. Just when I was about to have a "crisis of confidence," after the last one, Mr. Colangelo came over to me and said, "I don't get it. All my speeches are pretty much the same but you're here week after week. How come?" My answer was pretty simple and straightforward.

I said, "Mr. Colangelo, since the ordinary ways of getting to meet you didn't seem to be working, I thought I'd see if I could tickle your curiosity. If you've got a couple of minutes I'd like to introduce myself and tell you something about me."

Was this worth it? I'll let you be the judge. Mr. Colangelo ended up serving on two Honorary Boards of non-profits I ran, he donated money personally as did the teams he owned (the Arizona Diamondbacks had become part of his sports empire), he returned my e-mail messages and he still says hello when we meet at breakfasts or luncheons.

His Senior Vice President became one of my closest friends, has chaired one of my Boards and his teams continually contributed tickets to causes I was championing. And what did this cost me? Absolutely nothing. In fact, I got three free breakfasts from attending these speeches. To say that this was a good "investment" of my time would be to belabor the obvious.

This is further evidenced by what you are about to read.

A couple of years after meeting Jerry I decided to take a "risk" (I wish there was a type face that indicates sarcasm) by sending a solicitation letter to each member of the Suns team. I had forgotten all about it when, a couple of weeks later, I came back from a meeting to find an envelope on my desk. In it was a small card that included a note from one of the players, and his wife, telling me how appreciative they were of the work we were doing. I always save their notes and letters like this one – they are the perfect tonic to fend off a bad day. I went to put this card back in its envelope, so I could file it away, when I realized that I hadn't taken everything out. What I had missed was a check, made out to the West Valley Child Crisis Center – for $25,000. I'm a pretty emotional guy to begin with but, even if I wasn't, I don't think I would have been able not to cry. This pretty much defined the phrase "tears of joy."

(Note: This deserves another thank you to Mr. Colangelo as I'm sure that the player who made the donation first checked with him to assure himself that I was the "real deal").

There is No Such Thing as an Unreachable Person

(Note: This chapter is a continuation of the one that preceded it)

Back in the mid 1980's I held the title of "Vice President of Corporate Development" for a reasonably large advertising agency.

There was an account I wanted to "pitch" and believed that the best way to do this was to get to their CEO. The problem was that, as seemed to be par for the course, he was protected by several layers of assistants, vice presidents and secretaries. My typical New Yorker's tenacity got me nothing but a healthy dose of frustration.

However, in the process, I began to get to know the CEO's executive assistant who, I felt, was beginning to feel sorry for me (although that was not manifesting itself in me being able to get through to her boss). I decided to send her a bouquet of roses and followed that up with another phone call, this time asking for a seemingly unrelated favor. I told her that I was aware that their company had a major branch office in Chicago and that her boss made a couple of trips out there every month. A newspaper article mentioned that he didn't own a vehicle so he used a car service to take him to and from the airports.

(Note: He may not have been making enough money to afford the parking fees in NYC. When I left there, in 1991, there was already a garage that charged $800 per month, payable in advance for the year. Not only that, they required 24 hours notice if you wanted to use your car. This is a textbook example of "chutzpah." For those of you not familiar with that word, the best example is someone who kills both his parents and then asks for mercy from the court – because he is an orphan).

My request was that she let me know the next time he was going to be coming back from Chicago, including the airline he was flying, the flight number, and the name of the car service he used. The flowers must have done the trick as she agreed, although she added the caution that if anyone ever found out that she was the source of this information I would be in very serious trouble (I recall she mentioned something about it being life-threatening).

A week later she called to tell me that her boss would be returning from Chicago, the following morning, on United Airlines. His flight # was 820, it was due in at 11:00 A.M. and he was being picked up by Fugazy Limousine Service. The next day I called United at 11:15 A.M. and confirmed that the flight had landed on time. I waited another 15 minutes and then called Fugazy's dispatch office and explained that I was the CEO's stockbroker. I told them that he had an open order to buy 100,000 shares of a particular stock at 10 ½. The stock had dropped to 10 5/8 but I didn't think it was going any lower. I needed to speak to the CEO immediately so it was critical that they give me the number of the phone in the limo.

They didn't hesitate for a second and immediately provided me the information I needed. I called the car, got the driver and asked to speak to Mr. CEO. The driver handed him the phone and I was "in," as the CEO had none of his "armor" at hand. I immediately explained that I was employing this rather unusual method to reach him because he was so difficult to get a hold of. In fact, I added, he was the most difficult person to reach I had ever encountered, and I had a good frame of reference since I spent almost all of my days (and a few nights) trying to get in touch with hard-to-get-a-hold-of executives (I think the he was flattered by that comment).

I then planted the critical seed in the CEO's mind – that if I was able to get through to the "hardest person in the world to reach" think of what I could do, on the CEO's behalf, in reaching new customers for his business. It made as much sense to him as I hope it does to you and, a week later, my agency was retained.

Phones, or things related to them, seem to have played a major part in a number of my successes. About a year after the "call the limo" story I was faced with a similar situation. The CEO/President of the agency I was working for challenged me to figure out how to get in touch with another one of those "no-way-to-get-through-to-him" individuals.

I've always read a great deal, for both pleasure and business and, for some reason, seem to file away all sorts of trivial information. In my memory vault was a note that "Mr. Difficult" was someone who had to own the "latest and greatest" when it came to expensive gizmos and gadgets. In fact, he probably possessed every single item in the "Sharper Image" catalogue (those of you who are old enough will understand this reference).

On the same day my employer assigned me the task, there was a story on the front page of the Wall St. Journal, revealing the fact that Motorola had come out with the first "flip phone," the smallest and lightest mobile phone yet.

This set some gears clicking in my head. I recalled that when I was growing up, every phone in the world had its number somewhere on the instrument. However that wasn't, and still isn't, true for cell phones. In fact, the only person who knows the number of a particular cell phone is the person who bought it, not necessarily the one who has it in their possession. I pointed this out to my boss, telling him that, while it would be expensive I, on his behalf, could create a very interesting situation.

I was pretty sure that I could put a phone in Mr. Difficult's pocket where me, and my boss, would be the only ones knowing its number. To make another long story a bit shorter, the phone was purchased, gift-wrapped (more about that in the next story), and shipped via FedEx with a note that simply said, "Thought you would enjoy this." My boss waited until the next day and then called the recipient, who was shocked to hear his phone ring.

When he answered it my boss explained that he was the one who had sent the phone and why. The voice at the end of the line was so impressed at the creativity and, again, at that same message – if we can reach you we can reach anyone – that our agency was invited in the following week and were retained before the end of the month. The phone had been quite expensive, about $1,500 I think (remember, this was in 1989. Those of you who are old enough will recall the "Bomar Brain," a pocket calculator. The product which now can be bought just about anywhere, for less than $2.00, cost $175, back in 1967). However, the client gave our agency billings in seven figures (with no decimal point). My point is that if you think of anything you do as an investment, and then measure ROI (Return on Investment), something like this becomes a no-brainer.

Of course that's true only if it works, and that doesn't happen all the time. A bit later on I'll provide some of the ways to dramatically increase your odds.

It doesn't always have to cost nearly that much money. The final story in my "phone trilogy" set me back about $40, but was equally effective.

The company I worked for had picked up a rumor that a fairly large-size corporation was getting ready to ditch their current agency because they felt they were being "backburnered." They were not getting the top art and creative directors assigned to their account, their calls were not being returned promptly and there were a whole bunch of other things that spoke to less-than-ideal customer service. My job was to convince them that we were different

I went to a Radio Shack and purchased a small "princess" style phone, red in color. The only unique (at the time) feature this product possessed was that it could be programmed for speed dialing – up to nine numbers. The numbers I entered were the direct dial number for our CEO (the one that bypassed his secretary), his home number and the phone number in his car. I then punched in the same three numbers for our Senior Creative Director and Production Manager.

I had a very nice card designed that said, "This is our Agency Hotline (remember, it was red). If you need to reach our CEO just plug this into any phone outlet and hit #1. You'll go straight to his desk. If it's "after hours" just hit #2 and you'll get him at home and, if it's in-between, hit #3 and you'll reach him in his car." The same "menu" was then repeated with the contact information for those two other agency executives. The note concluded with the message "You are one button away from the

51

hottest agency on the East Coast. Our top people are as easy to reach as the tip of your finger."

Of course, the real message was that we understood service, that we were always accessible, and perfectly willing to operate under the client's schedule, rather than ours. I gift-wrapped the box, had it delivered by messenger and we had a new client two days later.

Going back a few days, when I was getting ready to program that "hotline" phone, our Production Manager expressed some concern about giving out his home phone number to a stranger. I assured him that there would be no problems; while keeping my fingers crossed that there would be no problems.

About a month later he came into my office to thank me, profusely. It seems that we were getting ready to print the first major job for our newest client. Since everything related to it were things we had done many times before, he felt that he didn't have to be onsite, especially since it was a Sunday. However, the client's CEO had never seen anything like this before so he was in attendance.

Soon after he arrived they handed him the press proof. He looked at it and thought that something didn't seem right, although he could not put his finger on it. He called our Production Manager and expressed some concern. Reluctantly he said he would be there in 20 minutes, although he did admit that he enjoyed screaming out "Stop the presses!" (which actually hadn't started running yet but no one decided to take his fun away).

When our man walked in the CEO apologized, saying that it was probably no big deal and, if he didn't have the Production Manager's phone number on hand, he wouldn't have said anything (we had suggested, to all of our major clients, that they bring our "hotline" phone with them, when they were out of the office, on a business-related matter).

Our guy took one look and immediately saw the problem. The mailing included a coupon that need to be filled out and sent back. Somehow that coupon was designed as a "reversal" meaning that it had a black background, with white type. The only way someone could fill it out was if they had a pen that used white ink.

Had this not been caught there would have been a press run of 2M pieces where one of two things would have happened, both of them very bad. If it was before the mailing took place, it could have been corrected and the 2M coupons would have had to be printed again. In this scenario there would have been a waste of a great deal of both time and money. The other possibility was that the mailing would have gone out with the error, and the recipients would have thought the client to be totally unprofessional - and they certainly wouldn't place any orders (I can count all the pens I've ever seen that use white ink using all the fingers on either of my hands – and then subtracting five).

As I said, our Production Manager couldn't thank me enough times. We would never find out, but he was convinced that if either of the two possibilities described above had occurred, heads would have rolled, beginning with his.

A couple of more points here. In a little while I will pass along some other examples about how incredibly important telephones can be in your life. But, for the moment, let me mention the magic of packages.

Consider this. Twenty-five years ago the FedEx driver was treated like a god. Activity in offices would come to a halt when the driver with the purple envelope came through the door. Now it's just another mail delivery.

Twenty years ago faxes received the "treat them like gold" reaction. Now they are, more often than not, menus from local restaurants and usually get ignored. Ten years ago the head of the "get your attention" class was taken over by e-mails. It didn't take long before our computer mailboxes were being clogged with a myriad of offers we had no interest in. However, there is one thing that will always work, and it goes to the fact that all of us are children at heart and often curious to a fault.

Send a box that is gift-wrapped, to the person you are trying to reach, and the odds are that you will get through directly to them. Secretaries will avoid opening the package for fear that it is something personal and the executive, who won't return your calls or answer your letters will, for a moment or two, think of birthdays and Christmas and want to know what's inside. I once suggested to a friend, looking for a job, that he send a sneaker, new of course, with a note that said. "I'm just trying to get a foot in the door." He did, but was not hired.

NUGGET

However, this leads to another interesting point. The person who interviewed him suggested that he trying getting in touch with a friend of his, and even offered to arrange for an introduction. That magnanimous gesture resulted in him getting hired. And so I suggest you treat this just like what I discuss in the subsequent "It Should Never Take More than Two Phone Calls" chapter. If you are rejected it can never hurt to ask if the person who said "no" has any suggestions as to who you might call.

If the Idea is Nice Use it Twice, or Even Thrice

The "Hot Line" idea can be used in any number of ways. I mentioned it to a friend who's a realtor, specializing in new construction. When she meets a potential customer for the first time, as they are about to part company, she makes a statement to the effect that "It's been my experience that a half an hour from now you'll come up with a handful of questions you wish you had thought of earlier. I want to make it as easy as possible for you to get those questions answered immediately."

She then gives them a pre-paid, pre-programmed, cell phone. It includes all her contact numbers, the numbers of a few good restaurants in the neighborhood and the number for the school their children would probably end up attending.

Once construction starts she takes back the phone and reprograms it. Her numbers stay in, this time accompanied by those of the contractor and all the subs – electric, plumbing, etc. She calls it a "Building Your New House" phone. Every single client has commented favorably on this "customer friendly" gesture and several have told friends who have become her customers.

Look at what she's accomplishing. She's providing service in a world where that entire concept is now hiding beneath a blanket of mediocrity – and people eat it up.

Curiosity Can Do a Lot More than Just Kill Cats

In my role as Vice President of Corporate Development creativity helped but success truly has come as a result of the "10% inspiration/90% perspiration" ratio. My tenacity, to the point of being out-and-out stubborn, probably was of far greater value than the clever things I occasionally came up with, although this next story involved pretty much no "sweat."

I had just concluded a stretch of having brought in several pieces of new business and was being questioned, by one of our agency account executives, as to what I thought were the reasons I was able to do so well. I was feeling a bit cocky that day (there are those who will suggest that this is how I wake up every morning) so I answered, "It's easier than most people think. In fact, I don't even have to go after them. I can get anyone I want to call me and initiate a conversation."

The account executive took this as being a pretty outlandish claim and before I knew it we made a bet (dinner for two at the Four Seasons restaurant in New York City).Since he had this suspicion that I was in the process of tricking him, I got him to make this bet by saying that he, the account executive, could pick the company. The only conditions were that they had a Vice President of Marketing and/or Sales, who was in his or her office (easily confirmable by a call to the company's switchboard) and a published fax number (e-mail wouldn't be invented, or discovered, for another five years or so).

I suggested that he take The Red Book (a directory of every company in the United States that has an advertising budget that exceeds $100,000 annually), and drop it on the floor. When it "landed" and opened to a particular page, the AE could cover his eyes and point his finger wherever he chose. That company would be my target.

The "drop" and the "point" then followed and I was free to proceed. Oh, by the way, I should add that a condition of the bet was that I had to get that person to call within 30 minutes

Once my clock was ticking I took a piece of agency letterhead and typed onto it "This fax consists of this cover sheet and two additional pages." It went on to add that if there was any problem in the receipt of the complete message the recipient should call the agency. I provided my direct-dial number.

I then sat down at my computer and opened a new document. On the top of the page I typed "Page Two" and began in the middle of a sentence – "and frankly Mr. Jones, if this is not the best way to add $10,000,000 to your bottom line profits for the first quarter of your next fiscal year, I sure would like to hear what would put it in second place." I added "Thank you for your time" and signed my name.

It was then off to the fax machine where this page went with the aforementioned cover sheet. Mr. Jones called in eight minutes. "Where is page one?" he wanted to know. I ended up explaining the story behind the transmission. Although Mr. Jones found it "cute" (I'm pretty sure that's the word he used), this was not a "happily-ever-after" story, at least insofar as his company becoming a client.

But it was a very happy ending for my taste buds (I did insist that the account executive join me. If he was going to have to pay for two people he might as well get a good meal out of it).

The origin of this "modus operandi" came from something I had read many years ago – before faxes or even telex machines. The author said that if you want to get someone's immediate attention just send them a telegram that reads "Urgent! Urgent! Urgent! Please disregard previous telegram." The fact of the matter is, while "curiosity may have killed the cat," it can also be an incredibly powerful marketing tool and technique.

If you give someone an envelope that reads, "Do not open until two weeks from the date of receipt," or "Do not open until Christmas," what do you think will happen? I saw a survey that indicated that more than 95% of the recipients would totally disregard the admonition. It's nothing more than Brer Rabbit pleading not to be thrown in the briar patch – the very place he wanted to be.

Taking Risks – as Long as They are in Good Taste

Whether you're selling a product or yourself, a lot of people are trying to get in the same door that you are. Try a different door, a different day, a different time, or a different method of delivery. Your risk is minimal, and the upside potential is enormous.

Putting our current economic issues aside for the moment, a perfect example of appropriate risk taking can be explained by any knowledgeable bank executive (assuming that's not an oxymoron).

They tell their loan officers that, if none of their transactions lead to a default, they are being too conservative. To wit:

Loan officer A loans $100,000, with a 10% interest rate, to ten different businesses or individuals. At the end of the first year all the loans are intact, and the bank has earned $100,000 in interest.

Loan office B eases the criteria for handing over money. He makes 15 similar loans and, during the first year, one of them defaults. The bank loses $100,000 and gets $140,000 in interest charges, for a net of $40,000.

In the second year the A loans generate another $100,000 in interest while the B loans bring in $140,000. At this point the cumulative interest earned for the A loans is $200,000 while the B loans have provided the bank with a cumulative $180,000 - but things are about to change.

The next year the total interest earned on the A loans reached $300,000. The figure for the B loans is now $320,000.

The wisdom of loan officer B is now obvious. In years four-ten the interest on the A loans total $700,000 while the B loans bring in $980,000. By the 10th anniversary, loan officer A has generated $1,000,000. His (temporary) peer has seen the bank's coffers increase by $1,300,000 – 30% more than A. At this point B gets a promotion while his counterpart now works at a branch office in Cheyenne, WY.

NUGGET

Much to the surprise of many, the words "prudent" and "risk" are not always mutually exclusive and can, in fact, become partners, instead of economic enemies.

The easiest way to insure that bad things don't happen is to do nothing. If that is what you opt for not even a branch in Cheyenne will welcome you.

Testing Your Ability to Handle a Short Burst of Fear

I have already mentioned the fact a lot of the bills you receive can be looked at as the start of a negotiation – subscriptions, cable fees, credit card rates, etc. Well, there's one more that may shock a number of you. I'm talking about what you pay in taxes.

When I lived back east my brother-in-law, a highly regarded CPA, did my returns. Before he began working on the first one he told me that I had two options – and that both began with the fact that he would never do anything he knew to be illegal.

- Option #1 – He would scrupulously follow the letter of every tax law.

- Option #2 – He would push the envelope that contained those laws – specifically related to those open to interpretation. He went on to warn me that, if he did that, I might get audited. He mentioned that because he knew of some people, including several of his clients, who could not deal with getting a letter from the IRS that began with the words, "Please visit us on......."

Before I could provide a choice he said, "All audits end up being negotiations. You will not get to use all the deductions you claim and the IRS will not collect on every thing they are questioning. Given that you are a "small fish" they are going to try to get fifty cents on the dollar. Yes, you will get hit with some interest and penalty charges but, if you pay them on time, what you save will far exceed those charges."

I've been audited three times. And, I will admit that the first time I saw an envelope from the IRS, my pulse began to race. However, after recalling what I had been told, I started looking for the receipts I would need.

I'm going to use some very round numbers here, since I don't remember the exact ones. These are based on the fact that I was in the 25% bracket.

In my first return that was audited I had claimed $4,000 in questionable deductions and, after meeting an agent with the IRS, I was told that only half of them were legitimate.

- So I had to pay taxes on $2,000 (taxes I would have to have paid under any scenario).

- I did not have to pay taxes on the other $2,000, thus saving $500 ($2,000 X 25%).

- My penalty and interest charges were 5% on the money owed. 5% X $2,000 equals $100.

- Subtracting the $100, from the $500 I saved, left me with a net savings of $400.

Over the next five years I was audited twice more (saving roughly the same amount each time) and my CPA turned out to be a profit. Technically the IRS won, because their "take" averaged 51% of the amount in question. However, had I not used this approach they would have gotten 100%.

(Note: If you have had heart trouble you may want to ignore this. My audits were in an office with cubicles. All three times I was there I heard people pleading and once I am quite sure I detected a sob or two. If only they had known, in advance, what to expect).

How to Turn $.20 into $200,000 (w/o Joining Amway)

This is not a story about buying a hot stock, or even a lottery ticket. It doesn't involve a Ponzi scheme, a chain letter or anything related to multi-level marketing. The $.20 referred to was the cost of a first class postage stamp 29 years ago and the $200,000 is the size of an order that was received – the finale in a sequence of events launched by a letter that got someone's attention.

In the early 1980's I was running the international division of Cliffdale Associates. My job was to take items that had been successful in mail order ads in this country and sell them overseas. At the time this story took place Cliffdale was doing business in about 20 countries, including South Africa and Finland.

Our biggest account was a "Scandinavian Fortune Top 10" Finnish conglomerate that was buying automobile polish from us. They were purchasing the product in a concentrated form, in 55-gallon drums weighing 500 pounds apiece. They had recently opened a letter of credit to buy 50 of these drums, at $4,000 each. Their order was being produced and was going to be shipped, by ocean, in about three weeks.

Concurrently, there were some documents I had to get to a client in South Africa. These were very time sensitive and, as I had done several times before, I called DHL who were a major player in the international air freight market, specializing in small packages (although they handled shipments of any size).

DHL assured me that the envelope would be delivered on time (for a fee of $95). DHL did not tell Cliffdale the truth.

I decided that rather than use the standard method of a complaining phone call, as well as a letter expressing my disappointment, I would try a slightly different approach and see if I could get my point across using a touch of humor. With that in mind, my correspondence to DHL was in the form of a fairy tale. Here's what it said:

March 5, 1982

Our Ref: PB/MS/DHL/82/3899
Mr. David Allen
President
DHL Corporation
1818 Gilbreth Street
Suite 252
Burlingame, California 94010

Dear Mr. Allen,

I would like to take a few minutes of your time to relate a short story. I ask that you read it carefully as there will be a quiz immediately following and I believe you have a vested interest in answering all the questions correctly.

Once upon a time there was a company called Cliffdale Associates (to make the story more readable we will call them "client"). The client had many occasions to make use of a courier service offered by a company called DHL (no need to simply that name).

On February 26, 1982 (Friday), at 11:00 A.M., the client called DHL and explained that they (the client) needed a small package of documents delivered to Johannesburg, South Africa by March 3rd (Wednesday). DHL assured the client saying, "Not to worry. We are a well-run efficient company and we will pick up your package later today. It will go on a flight on Monday, March 1st and be delivered, in Johannesburg, on March 3rd." The client felt very good.

At 3:30 P.M., on that same day, DHL called and explained that they were running late so the pick-up would not be made until the morning of March 1st but again, not to worry, as the package would get on the same flight.

The client, convinced that this efficient, well run, company knew whereof it spoke, had a quiet and peaceful weekend (how foolish of the client, as we shall soon see).

When no one had arrived at the client's office by 11:00 A.M. on Monday, March 1st, the client called DHL who, once again, offered the "not to worry" phrase.

DHL picked up the package at 12:09 P.M. on Monday, March 1st. After the pick-up the client called DHL to make sure that the package would still get on the flight. DHL said, "Maybe." "Maybe?" thought the client. What happened to "not to worry?"

At 3:10 P.M. on March 1st DHL called the client and said, "So sorry, but the package has just arrived here and missed the 3:00 P.M. cut-off. So sorry, but there is nothing we can do. So sorry but we can't put it on another flight to insure the same delivery date. But, here's the good news. We can put it on a flight leaving on Wednesday, March 3rd and deliver it on Friday, March 5th."

Poor client. The package urgently had to be there on Wednesday and the "service" organization that DHL purported to be turned out to be the screwer in a screwer/screwee affair. Sadder, but a good deal wiser, the client took out a piece of paper they had filed away entitled "The Three Greatest Lies in the World."

On that list it said:

1. "The check is in the mail."

2. "I'm from the government and I'm here to help you."

3. "It's on the truck."

The client carefully crossed out the number three in the title and changed it to a four. They then added:

4. "Not to worry – DHL."

Now for the quiz.

1. How do you think the client feels about this sordid affair?

   a. Happy

   b. Sad

   c. Angry
   (Note: more than one answer may be correct)

2. What type of future dealings do you think the client intends to have with DHL?

   a. Keep using them – the client is a masochist.

   b. Recommend them to others – the client is a sadist.

   c. Look elsewhere – the client is a realist.

3. What does DHL intend to do about this?

   a. Nothing – an appropriate answer in view of how this matter has been handled to date.

   b. Something – This requires some creativity since DHL will have to come up with an answer that is more than just a letter of the alphabet.

Mr. Allen, for your convenience I have attached an answer sheet and a self-addressed (you don't think we'd be dumb enough to pay the postage?) envelope.

If you will indicate your answers and return them quickly, we promise to grade your paper and indicate:

1. You flunked so badly that it's unlikely you will stay in business long enough to have this happen again.

2. You flunked but will probably be able to get away with pulling the same stunt on other naïve clients, or

3. You flunked on performance but passed the test and were able to come up with an answer to question three that will convince the client that history will not repeat itself and that some sort of amends are in order.

Good luck! Remember, there are others eager to take your place as a service provider to the client so your answers will determine whether or not the DHL folder stays in the client's active file.

Cordially,

Philip Barnett

Vice President, Export Operations

When I mailed this letter I really didn't know what to expect (if anything). It made me feel better to write it (over the years, the venting I do by writing, has probably saved me hours of time on an analyst's couch, not to mention a ton of money) but I didn't have any particular response in mind.

Three days later I got a call from Mr. Allen. He said, "Mr. Barnett, or do you prefer Philip? (he hit what I was hoping would be the first of many home runs by asking this question – more about this a bit farther down a subsequent road) I must admit that your letter made me laugh out loud. However, I understand that amusing me was not your purpose. We would really like to keep you as a client so, with your permission, I'd like to have the new person, who has just been hired by our New York office (I was in Connecticut), come up to see you tomorrow and see if we can get things back on track."

I said that I did not think myself to be unreasonable and so I agreed to an appointment the following day.

What happened next almost defies description but provided a lesson — that a unique form of communication can bring about truly incredible results.

The person DHL sent to see me was very young — a recent graduate, from an Ivy League school, with an MBA in International Business. It was pretty obvious that he had been told to do whatever it took to make me happy and get Cliffdale Associates back in the fold.

He began by apologizing and stating that there were no excuses for what happened (always the best way to begin). He then said that Cliffdale would not be charged for the shipment in question (pretty much what I thought he would say). And then he went on to add that DHL would handle the next air overseas shipment at no charge. Fair enough I remembered thinking. This was about as much as we could expect. DHL had, up until then, been a good vendor, and my anger was gone after I wrote the letter, so I was willing to give them another chance.

At that exact moment something happened that I'm sure the DHL rep thought had to have been a set-up. However, I swore then, and have ever since, that it was a coincidence.

My assistant walked into my office and handed me a telex (this was in pre-fax or e-mail days). It was from our client in Finland, explaining that they were going to be amending their letter of credit. It turned out that they had planned a major television campaign, featuring the automobile polish they were buying from us, and that having the product sent by ocean was not going to get it to them on time. Thus they were filing the documents that would allow Cliffdale to ship it by air, at their expense.

I read the telex quickly and related it to what the DHL rep had just told me. In fact, I confirmed it by asking him, "So, if I understand you correctly, DHL will handle our next air shipment at no charge?" "That's exactly right Mr. Barnett" was his response.

"Well," I said, "it turns out we have a shipment we need to get to Helsinki by air. It's 50 55-gallon drums of an automobile polish concentrate, each one weighing 500 pounds. The total is 25,000 pounds."

For a moment I thought the DHL rep was going to have a heart attack. After all, he was thinking about a small package weighing no more than a pound or two and I was hitting him up for twelve and a half tons of chemicals.

His skin tone rapidly changed color, to the point that I felt as if I was conversing with a ghost. I became so concerned that he was going to be seriously ill that I quickly interjected that I would never do something like that to him and that I had only been joking. Yes, Cliffdale did have this airfreight shipment to go out but would save the DHL "freebie" for the next time we needed to send documents. The DHL new employee's relief was both immediate and obvious.

I thought the matter was over and done with until the next day. That afternoon I received a call from Mr. Allen in California. He said, "Philip, I heard what happened yesterday and wanted to thank you for quickly telling my employee that you were kidding him. From the way he told me the story, he was already getting ready to update his resume. I'm glad we're going to keep doing business together. In fact, I'm so pleased that I have a proposition for you.

I know that we're not competitive on large bulk shipments so I doubt that we'd ever get that order going to Helsinki. However we do have flights going there three times a week and they are almost never full. If you would let us split your shipment and send it over a seven-day period we'll handle it at no charge."

Two things came immediately to mind. Mr. Allen understood customer service and I was in a position to look like a hero to our client in Finland. I graciously accepted Mr. Allen's offer and immediately sent a telex to Helsinki. It read, "We are so supportive of your television campaign that we are prepared to absorb the additional costs related to shipping the product by air, rather than ocean."

The next day I received a phone call from their Managing Director (Europe's equivalent of our CEO). He told me that, "We have been doing business with American companies for more than 40 years and are licensees for some of your major corporations. Your gesture was the most generous offer we have ever received from anyone, at any time. We are so appreciative that we have decided to double our media budget and therefore double the size of our purchase. Please ship the 50 drums by air and an additional 50 drums by ocean. We've already advised our bank to forward you a second letter of credit for an additional $200,000."

This is about as "happily ever after" as one can get. For the cost of that stamp, and a little bit of creative thinking, Cliffdale got a return on investment that is almost unprecedented (The ROI was one million times the amount of money invested – beat that Jim Kramer).

How to Turn $100,000 into $1,300 (w/o Investing in Real Estate)

During the second year of serving as the Executive Director of the Child Crisis Center, the decision was made to build a "Kids' Campus." Since I was also the Director of Development it was my job to try to raise $1M (I ended up bringing in just over $2M). My contract said that I was to get a bonus, based on the amount of money I raised. This was offered, before I could ask, because I was told that non-profit jobs don't pay very well (no kidding – I took a 30% pay cut when I assumed this position). However, I had no problem with being told (pick your favorite cliché - to put my money where my mouth is, to put up or shut up, or to walk the walk) that a good deal of my income would be based on performance.

The formula was that I would receive bonuses based on the amount of money I raised, over and above the average of what was brought in over the three previous years ($108,000). In my first year I got $297,000 in contributions. My bonus brought my income up to where it would have been in the for-profit world. So far, so good.

A month before my second year contract expired, when there was $2M more money, in donations and pledges, I was told my contract would not be renewed. For all intents and purposes I was fired. You may ask (I certainly did) how could this have possibly been warranted?

Well, they were legally within their rights. Arizona is at "at will" state which means anyone's non-union employment can be terminated without showing cause.

Almost all of the $2M was in pledges that we knew would be honored. First of all they were in writing and second they came from companies/organizations such as Rotary International, Home Depot and Honeywell. We didn't need most of the money for at least six months, which was when the groundbreaking would take place.

A month after I was terminated I called and asked for the status of my bonus check. I relaxed when I was told that it had already been mailed. So, imagine my shock when I opened the envelope and removed their check, in the amount of $1,300.

When I called to ask what was going on I was told that since I no longer worked there I was not entitled to any bonuses for pledges not yet paid (almost all of them). With the exception of one, all of these pledges had been solicited and closed by me.

Think about this for a minute. You're a car salesman, who gets a 10% bonus on every sale you make. A customer comes in on Monday, and buys a car for $50,000. He explains that he has sold some stock and will have enough money to pay for the car on Friday. In the meantime he puts down $1,000. Your boss then fires you on Wednesday and hands you a check for $100. When you start to protest he tells you that he doesn't owe you any commission on the other $49,000 because you won't be an employee when that money is paid.

I'm not sure what would happen in that case, but I know what did in mine. I immediately called a lawyer, and then met with him to provide the details. He told me that if it went to court the likelihood of a verdict favoring me was about 98%. However, it would cost me roughly $50,000 in legal fees and while I would probably recover all of that, when I won, that retainer would have to be paid upfront. Conversations with two other attorneys confirmed what he told me.

Since $50,000 was so far out of my ballpark that it couldn't be seen by anyone sitting in the stands (I'm sure they knew that), I was pure out of luck. Who knows, I might have helped dig my own grave in that, more than once, I explained a suggestion by reminding the Board, "No risk, no reward." Here their risk was believing I would not be able to afford pursuing this while their reward would be approximately $100,000. They took the risk, they got the reward, and I got screwed.

Given my age, what I learned will probably never come into play for me again, but that's not necessarily true for any of you reading this. So, here's my advice.

NUGGET

If you are intending to get a "white collar" job, in an "at will" state, insist that any contract includes a statement the only reason you can be terminated is for cause. And, if possible, try to get a multi-year deal. While both of these suggestions should be acted on, one is better than none, especially given today's economy (I doubt it will have gotten better by the time this book is published (if I ever finish writing it), in early 2012.

Taking the Wind Out of Their Sails (a Perspective on Customer Service)

One of my many jobs was running a manufacturing division. There were occasions when we would get a call from a customer who was, shall we say, less than pleased. My two assistants were instructed to try to mollify or reason with the angry person. However, I told them that they did not have to put up with obscenities and that, if they hung up because of verbal abuse, I would fully understand. That being said, I asked that if it got to that point they should give the call to me and I would deal with it. Once or twice a year one of them would come into my office to tell me that there was a raving maniac on the phone, someone who could not be reasoned with.

I would pick up the receiver and say the following, "Mr. Jones, I understand that there is a problem and my job is to solve it and make you happy. However, before I do that let me tell you that you are the best thing to have happened to me today.

On the way to work I got not one, but two flat tires. Of course I only had one spare. When I arrived here there was an envelope from the IRS telling me that they are auditing me for the last three years. And, five minutes before you called, I was contacted by my son's school. They wanted to let me know that he had punched a teacher and was being suspended for a month. OK, let's talk about your problems."

I could, quite literally, hear a whoosh of air at the other end of the line, as the wind went out of his sails. I'm sure that Mr. Jones' immediate thought was "Wow, I thought I had it bad – that poor man."

What I had done here was nothing more than put things in perspective and plant a "there but for the grace of God go I" seed in the customer's mind. This got him to calm down and stop yelling. Once that was accomplished, solving the problem was usually the proverbial piece of cake.

And, by the way, very often the easiest first-step-towards-a-solution is to simply ask the customer what they would like to see happen. I grew up playing tennis competitively and, if given the option in the first game, I would always choose to return serve. In life, as in business, I like to know what I am up against before I have to make my first move. The funny thing here is that the customer will usually suggest something less generous than you were prepared to offer. Empowerment can be a wonderful tool.

NUGGET

Perspective - To a colony of ant a drop of dew is a tidal wave.

Onions and Orchards

When my former wife worked as a flight attendant, she told me about "Onion" and "Orchard" letters – those that came from angry passengers along with ones from those who believed they had received exceptional service. I'm sure that you've already figured out which name went with each grouping.

As you can probably guess, I write lots of letters, and most of them are the type that bring tears to my eyes, rather than ones on flower scented paper. The out-of-balance ratio, that seems to get worse with each passing year, is a reflection of the decline in customer service and/or product quality.

Nonetheless, I feel obligated to speak up, on those occasions when I find myself dealing with someone I would try to hire, if I had a job opening. And it wouldn't matter what their skills are. Skills can be taught – attitude can't.

And, to prove that the positive comments I make don't just end up in a file folder, there have been three times

74

when the person I had been talking to got in touch with me (I would blind copy them on the e-mails I sent), in order to let me know that, shortly after we spoke, they received a promotion.

I'm sure this had nothing to do with the "luck of the draw," and here's why.

-   When our conversation was about to end I explained that I'd like to speak to their supervisor. That person then gets to hear the plaudits that had been earned.

-   After hanging up I call back, and ask to speak to their Human Resources Director. I tell that person that they deserve praise as well, since they had been smart enough to hire the individual who had helped me.

-   My final conversation takes place with the person who trains their customer service staff. Once again I offer applause since the job is one almost no one comes naturally to. Therefore, the quality of their performance is directly related to the quality of their teacher(s).

Now, when I have negative experiences I don't go this far, as there is no point in talking to anyone but a supervisor.

There are a couple of reasons why I've written this chapter – things I refer to elsewhere in this book.

-   If you are a business owner beware of the damage that can be done by one or two "rogue" customer service employees. These days, almost every recording we hear begins with, "This call may be recorded for quality purposes." Of course, that admonition means nothing if nobody listens to them, and then acts accordingly.

- If you are a consumer (and just about every one of us is) you can do something if you would like to see the quality of customer service become enhanced. You have to make your feelings known, whether they be good or bad. One person can't make a difference you say? Well, think about this. Anyone running for political office will tell you that two people represent an audience, six people are a crowd and ten equal a throng. And it took only me, along with four other friends, to get our local newspaper to change one of their guidelines dramatically. They heard from each of us at least once a week and, as result, there are no more "smut" headlines above their gossip column. Five people caused a change in a newspaper with a circulation of more than 300,000. And none of us spent a penny.

(Note: Aside from those "quality assurance" messages we also hear, "Please listen carefully as our menu has recently changed." If you know someone looking for a job, with great growth potential, tell them to get into the "changing menus" business as there is obviously a huge demand. Either that or the word "recently" has been redefined. One of my insurance companies keeps telling me to "listen carefully" and I have – for at least three years. I guess that "recently" means within the last decade).

Where There's a Will There's a Way (and Usually Several Relatives).

Sometimes I think that there is nothing that I enjoy more than hearing someone say, "There's no way you can ever do that." If there is anything I live for it is to be challenged (unless it has to do with my car, my computer, spatial relations and assembling anything that has more than two parts). Three stories will illustrate this fact. While none of them involve earthshaking events they will give you some insight into my mindset and, perhaps, encourage you to not be discouraged when faced with odds that appear to be not in your favor.

1) When I was a junior in college, my girlfriend and I got invited to a first year anniversary dinner being thrown for a close friend and his wife. We decided that the appropriate gift would be a bottle of champagne. However, there was a problem. It was a Sunday, in a small town in upstate New York, and the way the laws existed back then, you couldn't buy champagne on that day of the week. Wine and liquor were only sold in liquor stores which were not open on Sundays. A quick check with a restaurant told me that they couldn't be of assistance, since an establishment such as theirs could lose their license, to serve alcoholic beverages, if they sold bottles "to go."

After about ten minutes of concentrated thought I figured out what to do. We drove downtown to the one and only hotel within 10 miles. We checked in (I won't tell you how long ago this was but the room was $8 per night) and went upstairs. Upon entering the room I went straight for the phone, called room service and asked that a bottle of champagne be delivered as soon as possible. Ten minutes later a waiter knocked on the door. I tipped him $2, grabbed the champagne (and my girlfriend) and headed back down to the front desk where I informed the very startled clerk that we were ready to check out. I paid the for the room, the champagne ($10) and we were out of there – a total of 12 minutes, $20 spent and a bottle of champagne to bring to the party. To this day that clerk probably thinks we hold the record for the quickest quickie.

2) About midway through what turned out to be 17 years of marriage we were having eight guests for Thanksgiving dinner, with the company due at 3:00 P.M. It was about noon and I was helping make the house look a bit more presentable when I heard a scream from the kitchen. I had been married long enough to recognize this as a scream of anger, not pain.

I came downstairs to find my wife stomping around the kitchen muttering that she had forgotten to buy sweet potatoes. She's remembered everything that went with them – the marshmallows, cranberries and walnuts – but not the main ingredient.

I calmed her down and told her not to worry, that I would go to the store and get some.

I jumped in my car and raced over to the supermarket, arriving at 12:05 P.M., only to be greeted with a sign that said, "Closing at 12 Noon on Thanksgiving Day." I realized that I couldn't ask my neighbors since they were also entertaining, so I headed for the local 7-11. You can probably already figure out what happened there, as the request for sweet potatoes was greeted with a "you've got to be kidding" stare.

I got back in the car and headed in the general direction of our house, still determined to figure something out. I was on the turnpike and pulled off to get gas, at the Howard Johnson rest stop. While filling up the tank the solution came to me and, once I figured it out, I could not resist the impulse to play it to the hilt.

I drove the 50 yards to the adjoining restaurant, walked in, and advised the hostess that I was a party of one. I got seated in a booth and was handed a menu. A couple of minutes later a waitress came over and asked if I was ready to order. I paused for a minute and said, "Yes, I'd like 20 orders of sweet potatoes, served in a large bowl."

(Note: "Yikes." I just started five consecutive paragraphs with the word "I").

The waitress looked at me as if I'd lost my mind but, when she realized I was serious, headed for the kitchen. Ten minutes later she reappeared with what looked like a soup terrine, put it down on my table and stared at me as if I were an alien from another planet.

I took my fork, dug in, and took a large bite. I then put down the fork, wiped my mouth with the napkin, turned to the waitress, and said, "That was delicious but I am stuffed. So I'd really appreciate it if you could take what's left and put it in a doggy bag."

When she returned with my "remains" I paid the $40 bill, left a $5 tip, got back in my car and headed home. I walked through our front door exactly 30 minutes after I had left, handed my wife a paper bag and said, "Here you go." Her response was, "I'm afraid to ask you where you got this but thank you." It wasn't until five years later that she got around to inquiring how I had become her "sweet potato man."

3) My third challenge came after I was divorced. And, once again, it involved nourishment of a kind (I never did investigate the possibility that my greatest pleasures come from telephonic, food and beverage challenges).

I had invited a date over to dinner at my Connecticut house. Before she arrived it had begun to snow and by the time we were halfway through the meal it was a full-fledged blizzard.

For some reason, in the middle of the meal, I decided that Crème Brulee (there are a few variations when it comes to the spelling of this word – sometimes the "B" is capitalized and other times it's not, sometimes there are two "e's" and sometimes one, and there are a bunch of accent marks that I can't find. However, even with all these possibilities I'm sure it doesn't matter, since you know what I'm referring to) would make for the perfect dessert. There were only a few minor stumbling blocks. I had none of the ingredients (and, even if I did, I had no idea how to make this delicacy). And, while there was a wonderful French restaurant in the next town, there was no way in the world I was going to drive in that weather and the restaurant was not the type that offered delivery service.

It only took a couple of minutes of heavy thinking (and one more glass of wine) to come up with the answer. I called the restaurant and confirmed that they would make the dessert available for pick up. I then called Domino's (across the street from them) and asked, if I ordered a pizza, could the driver go out of his way, by about 25 yards. When I was told "no problem," I was back on the phone with the restaurant, gave them my order, along with my credit card number, and told them that a kid will be there, in about 10 minutes. No more than 20 minutes later a car pulled up and the driver knocked on my front door, carrying a piping hot pizza and two exquisitely crafted desserts. A $5 tip and my date and I topped off a perfect meal. The snow got so heavy that she had to stay over (what a shame) and we ended up breakfasting on micro-waved pepperoni and sausage pizza.

NUGGET

I guess it's that there's more than one way to skin a cat, drink champagne, buy sweet potatoes or dine on Crème Brulee. One of the more popular suggestions, in this day and age, is to "Think outside the box." Since no one ever bothers to tell you where the box is, or what it looks like,

I will translate that to read "DON'T EVER BE AFRAID OF YOUR OWN CREATIVITY AND IMAGINATION!"

Killing Two (Or More) Birds (Figuratively, Not Literally) With One Car

There's a very nice side story here that has all sorts of business implications – specifically regarding how to increase your revenues, without adding expenses.

The day after the "French custard" experience I drove over to the restaurant (to return their two ceramic dishes) and then to the pizza place to personally thank their manager (the roads had been cleared). While we were talking I noticed that there was a Blockbuster, a couple of stores away. I suggested that they try running an ad that said "A pizza and a movie for only $10.They would pick up the movie and deliver it with the pizza (it would be the customers responsibility to return the video).

I knew the idea was working when I saw their ad, featuring this offer, running week after week, in our local paper. After a couple of months I decided that the manager had an exceptionally bright future in the world of business. He had added on the fact that if the customer used the dry-cleaning facility, in the same strip mall, he would pick up their clothing for no charge. He even went so far as to reverse the process, giving the Blockbuster and dry cleaner discount coupons for his store. I don't know where he is now, but we could sure use him in Washington, DC.

Sometimes the Adage is Wrong

From the time that most of us are children we are told, "Tis better to give than receive." I have grown to believe that this is true and, hopefully, have "indoctrinated" my son to think the same way. However, I know of at least one instance when it was wrong.

Let me set a scenario.

You are attending a trade show, Chamber of Commerce meeting, etc. Just think of any event that will be attended by a number of people you would like to have as customers. Having them all in the same room is the good news. The bad news is the fact that there will be a couple of dozen other people, just like you, hoping to land a "big fish" or two.

If you stroll around for a few minutes, it won't take long for you to hear the same phrase, over and over – "Let me give you my card."

Now, flash forward to the next morning. Picture a potential buyer/client sitting at his or her desk, faced with 24 business cards and a small mountain of brochures. When they look at the cards they will have a great deal of trouble matching up faces to names. In fact, they will probably be trying to figure out why they have your card at all.

Ok, it's time to flash backwards 14 hours. Before you approach someone "hang out" in their vicinity for a few minutes – and do some unobtrusive eavesdropping. When you do get to talk to them, even it it's only for a minute, try to mention a fact or two you "overheard" and then – and this is the key – ask them for their card. As soon as possible after doing that, walk away, turn over the card, and jot down a few meaningful notes.

Here is how it played out in real life.

As you will learn later I was doing some consulting work for a chain of automotive repair shops – nine locations plus two that did body work. They felt that their business was stagnating so they wanted to tap into some new markets.

There was a big tri-city (Phoenix, Scottsdale and Tempe, AZ) Chamber of Commerce event, where representatives of most of the major businesses in the area would be in attendance.

I wandered around with my client, just to make sure he was doing what I told him was necessary. Specifically he was to ask anyone he talked to if their business had any company vehicles and, if so, how many. As soon as he had 10 seconds of "all-alone-time" available he was to put that number on the back of their card.

I sat down with him, the next day. He had 21 cards, with numbers ranging from four to 23 (most of the people he talked to didn't qualify, but that should never slow you down. Remember, in major league baseball, if you are right three out of every ten times - three hits in ten at bats - you will get paid several million dollars a year).

Here is the letter he sent out that same day:

Dear Mr. (Ms.) Jones (by the way, the reason I've decided on the "generic" Jones is that I believe that Mr. or Ms. Smith must be exhausted by now),

It was a pleasure meeting you at the Chamber of Commerce event yesterday.

You mentioned that you have 16 company-owned vehicles and I'm sure they have to be serviced frequently, as it goes without saying that you don't want them to become rapidly depreciating assets. Well, to paraphrase all those television infomercials, "Have we got a deal for you." For each car or truck of yours that we service you will get a 1% discount. If we handle all 16 that will cut your expenses by 16% - on each and every vehicle. That's 16% on parts and 16% on labor.

And, to make things even better, we have a facility in your area so we would be pleased to pick up your vehicles and deliver them back to you, the same day – and there's no extra charge for this service.

Still thinking about it? We'll toss in the fact that all of your employees qualify for the same discount you receive.

It would be easy to provide you with a myriad of testimonials but I think I can sum them up in one simple statistic. 94% of our customers come back again, and we're pretty sure that at least 3% of them moved, before it was time for their next oil change.

I will call you in a few days to see how we might move forward. If this turns out to be the type of decision that is below your pay grade, I'm sure you will be able to pass it down, so that the right person and I can talk.

Naturally, if you have any questions, or require any additional information, please do not hesitate to call,

Thank you for your time and consideration.

Cordially,

etc.

These letters were individually signed and sent out in hand-addressed envelopes where the name and address were printed directly on them (no labels). And stamps, not meters, were used for postage – and not one of those "universal" generic ones such as the Liberty Bell or American Flag (I mention this several times, because these stamps are now seen to be on the envelope of some type of "junk" mail).

I was so confident in what was going to happen next that I waived my fee of $5,000 for this job. Instead, I was willing to "bet on the come" by only getting paid if I was right.

Here's what happened.

Over the course of the next six months he serviced 113 cars, from 17 companies and/or their employees (almost all of them more than once). My agreement was that I would get paid $10 the first time a vehicle came in, $50 the second time and $10 thereafter. Since his retention rate was 93% this worked out quite well – for both of us. Their initial visits paid me $1,130 but the 2nd ones brought in $4,650 (113 vehicles X 93% X $50). So I was already $780 (15.6%) ahead of the game (my standard $5,000 fee). When I told him that I was moving to Arizona he asked if he could "buy out" the balance of our agreement, for $5,000. When I said yes, it meant that I had netted $10,780 - more than double what I would have otherwise received.

NUGGET

Sometimes it's OK to do the asking, and clients like it when you are willing to bet on being right since that creates a true win/win (or lose/lose) situation. And remember, it's the second order/purchase/servicing that is the most critical. The first one is often nothing more than a "let's-see-what-they've-got" transaction. Hurdle that cleanly and promptly and you will likely have a CFL (Customer for Life).

Career Choices – Where Do I Go From Here?

One of the first youngsters I knew who needed mentoring was my son. I am a single dad and learned that Justin tended to take the things I would suggest to him with the proverbial "grain of salt" (why is it never called "a grain of pepper?"). I'm convinced he believed that I had read a book on parenting and was simply regurgitating the mantras of one or more authors. It wasn't so much that he thought I was lying to him but rather that I was simply saying things because I was required to. Whatever the reason, he rarely listened.

That's why the concept of "disinterested third party intervention" quickly became appealing. If Justin was told something by a person with no apparent vested interest in him, it was much more likely to sink in.

There is a tendency, among all parents I suppose, to treat the future of our child, or children, with a degree of urgency. Who among us has not questioned an offspring about what they are planning after graduation? For the person on the receiving end of the question it can get a bit daunting.

Justin had finally settled on a major of Hotel and Restaurant Management but did not exactly understand why, at least using reasons he was able/willing to express to me. Once I realized this I asked John, my next-door neighbor, closer in age to my son than he was to me, to step in.

So he sat down with Justin and told him that he was Justin's genie and that he was there to grant him one wish – that in 15 years, when he was 36, Justin would be able to have any job he wanted. Assuming that were true, John wanted to know what Justin would opt for.

My son's answer, quite reasonable considering his schooling, was that in 15 years he would like to own his own restaurant.

John then began a trip backwards, believing that it's much easier to return from a destination than it is to get there in the first place, when you must spend a good deal of time just figuring out what station to go to, let alone which train to get on.

John then said to Justin, "That sounds like a good idea to me. Now, if you want to own your own restaurant in 15 years what will you have to be doing, 12 years from now, that will give you the necessary experience needed to take that last step?"

Justin thought for a minute and said, "I'd probably need to be running a restaurant, like as a General Manager, for three years."

John, quoting Richard Dawson (for all you former "Match Game" addicts) said, "Good answer. Now, what job should you have nine years from now to get hired as a General Manager?"

Justin's answer? "Assistant General Manager."

You can see where things are headed. It only took a few more questions for Justin to have a pretty good timeline in front of him and realize that taking a job as a waiter was not only a good idea but part of an overall plan, something he hadn't had before. Justin's life, and future, suddenly were a whole lot less confusing.

There are two lessons to be learned here. First, you may not always be the best person to get a point across. The very simple fact that you have a personal interest in the relationship (i.e. agency to client, manufacturer to buyer) may eventually mean that you will start being tuned out. This is why professional sports teams often change managers/coaches. It's hard to get "buy in" from a player who has been hearing the same pep talk for seven years. College coaches don't face that same problem because players are constantly rotating through the system. Of course all this reasoning pales before the most important consideration – winning often, sad to say, at all costs.

If the point you're trying to make is really important, provide it to one of the people who reports to your client, or a friend of theirs. Once again, try to remember what Harry Truman once said "It is amazing what you can accomplish if you do not care who gets the credit."

The second thing to understand is that "if you don't know where you are going, any train will get you there." There is an ancient proverb that says, "The journey of 1,000 miles begins with but a single step." While that is certainly true, the problem is that, if it's in the opposite direction it should be, you might end up 2,000 miles away from your goal.

So, before you take that first step make sure that, if it's a client, they tell you their specific goal(s). Do they want sales to increase by 25% a year, for the next five years? Do they want to have the size of their donor database double in three?

A word of caution here. Don't let those goals be too short-term. One reason the Japanese were able to get a strong foothold in this country is that they understood that it was not necessary to make a profit immediately. Far too often, in the U.S., in order to satisfy shareholders and analysts, businesses want results in one or two fiscal quarters and that may not be possible.

Sometimes it really is a "two steps forward, one step back" process and, with equal frequency, the one-step-back part comes first. I was consulting for a non-profit who had that donor goal I just mentioned. The first thing I did was reduce the size of their existing list, something they had never done. They believed that "Once a donor always a donor." Of course this didn't take into account that people do die and others haven't given money in 20 years. They weren't even aware of the fact that, twice a year, they should run their list against the NCOA (National Change of Address) file and make the corrections and deletions accordingly.

At the end of the first three months I told them that there was both bad news and good news. I had reduced the size of their list by 30% (bad) but I had cut their expenses (printing and postage) by an equal amount. The last sentence in my report said that you should never try to erect a building until you're sure the foundation is solid.

Fortunately (for both of us) they accepted my explanation and it only took two years to double the size of their list – and this time it consisted of meaningful names.

(Note: In the case of my son, while the backwards thinking didn't work out as planned, he did start out as a waiter, in Vail, CO. While doing that job he met someone who pointed out that Justin could take his real love, and turn it into a career. This is evidenced by the fact that it's 15 years later and Justin still does not own a restaurant. Instead he is a reggae disc jockey, with his own radio show and several awards won – and it's highly unlikely that this would have happened had taken a different first step).

A Surprising Window of Opportunity

Since I just mentioned non-profits I thought this would be a good time to point out something that most people in the fundraising business seem unaware of – a "window of opportunity" that, at first glance, doesn't seem to make much sense.

When I was the "Big Cheese" (sorry, I could resist from using this term) of three 501(c) (3) organizations, I made sure that we mailed out solicitation letters on Dec. 24th. There are two reasons why these are so successful. First, they arrive before the recipients get their credit card bills – the ones that reflect how much they spent for presents. And second, they can use guilt as the primary message – something to the effect that "Now that you're enjoying all the things you received during the holiday season, why not do something to help those who were not so fortunate."

We compared the results against mailings done at other times of the year, and the donations we received, from Dec. 27th – January 10th, consistently beat any other two week period – and usually by a lot.

Can't Fall asleep? Do You Toss and Turn All Night? Try Reading a Stack of Resumes

One day I was sitting in our HR Director's office when she pointed to a foot-high stack of papers on her desk. She told me that there were a couple of people out sick in her department and asked if I could help out by screening a stack of resumes and picking out the ones I felt represented qualified applicants. She then added that I might find this to be the equivalent of intellectual root canal.

To prove her point she pulled the top dozen off the pile. She told me that she and her HR associates spend two-three minutes reading a resume for the first time. I was asked to do the same and so I spent the next 30 minutes looking through what she handed me.

What she didn't tell me was that there was going to be a test when I was finished, one that proved somewhat

embarrassing to me and should have been highly
disturbing to the 12 people whose futures I possibly held
in my hand.

After I completed my assigned task she asked me to
wait for a half an hour and see if I could remember a
single person's name. I could only recall one (probably
because he was also a Philip). She then inquired what I
could remember about one or more of the applicants.
There were a couple of minor things but I could not, for
the life of me, tell her which person had done what.

She pointed out that the original stack held 115 such
documents and that this was a typical response to an ad
offering an employment opportunity. And, she added,
every one of the remaining 103 "curriculum vitae" looked
and read exactly the same as the ones I had attempted
to digest. They all used exactly the same language (she
called it "resumespeak") and they all seemed incredibly
determined to convince the reader that the applicant
was identical to everyone they were competing with.

We then sat down with our Vice President - HR to get a
bit more information. She confirmed that they averaged
about 100 applications per opening and added that, at
least in the case of their company, roughly 50% of them
came from people who appeared to be qualified. This
meant that, even if yours was among those selected for
re-examination, your odds on getting the job were about
one in fifty.

She went on to add a number of things that might, or
might not, impact a decision – her ability to concentrate
on what she was reading, her mood at the time and,
perhaps of greatest importance, the quality of the
resumes that she read directly before she got to yours.
If you can figure out how to do this you should get
your resume directly under some very inferior ones. The

problem here is if the evaluator gets disgusted and stops reading, just when he or she is about to read yours. The next time, when they pick up where they left off, you will have lost your "competitive edge."

She and I then went out to lunch and she asked me what I had learned from this. When I stumbled a bit with my answer she suggested that I consider the adage I mentioned earlier – "In the land of the blind the one eyed man is king." This is the perfect place to add a revelation (at least for me). For years, when using this quote, I attributed it to Mark Twain – it does sound like something he would have said. However, when proofreading and fact checking this manuscript, I discovered that it was originally said by Erasmus, some 400 years before Mr. Twain was born.

"Look," she said, "if the odds of you getting a job are as bad as they obviously are, why not take some risks. I mean what's the worst thing that can happen – that you won't get a job you probably weren't going to get anyhow? I'm not suggesting that someone do anything in bad taste but do something that sets you apart from what looks like a flock of sheep."

I think this goes back to something I mentioned earlier - that I never believe in competing on a level playing field.

She asked me what I could tell her about the 12 people whose resumes I had read – not about where they went to school or the jobs they had held but about the types of people they were. It didn't take any heavy thinking to conclude that I knew absolutely nothing about what made them tick.

That night I spent a great deal of time thinking about this, especially in light of the fact that, the next day, I had a meeting with the three about-to-be college graduates I was mentoring. Appropriately enough, the subject matter for that get-together was going to be resumes. Thus was born the idea of the "alternative" version.

The three youngsters I met with were a young lady who was looking for an entry-level position with a non-profit, another young lady who wished to pursue a career in sports management and a young man who was after a job as the computer expert, for a company who, when it came to technology, was "lost in cyber-space."

The sports-related job would be the most difficult. Almost every person in that field was male, so she had to convince them that, when it came to sports, she could be one of the guys. The computer geek did not have to really worry about speaking the language of the employer he was interested in because, when it came to technology, their vocabulary was very limited. However, he should expect that they might show what he submitted to some people with expertise in the field and ask them, "Does this kid know what he's talking about?"

We went over the resumes they were currently using. It didn't take long to conclude that they had read the same "How to Write a Resume" book that had been the basis for everything I had looked at the day before. Yes, the "Three E's" were there – education, experience and expertise - but not much else. I recently read a Human Resources Director equate trying to get to know the "real" person, whose name is on the top of a standard resume, with being able to determine someone's hair color, once you know their height.

I suggested to them that while it is important to submit a resume such as the one's they had already written, I thought that they should consider drafting a second one as well - an "alternative" version.

Here's what I proposed. Write down things that reflect your personality, that suggest you have a sense of humor, that emphasize your work ethic and the fact that you'd probably be fun to be around – not in a frivolous sense but with language that should make people smile. I can tell you, from having been a member of several search committees, if you did a word-association test, and asked people the first word they think of when they hear "resume," the word "smile" would never be heard ("boring" would be in everyone's top three).

Get across the point that you will fit in easily, that you're a team player and that, especially in the case of the sports and computer jobs, you speak their language. And again, don't shy away from showing that you have a sense of humor. A number of people are afraid of doing this for fear that no one will get the joke. But, as you are about to read, I'm not talking about things with punch lines (unless you're auditioning for "The Improv"). Finally, I told them to keep their sentences very short (unlike what you're reading right now) so that the document can be easily read, even by someone with little time, who is tired, or who is being distracted.

I tossed out a few ideas and then let them have at it. When they finished, I made copies of everyone's results and passed them out. The group, including me, then made editorial comments and took phrases that someone else had come up with, that they really liked, and worked them into their own versions (I feels strongly that one should always use the BASE system – Borrow And Steal Everything – not really everything, although I do subscribe to the fact that, in certain cases, once you have obtained permission, plagiarism is the highest form of flattery).

Here now are the final versions of the three "alternative" approaches. Each was submitted with a standard version, references and a short covering letter. After you've had a chance to read them (and it won't take long), I'll fill you in on the results.

Telling Them Who You Really Are

ALTERNATIVE RESUME #1 –
Entry level position with a non-profit

I collate.	I say please
I staple.	I say thank you
I stuff envelopes.	I send e-mails
I lick stamps.	I proofread
I empty wastepaper baskets.	I do windows
I alphabetize.	I file.
I balance my checkbook.	I follow directions.
I pick up.	I deliver.
I arrive early.	I stay late.
I can work Saturdays.	I can work Sundays.
I can work holidays.	I look good in a team uniform.
I do what it takes.	I write thank you notes.
I edit (first drafts)	I edit (subsequent drafts)
I pitch in	I help out
I get excited	I stay calm.

95

I never quit

I'm not picky

I appreciate kindness.

I can have four pots
cooking on the stove
without burning anything.

I know when to say when.

I almost never repeat
myself.

I respect those older
than me and try to
learn from them.

I love my parents.

My parents love me.

I give credit – when
credit is due.

I know how to follow.

I volunteer.

I cry.

I care

I almost never say never

I'm very choosy

I can juggle at least three
things at the same time.

I love to brag about
where I work.

I almost never get sick.

I almost never repeat
myself.

I respect those younger
than me and hope to
mentor them.

I like my parents.

My parents like me.

I know when to lead.

I type.

I smile.

I laugh.

I know there is no "i" in
team, boast or me.

I am a work in progress who is a lot closer to attaining my
goals than to the station my train pulled out of. I believe
that my voyage would move measurably faster as part of
your organization and hope you feel the same way.

ALTERNATIVE RESUME #2 – Sports Marketing

1. I do not have an agent.
2. I won't cause any salary cap concerns.
3. I do not require a signing bonus.
4. I will not force you into paying a luxury tax.
5. I report on time, ready to play, from day one.
6. I attend mini-camps without complaint.
7. My favorite four-letter word is ESPN.
8. I show up early for spring training.
9. The only time I've ever been in jail was in a Monopoly game.
10. I only need to be given directions once – whether it is on how to do my job or find the event/ballpark/luncheon/dinner/seminar/printer/meeting, etc.
11. When my computer crashes I can serve as crash control.
12. I volunteer for community service projects without being asked.
13. The only thing in my medicine cabinet is aspirin.
14. I would never miss an "optional" practice.
15. I'd need a map to find the trainer's room.
16. If I dislocate a finger I snap it back into place and get back in the game.
17. I understand that if you're five minutes early, you're late.
18. I can wash, and repair, my own uniforms.
19. I don't say stupid things to the media.

20. I willingly sign autographs.

21. I do not require first class airfare or a hotel suite.

22. I don't sulk if I'm not starting.

23. I will not only get the coffee, I can make the coffee.

24. I always vote for my teammates on All-Star ballots.

25. I have no tattoos.

26. I'm very coachable.

27. I play multiple positions.

28. I'm never on injured reserve.

29. I dress properly on the road.

30. I won't demand to renegotiate my contract.

31. I can speak for five minutes without saying "like y' know" even once.

32. I will never fall over from the weight of my own jewelry.

33. I will never ask, "What hours am I expected to work?" because it makes absolutely no difference to me. The only reason I wear a watch is to make sure I'm on time for appointments, meetings or practices.

34. I am a textbook definition of a team player. Individual victories mean nothing when it comes to determining who wins and who loses.

35. I tend to win because winning is important and I care so much. But I only win as part of a team.

36. I'm arrogant enough to be occasionally cocky but humble enough to know that I've still got a lot

to learn. I am a work in progress well past rookie camp.

37. I don't want just any job. I want to work for you.

38. My sneakers are laced up, my cap is on straight and I am truly ready to hit the ground running.

ALTERNATIVE RESUME #3 – Technical Support

- I install.

- I re-install.

- I uninstall.

- I network.

- I network networkers.

- I never panic.

- I calm down people who do panic.

- I create files and folders.

- I know the difference between a file and a folder.

- I download.

- I upload.

- I communicate with hardware and software companies.

- I speak their language.

- I translate their language to your language.

- I bring the coffee.

- I can make the coffee.

- I configure.

- I reconfigure.

- I eat hackers for breakfast.

- I spit them out before lunch.

- I hook up.

- I manage crashes.

- I install firewalls.

- I delete the cookies (and caches) – but never touch the Oreos.

- I read the directions.

- I write the directions.

- I program.

- I input.

- I'm comfortable with mice and modems.

- I know that Control, Alt, Delete is not a law firm.

- I'm conversant in MS Word, Excel, Access, PowerPoint, QuarkXpress, Adobe Illustrator, Photoshop and every variation of Windows you might have in your office.

- I do what it takes to get the job done.

- **If I look at my watch it's too much like work. The only reason I wear one is to make sure that I'm on time for appointments.**

- **I can speak entire sentences without saying "like y'know" even once.**

- **I have no tattoos.**

- **I won't fall over from the weight of my own jewelry.**

- **The only time I've ever been in jail was in a Monopoly game.**

- **My idea of a strong drug is a baby aspirin.**

- **I've been called a geek and a nerd.**

- **I am a geek and a nerd.**

- **Companies with no geeks and nerds will face extinction a whole lot faster than the dinosaurs did, possibly in less than a year.**

So, how did these three stories turn out?

- The young lady, looking for a job with a non-profit, called me a week after sending in her first job applications. She could barely contain her delight as one of her "targeted organizations" offered her a position with a slightly higher salary than she had hoped for. Two days later she was calling again, this time with a bit of a problem. It seems that the second organization where she had applied wanted to hire her as well. And, within 24 hours she got an offer from the third place she had submitted her resumes to. All three were outstanding opportunities and all three mentioned how impressed they were with her unique approach. Wouldn't you love to be faced with her kind of problem?

- The sports marketing person ended up with a shorter time frame. She faxed in her material to the "I would kill to get a job with" organization, was interviewed the next day and offered that job the following morning.

- The fastest response occurred with the young man looking to provide technical support for a company desperately in need of a "computer doctor." He also faxed in his resumes and, an hour after doing so, got a call asking if I had sent this to anyone else and, even if he did, could he start the next day.

After each of them had been working for a few months, I got their permission to interview their respective HR Departments. What I wanted to know was what it was that caused them to respond so positively, and quickly, to these three applicants?

The answers I got were almost identical – we liked the idea that they spoke our language, that they seemed to be the type of person who wouldn't bitch and moan if asked to do something trivial and that they appeared to possess all those qualities that are almost impossible to teach.

Perhaps the most flattering thing of all was that two of the HR directors asked if they could "borrow" the alternative style, one for a daughter and one for a nephew. A few months later I got a call from each of them, letting me know that both the daughter and nephew had gotten the jobs they wanted.

Now, please understand, this was not designed to work for every person or be suitable for every opportunity. In fact, when I presented this idea at a seminar, a fellow panelist suggested that if he ever received something like this in the mail he would toss it in the garbage as he found it to be totally unprofessional. After the session broke up, several members of the audience came up to me and pointed out that his comment could be an indirect form of self-selection, since none of them would ever want to work for a company that couldn't enjoy and appreciate the alternative type of approach.

There is one other scenario I developed that I would encourage readers (or their children, looking for gainful employment) to consider. It relates to the fact that we live in an increasingly visual world where there is more and more demand for "15 second photo/sound bites." If you accept this to be true, how might you present a "picture" of yourself – something that would, almost instantly, allow someone to have a sense of who you are, what you do, what you believe in and how hard you're willing to word? I suggest a one-week calendar "visual."

	Sun	Mon	Tue	Wed	Thu	Fri	Sat
Mon. - pick up donuts @ 7 AM / Mon. –Drycleaners / Tues - 12 PM – Lunch w/Ed / Wed – 1 PM – Dentist / Thur. 7 PM – Rotary speech / Fri. 2 PM – proof read brochure	1	2	3	4	5	6	7
	9 AM – Church / Dad's Birthday	Staff Mtg – 8 AM / 8 PM – Race for the Cure Mtg	7 AM – Printers / 3 PM – take client to airport	7:30 AM – Client / 7 PM – Gym	7 AM – Excel Training / 5 PM – oil change	9 AM – Creative / Staff Mtg / 8 PM – Gym	9 AM – Habitat for Humanity / 12 PM – Trade show
	Make airline reservations for Thanksgiving.	Order DVDs w/ Amazon.	Give spare key to Suzanne.	Sent get well card to Alice.	Get baby shower gift.		

I suggest you make note of a number of things.

- It indicates that the individual whose life is being described has no problem coming in early, staying late or working on weekends.

- Entries such as the one related to Habitat for Humanity suggest a community-minded person.

- There is the human touch of remembering someone's birthday.

- Everything that's on the outside should have a line, ending with an arrow, taking it to the appropriate day.

- Use Magic Markers of different colors – but not too many because making this look like a rainbow can be too distracting. I would have done that here but just one page of color almost doubles the cost of printing.

- Unlike what you see here, your entries should be handwritten and they should not look as if you spent a lot of time "lining things up." This is intended to depict someone who thrives on staying busy.

The suggestion is that this be used as a possible "closer," when you are (hopefully) being interviewed. The person you are talking to has already seen all your printed material so you might, at some point in the conversation, hand this to them and say, "let me tell you a little bit more about myself by having you look at this."

Again, is the appropriate 100% of the time? Of course not. Will it be helpful more often than not? Absolutely!

While the examples I've given were intended for use by individuals, there is no reason they can't be employed in the world of business. For example your "alternative qualifications" might look like this.

- If we show up five minutes early we're late.

- If we don't beat your deadline fire us.

- If our product/service doesn't meet your specifications, what you said wasn't what we heard, and we should have asked for clarifications.

- If we don't come in at least 5% under budget we need a refresher course in math.

- We believe that "no can do" is a dessert listed on the menu at a Chinese restaurant.

- If you want "soup," we'll give you soup.

- If you want "nuts," nuts are what you'll receive.

- If you want both you will get both – and everything in between.

- We offer steak, not sizzle; quality in lieu of quantity and show more than tell.

- We always wear sneakers because we not only walk the walk, we often hit the ground running.

- We expect that you will tell your competitors how terrible we are. If you don't they may try to "swipe" us, although that almost never happens, because we believe in loyalty.

- Finally, we ask for loyalty in return, but only as long as we get the job done, using the highest standards (yours and ours). Remember, "The flavor of the month" only lasts for 28, 29, 30 or 31 days.

NUGGET

There is an acronym that is very appropriate here WYRIATI – "What you read is all there is." While in most cases this is not true consider it in terms of a resume. As far as an evaluator is concerned this is all they know about you and, when that's the case "all they know" should be as much of you as is possible – and a standard resume doesn't come close to accomplishing that,

A suggestion:

If you are the one doing the hiring ask every applicant to create an "Alternative Resume" in addition to the standard one where all you really learn is if they have those "Three E's" – experience, education and expertise. When they ask for clarification, as they surely will, hand them an example of one – as written by an eight-year-old.

- I make my bed.

- I walk the dog.

- I say please.

- I say thank you.

- I do my homework.

- I brush my teeth.

- I rake the leaves.

- I don't ask for pizza – more than once a week.

- I don't lie.

- I don't bully.

- I don't use bad words.

- I don't talk to strangers.

- I give 10% of my allowance to a charity.

- I put 10% of my allowance in my piggy bank.

And, if there's a way to do this, give each applicant a writing "test." This will reveal a great deal about an applicant's skills – their ability to think on their feet (while sitting down), how they deal with pressure and how creative they can be. I'm convinced that two of the jobs I got, with non-profits, were a result of the fundraising letter I produced (as if I've not given you enough to read, I'm including one). In many ways I think this is the best thing I've ever written, in part because I was able to produce it in 30 minutes and in part because the idea I came up with converted me from being an atheist into an agnostic – my religious friends say that this proves there's still hope for me. What follows is known as a "long form" (surprise, surprise) solicitation which can be very appropriate in certain situations.

MAKE-A-WISH FOUNDATION LETTERHEAD

Dear ,

The letter that is enclosed will require about five minutes of your time. We hope that you find the message both a bit different and equally compelling.

However, should that not be the case, please mail back the form anyhow (we pay the postage), with an indication that you would like to have your name removed from our database. The last thing we want is to be intrusive or waste your time, or our time and money. Please be assured that we will follow your wishes.

However, if what we say makes sense to you, please respond accordingly. The support you provide will come pretty close to working some miracles and will help change the lives of everyone we are able to help.

Cordially,

XXX

Executive Director

Make-A-Wish Foundation

MAKE-A-WISH FOUNDATION LETTERHEAD

Dear (personalized),

During a recent conversation among friends, one that became rather animated at times, each of us was asked to explain the reason we gave time and/or money to a particular worthwhile cause. We each put $10 on the table with the plan being that, after all of us had told our stories, there would be a secret ballot. The charity being "pitched" by the person who got the most votes would receive all the money.

When the votes were tabulated there was little doubt as to the winner. Actually there was no doubt, as eight out of ten had my organization's name on a piece of paper (there would have been nine except you were not allowed to vote for yourself).

Especially impressive was the fact that I was up against a myriad of worthwhile causes, ranging from those who assisted the elderly to others targeted at newborns. My competition also included charities raising funds for critical research and those trying to bring aid and comfort to abused children and women. And yet, for all intents and purposes, I received almost every vote.

Until the "presentations" began I had really not given much thought to the matter. As with my friends, I look at volunteering as a way of paying rent for living on the planet. We all supported groups that we felt were accomplishing important things and so my intent was to simply explain the things my organization was trying to do and the resulting impact.

Then, while listening to someone give an impassioned, and quite persuasive, plea for their charity, I was struck with a reason that seemed compelling beyond anything I had previously thought of.

However, my initial internal reaction was that I was simply being pleased with myself and that, when exposed to the scrutiny of others, my "revelation" might prove to have a bit less appeal than my ego was leading me to believe. Suffice it to say, the rationale touched just about everyone so I would like to share it with you and explain **why the Make-A-Wish Foundation is, perhaps, a bit more important than you might have previously thought.**

I have never thought of myself as being a particularly religious person. Every time I think seriously about the subject I find myself more and more confused. When pressed on the subject I explain that I see myself as a humanist and quote a line from a song in "Les Miserables" as an explanation – "To love another person is to see the face of God."

I have come to no conclusion as to what happens after someone dies. I have heard several possibilities and continue to evaluate all of them. One of the most intriguing is that you travel to a world where you get to spend eternity re-living one day from your previous life. Each second of that day would take more than a trillion years to experience again. It's almost too delicious to contemplate.

Now, most of us would probably have no trouble picking out that day. In fact, our biggest problem would be in choosing only one among many – was it the day of the winning touchdown, the prom date, the big promotion? It might be the first time we fell in love, or got married, or became a parent. What a wonderful dilemma, to be faced with so many terrific choices.

Well, for a Make-A-Wish child the day of choice had not happened yet and, unless a lot of people act pretty quickly, it probably never will.

I'm sure there is no need to describe what this rather extraordinary organization does - its mission is in it name. I'm simply trying to point out that the importance may be far greater than you thought.

I was a Make-A-Wish grantor for a teen-age boy whose only request was to see Michael Jordan play basketball. This was accomplished, beyond his wildest imagination. He got to fly to Chicago to see a playoff final, culminating with Mr. Jordan giving Kevin a personally autographed ball and jersey. From that day forward Kevin slept with his gifts. His mom told me that not a day went by that her son's face didn't light up from the memory. And, when he passed away, the jersey and ball were buried with him. I think it took me two days to stop crying.

I would like to believe that this theory about a "next life" is correct. If it is, your contribution will not only let a child's dream come true in his or her lifetime but, perhaps, forever. And, if that occurs, think of how well you will sleep, knowing that you helped make it happen.

Cordially,

etc.

One (of many) slight diversions.

When I was interviewing for a job I was asked to take a "Personality Test" (it was one of the standard ones although I can't remember which). I was put in a conference room, by myself, and was told that I had 30 minutes to complete my answers. Two minutes into my "exam" the lights went out. Since I was pretty sure that they weren't trying to see if I could fill in boxes in the dark, I decided that this was being done to test my "creative problem solving."

As good as I think I am at that sort of thing I kept drawing blanks. So, I stood up in order to find someone to ask what to do. As soon as I did that the lights came back on. It turns out that the room had a motion sensor and, if there was no movement for two minutes, the lights were automatically turned off (they were way ahead of their time as far as "Green" solutions are concerned). But it did provide proof to those who say I can never focus on one thing for very long – after all, I went 120 seconds without moving more than an inch or two.

The Interview

If you are interviewing for a job, do everything possible to be the first or last person they talk to. There are advantages and disadvantages to both.

If you are first, you set the standard against which everyone else will be judged. But, given the time frame involved, this may make you the easiest to forget.

If you go last, you will be the easiest to remember when the search committee does their reviewing. However, it is possible that, by the time they get to you, they will be tired and thus not paying full attention when you tell your story.

Here's one hint if you do go last (or just late in the process). Bring a box of donuts and make some comment to the effect that you know they've put in a long day and are probably tired and hungry. Besides, you wanted to re-energize the room with a sugar rush, before they begin to learn more about you.

And, no matter what position you're in, make sure you get the name and e-mail address of everyone in the room. Before the day of your interview ends, send thank you notes. Tell them you appreciate their attention, the quality and scope of their questions and the latitude they allowed you in answering them. Close by saying how much you look forward the next step in their hiring process and to the possibility of joining their team.

Normally I would suggest that these notes be handwritten but you want to differentiate yourself from other applicants, as quickly as possible, so in this case I recommend using e-mails. Having said that, if you can get handwritten notes delivered the same day, that would be preferable.

(Note: Earlier today I came across a statistic that absolutely amazed me. Prisoners whose parole hearings are in the morning are successful 70% of the time. For those sitting in front of a parole board in the afternoon? 10%. That "amazement" was quickly tempered, when I started to think about it. It's very possible that these

Boards historically have a certain number of paroles that get granted, each time they meet. Since it is obvious, based on these statistics, that they hear enough compelling cases that result in them reaching that number before lunch, the afternoon prisoners have little chance for success.

While I don't think this holds true for job interviews - no matter how good someone being interviewed might be, the committee will almost always meet with those people who have scheduled appointments - it certainly might when it comes to evaluating scholarship applications).

Your Mind is Your Car - Your Words are the Wheels

Your head may be filled with enough good ideas to make you wealthy, beyond your imagination. However, unless that cranial car can move forward, all of that brain power will mean nothing.

You must learn how to clearly express yourself – orally, on pieces of paper and electronically. Your peers may be OK with LOL or "Like 'y knows" but, if you use those in an interview or on an application, you will never be taken seriously.

The only way to improve in these disciplines is to:

- Read things that are well written. You won't learn anything from video games, "tweets" or Facebook postings. YouTube is a non-entity and texting serves little purpose. And any material available at the checkout counter in a supermarket is not worth the paper it's printed on.

- You have to be able to read and absorb. It doesn't have to be Shakespeare but it should be a major newspaper, such as the Wall St. Journal or the New York Times. It doesn't have to be the "National Review" but it should be Time or Newsweek (it never can hurt you to know what's going on in the world).

- Practice talking and no, this does not mean on the telephone. If possible take a course in public speaking, join the debate team or sign up for a school or community theater group. Being able to stand up in front of an audience, and express yourself clearly, with no evidence of stage fright, will put you markedly ahead of 98% of the general public.

- And finally take a course in advanced English composition and/or creative writing.

Your goal should be to reach a point where you can stand in front of a dozen people you don't know, and do a 15-20 minute presentation, without stumbling (this is one of the advantages of using PowerPoint as you can use the words on the screen as your "notes" (a word of warning here – use the "scroll" feature to show only one point at a time, so people can't read ahead – which they always do if you let them – and thus not be paying attention to what you are saying).

And, when they mention that there were two people unable to attend the meeting, make sure you have a "leave behind" for them (as well as for those who were present). These are really easy to do as all you have to do is write a covering letter and then print off the PowerPoint display.

(Note: If you have children looking to enter the job market, or getting ready to apply to college, show them the previous two chapters. My guess is that, one day, they will thank you).

My Time May Not Be Your Time

Franklin D. Roosevelt once pointed out that it took him about an hour to write a one-hour speech. A 30-minute one took two hours, a 15-minute speech required four hours. It eventually got down the point that if all he had available was two minutes, he might require an entire day, to get it just right.

You should definitely spend time creating a two-three minute presentation (the subject matter can be of your own choosing) and practicing delivering it without the use of notes (the best thing to do is either stand in front of a mirror, or a small audience of friends or family members).

A word of caution here. If you are given a time deadline make sure you practice with a stop watch in hand – but even that may not be enough.

Several years ago Jerry Colangelo was kind enough to agree to do a one-minute PSA (Public Service Announcement) for the Crisis Center I was running. The condition was that I write the copy. I certainly understood where FDR was coming from because this task took me several days to complete (I was able to put in more time since I had no presidential duties to worry about).

The sound crew from a local radio station met me in Jerry's office. I handed him the script, he looked at it and said to me, "Philip, you've got to be kidding." When I asked what it was he objected to he didn't bother to answer me. Instead he turned to one of the engineers and said, "Let's do a first take, just to check the volume." Then he added, "Philip, why don't you time this."

When Jerry finished my stopwatch read 2:03 – two minutes and three seconds. I immediately understood what the "you've got to be kidding me" comment meant. Jerry's delivery is slow and deliberate whereas mine resembles almost anyone who grew up in New York City.

And so the editing process started – knocking off ten seconds, then another ten, etc. When it got down to Jerry's time being 1:09 I convinced him to talk just a little bit faster. That caused him to stumble over a few words but, after four more "takes" it was finally a "wrap."

The teaching moment? The phrase "my time is your time" is not always correct. When I did this again, a few years later, I first attended a speech being given by the person who was going to be helping us out. I recorded it and, once I counted his average words-per-minute, I had guidelines that put me in far better shape. This is demonstrated by the fact that the second PSA only needed to be recorded twice.

There's actually another very important lesson to be garnered from this. I was very fortunate in that I knew Jerry fairly well. Had I not, needing an hour to create a one-minute ad would not have been the best way to establish a positive relationship.

NUGGET
(totally unrelated to what you've just read)

Never pretend to know something when you don't. The best thing to say is something to this effect. "At the moment I don't know the answer to that question. However, I know exactly where to find the necessary information so is it OK if I get back to you within the hour?" (And it's fine if you consider Google to be the "where"). But be careful. More than one interviewer has been known to ask a question they already know the answer to, in order to judge your response. Getting caught trying to bluff is never a good thing.

Michelle's Story

Before departing from the subject of applying for a job, there is one other scenario I was involved with that may be of some value, depending on what it is you are trying to accomplish. I'm going to go into some depth here for a couple of reasons. First, my notes are extensive and address something I considered very important – getting a potential customer to understand that you have some in-depth insights into their business. And second, from the moment I met Michelle I developed an "attitude crush" and, to this day, she remains a close friend. The amount of material here is a tribute to the fact that you don't have to have a doctorate, or a master's degree or even a college diploma to succeed. If you have the desire, and a sense of the way things are supposed to be, good things will happen, far more often than not.

Michelle was the first person I ever mentored. She was an absolutely delightful transplanted West Coaster, hoping to make a name for herself in the New York metropolitan area. She did not have much schooling, but was incredibly eager to learn. And she was about to enter the next phase of her life with some real strengths - her infectious and engaging personality, her innate understanding of customer service, even though she had no training in that area and, while not stunning, she was "easy on the eyes." I hope nobody takes that last comment as being sexist, or politically incorrect, so let me see if I can put that another way. Nope, I can't.

After she and I had became friends, I directed her towards Mercedes Benz, where I had a contact. I was quite sure that Michelle would be perfect to serve as a model/spokesperson at the auto shows where Mercedes exhibited.

I'll shorten a story that's several years in length by telling you that this was truly a "duck to water" situation. Michelle loved the job and Mercedes loved Michelle – to the point that they kept giving her more and more responsibilities.

Before long, Michelle was the person in charge. She was hiring the people to work in the Mercedes booths, she was training them and she was developing and implanting policies that Mercedes totally and enthusiastically supported.

There then reached the point that Michelle decided that she wanted to do more with her life. She wanted to own her own business and she asked me for advice.

It only took about five minutes to conclude that Michelle wanted to continue with what she was doing, except that she wanted something that was hers, with her name on the letterhead. This fit one of my rules perfectly that, with all other things being equal, people should do what they are good at.

Within a couple of hours we had outlined a plan – a business that could be used by any automobile manufacturer (in fact, by any company) who exhibited their products. The idea would be to offer them a service on an outsource basis – one that would be of higher quality, and less expensive than what they were currently doing. The name of the business would be **P³** (P cubed or P to the 3rd power) – Professional Product Presentations.

The challenge was going to be to get perspective clients to understand how well Michelle understood their business and how that would translate into to benefits for them. It would be somewhat like submitting a resume, except with some significant differences, the major one being that there was only one thing of real importance – that Michelle represented an improvement over whatever status quo existed because she was so knowledgeable.

She asked for my help in composing a letter. Michelle knew what she wanted to say but was not at all comfortable that she knew how to put those thoughts into words. She was very aware of the fact that I am a reasonably good writer. Furthermore, from our conversations, and the fact that I had attended several shows where she was working, she was very comfortable that I understood her job and what made her so good at it (Michelle did not have an iota of experience in one of the disciplines I mentioned earlier – cohesive writing. This observation is not intended to be pointing a finger as nothing in the work was doing required this skill set).

I am never one who could resist having his ego stroked so when Michelle told me that she couldn't think of anyone who could do a better job in getting **P³** launched, there was no way I could turn her down. This is the letter I composed on her behalf.

Dear Automobile Company Executive (the actual letter would be personalized),

The first few paragraphs of this letter may seem like a strange way to initiate a dialogue but, I believe, they will tell you a great deal about my organization - and me.

I have just concluded a ten-year stint as the Field Supervisor for Mercedes Benz. For all intents and purposes I was in charge of their "space" at every major auto show in the country.

If you ever wanted to find me at one of these exhibitions, all you had to do was come to our area of the hall and observe for five or ten minutes. I would be the well-dressed young lady who was emptying the wastepaper basket.

Why, you might ask, is the person in charge doing a job that appears to be menial, to say the least, and one that Mercedes had surely contracted for? Amazingly, for such a simple question there are three answers.

1. The wastepaper basket needed emptying.

2. Arena maintenance only comes by once an hour and I refuse to allow things to look less than perfect in the interim.

3. I would never ask a member of my staff to do something I had not demonstrated a willingness to do myself ("Do as I do," not "Do as I say").

Having introduced you to a bit of my personal philosophy, please allow me a few additional minutes to explain why I have created **P³ – Professional Product Presentations** (or, as a business associate has affectionately dubbed us, **"Maitre d' Automobiles"**) and why this can be of great benefit to (fill in name of company).

Have you ever gone out to dinner, only to find yourself with a 15-minute wait accompanied by treatment that was less than attentive or, even worse, rude or discourteous? My guess is that even if they had an award-winning gourmet chef the food would not taste all that good.

The fact is, your emotions affect your taste buds and so your entire dining experience is enormously influenced by how you are treated when you first arrive. At the very top of the list of truisms of customer satisfaction is the often repeated adage – "you never get a second chance to make a first impression."

Well, the same holds true at an automobile show. No matter how attractive your vehicles, no matter how appealing their styles and colors, it won't count for much if your staff does not act in a professional manner that creates and maintains a positive mindset in the potential buyer.

My decision to establish **P³** wasn't random, blind or uninformed. I'm not coming to you with what I think is a good idea to fill a perceived need. This was an educated decision, based on years of experience. I know it makes sense and I am equally confident that the need has never been greater.

For the past 10 years I have been with Mercedes Benz, first as a floor team member, then a Regional Manager and finally the Field Supervisor. I have hired and trained staff, worked with exhibition hall managers, interacted with local sales forces and convinced truck drivers to put a priority on deliveries to my location.

Let's face it – with the exception of a few technical gadgets, cars can't talk. And, they most certainly cannot answer questions or assess customer interest. They lack the ability to smile, direct, assist, inform, interact, or solve problems.

The people who work for me do all that and more. They enjoy their work and they communicate that feeling to anyone in their "neighborhood." Both the serious customers and window shoppers love coming into areas staffed by my people because my people are happy to be there and everyone wants to share in that experience.

And, the **P³** personnel appreciate the fact that those who attend the show in the first few hours of opening day are no more important than the last stragglers, still asking questions during the final few minutes of getaway day. My employees may be saying the same things 100 times a day but we are well aware that the person listening has not heard it before.

We fully understand that "the cars are the stars" and we never act in a way to detract from the reason people attend these shows. However, we also know that you need more that statuettes handing out literature and that, very often, a smile and friendly voice converts a skeptic, standing 10 feet away, to an interested party sitting in the front seat of this year's model.

You invest an enormous amount of money in your shows throughout country. **P³** provides you with a way to protect, insure and enhance that investment. We do all your paperwork, we file any reports you need and we keep track of literature inventories. We set things up and we break things down and we arrive early and stay late, without you having to worry about overtime. You do not have to concern yourself with FICA, withholding, benefits, disability or unemployment insurance, laying people off, hiring or firing.

We are familiar with all the exposition halls and their managements. We anticipate problems before they become problems and we work with your marketing arm to maximize the efficiency and effectiveness of your presentation. We are, for all intents and purposes, "soup to nuts."

I invite you to take advantage of the fact that I am constantly being teased for being such a perfectionist. Part of it is the nature of my personality and the rest the result of having earned the equivalent of a doctorate from Mercedes University. There are a number of people who believe that putting on really great shows involves an element of luck but my associates and I all are aware that luck is the residue of design.

Our job it to make your job a good deal easier and a lot less stressful. One of the things you contract for with **P³** is for us to do the worrying. As a result you will get more sleep and see your blood pressure lowered. We will have visitors, at every show where you exhibit, thinking that the folks at (fill in brand name) really have their act together and, if their people are that sharp, it says a lot about their products.

We know what we're doing, we do it very, very well and we would like to do it for (fill in brand name) I will be calling you within the next couple of weeks with the intent of setting up an appointment where we can discuss this in greater detail. If you would like to get in touch before that, please do not hesitate to do so, using the contact information on the letterhead.

Thank you, so very much, for your time, consideration and interest.

Cordially,

Michelle Corpus
President & Chief Executive Officer
Professional Product Presentations

P.S. I have attached two letters directed at the management of an exposition hall. Since these are the people who can make or break your exhibit, I have always found it very helpful to first flatter them by asking for their opinions and then thank them profusely. At the cost of a couple of postage stamps, some serious ego stroking can be employed for your benefit.

P.P.S. I probably misled you a bit at the beginning of this letter. If you would like to find me at a particular auto show you will have to ask for me by name. Everyone who works for me empties wastepaper baskets.

That was the "letter of introduction." The two enclosures were as follows:

Dear Exposition Hall Manager (sent two-three weeks prior to the opening of the show).

In a few weeks my team will be coming to (fill in name of city) to work for (fill in brand name) at your automobile show. Since we are continually growing, and adding new staff, a number of my co-workers will be visiting your city for the first time.

They are always asking me for recommendations of restaurants and other attractions in the immediate area of (fill in name of hotel). I am certainly no expert on these subjects so I thought it would be a good idea to ask someone who knows a good deal more than I do.

With that in mind I would appreciate it if you might take a couple of minutes and fill out the form I have enclosed and return it using the postage paid envelope that I have included. The information you provide will certainly go a long way towards making our stay in your city more enjoyable – and, hopefully, not too fattening.

Thank you so much for your input. We look forward to seeing you, and working with you, very shortly.

Cordially,

etc.

Dear Exposition Hall Manager (sent no more than 48 hours after a show ends),

My teams and I spend about 48 weeks, out of every year, on the road. After a while it becomes hard to differentiate between cities, hotels and show sites.

However, there are certain locales that stand out. It's not the building per se and certainly not the weather, as we rarely get to experience much time outside. What makes a particular location special to us is the way we are treated by the show's management – the fact that we are respected for the job we do and readily assisted when help is necessary.

It is for that reason that (fill in name of city) is a very special market for us at **P³** (Professional Product Presentations) and it is why I am writing to say thank you.

Your staff made our stay comfortable. You created an environment that was pleasant and your people were there when we needed them, treating us as colleagues and not just hired hands. We always got straight answers and accurate information. In the world we live in this is incredibly important and equally rare.

When we do our scheduling it is easy to see why everyone wants to work the show in (fill in name of city). And it is why, whenever anyone asks me who should serve as a model for the way things should get done, I always point them in your direction.

You have our gratitude and appreciation. We look forward to seeing you again next year.

Cordially,

etc.

(Note: If the same person is in charge the following year you can send cards that begin with "We are looking forward to working with you again" and "Once again, thank you."

That was the "package." And I took it a couple of steps further, writing a different variation of the basic letter and a reference letter for Michelle to use as she saw fit. These letters follow:

Dear (fill in name of brand Marketing Manager)

Do you know the answers to the following three questions?

- What is the most frequently asked question at an automobile show?

- What is the best, and fastest, way to get additional literature delivered to a booth?

- If a light bulb in a display burns out, what is the quickest way to get it replaced?

(Note: The answers appear at the end of this letter).

Our job at **P³ (Professional Product Presentations)** is to know the accurate responses to all these questions, and hundreds more. The reason we know them is not so much because we are so smart (although the people who work for me are exceptionally bright).

Instead, it is because we have "been there and done that." We have a wealth of experience that allows us to anticipate problems before they occur and questions before they get asked. If it has happened before it has happened to us. We may not have known exactly how to respond the first time but we certainly know now.

As far as an auto show is concerned we are aware that, if possible, it is a good idea to "empower" the customer. Many of the people in attendance are "experts" (or at least they think of themselves that way) and it never hurts to allow them to demonstrate their expertise. It makes them feel good and, when they do, they tend to want to stay where they are. If they state something we know to be factually incorrect we will diplomatically address the issue and we will certainly fill in any blanks – but we never steal their thunder.

We understand that the relationship between an individual and a car is unique and our job is certainly not to get in the way of that. On the other hand, we want to insure that the introduction of man (or woman) to machine goes as smoothly as possible, so we are available to assist at any time.

Aside from our experience there is something else that will work for your benefit. My staff truly likes what they do and they communicate that feeling to everyone who comes by, from the casual observer to the under-the-hood fanatic. We know that our performance not only impacts your results, it reflects right back on us and determines the future success of our own business.

We invite you to allow **P³** to present your products professionally. It will probably cost you a good deal less than you are currently spending, you will be assured of consistent quality and your cars, trucks and SUV's will get the "packaging" they deserve. When people are asked, as they are leaving a show, which booth stands out in their mind, it is very likely that they will mention the one staffed by **P³** personnel, talking about your vehicles.

I look forward to speaking with you shortly and to working with, and for, you in the near future.

Cordially,

etc.

P.S. The answers to the questions are:

- Where is the nearest restroom?

- Introduce yourself to the administrative assistant in the show management office and have everything addressed to his or her attention. Make sure that person has your cell phone and pager numbers and that you have theirs. And, if you make use of their services, always send a short thank you note.

- On set-up day locate the head electrician and get the name, pager number and cell phone number of their senior person who will be working each day of the show. However, also be sure that you have a couple of spare bulbs in all the appropriate sizes and that you know where the ladders are stored.

As I said earlier, Michelle became a friend, as well as a mentee, so when she asked me if he might consider writing a letter of recommendation I was delighted. This is what got included in Michelle's mailings:

Dear Brand Manager,

I am delighted at being afforded this opportunity to write a letter of recommendation on behalf of Michelle Corpus and her organization – Professional Product Presentations.

I have been in the marketing arena for almost 40 years. Since my area of specialization has been customer service I believe that I am almost uniquely qualified to pass judgment on an operation that deals primarily with that discipline.

I have worked with dozens of companies and lectured to thousands of employees during my career. While I get a lot of lip service agreement, and head-nodding acquiescence, the reality is that most people don't get it. In fact, most would have trouble explaining what "it" is.

I suppose that resumes have their place, as do letters like this, but the real test, the one factor that separates the wheat from the chaff, comes from performance. And, I'm not just talking about the first hour of the first day, when everyone is fresh, well rested and on their toes, knowing that they are being observed or evaluated.

I first met Ms. Corpus quite by accident. About 10 years ago I was attending an auto show. It was the eighth or ninth day the exposition was running and I was waiting to meet an associate, late in the afternoon.

I was standing off to the side of the information desk at the Mercedes booth. Although I was looking away (trying to spot my friend), I could hear the voice of the person behind me. People were asking questions, some pertinent and some rather inane. And yet, no matter how trivial the request was it was met with the same level of interest and enthusiasm. My guess is that you understand what I mean when I say that I could hear the smile.

I have worked well over 100 trade shows. I have spent 10 days in a booth at McCormick Place in Chicago, two weeks at the fairgrounds in Hanover, Germany and enough time at the Javitts Center in New York to qualify for my own locker. The hardest single task, at any of those events, was convincing my staff (and me) that no matter how often we were saying the same thing, it was all new to the person on the receiving end.

My friend was a half hour late that day so I got to listen to 30 minutes of the magic that Ms. Corpus wove – not by doing anything complicated or technical but rather by making each person who talked to her feel as if they were the only one is the exposition hall.

If you've ever watched Tiger Woods play golf, Michael Jordan dunk a basketball, or listened to Pavarotti sing an aria, you recognize that you are in the presence of something very special. While manning a booth at an auto show may not be as high profile, and certainly not as glamorous or well paying, the fact of the matter is, talent is talent.

Because I understood and appreciated that, I made it my business to get to know Ms. Corpus and have had the privilege of watching her progress in the profession she practices. I don't think I'm overstating it even one iota when I tell you that she is as much as the top of the game she plays as Mr. Woods, Jordan or Pavarotti are at theirs.

In the real estate business there is an often-used phrase – "curbside appeal." It relates to the first feelings that a potential client has when her or she approaches a property. That reaction has an enormous influence on any purchasing decisions they will make down the road.

Ms. Corpus understands that far, far better than most. She is aware that she and her staff are the "gatekeepers" to your products and they take that responsibility very seriously.

I am proud to say that Michelle is a friend but I would not be writing this if that was all this is about. I am very protective of my own reputation so the letters of recommendation I write are very few and very far between.

I insist that people judge me by the company I keep so, I suppose, you might say there are some selfish motives behind this. Who knows? One day I might want to do business with you and the likelihood of that happening will be enhanced based on your previous experiences with what I've had to say. And, even if that doesn't happen, save this letter. If you do end up retaining her company you will probably want to send me a thank you note.

Cordially,

Philip Barnett

If you can find someone to compose a letter of recommendation similar to this one, written about you, you may not need to read anything else in this book. Yes, I know, I just congratulated myself for a job well done. But, the fact of the matter is, I've written 11 similar letters in the course of my life and 10 of them have been instrumental insofar as a person either getting the job they wanted or the acceptance letter they sought. In the words of baseball legend Dizzy Dean, "It ain't bragging if you can do it."

Michelle ended up creating a "package." The covering letter combined the copy points in the two samples cited earlier. It went with the letters to the exposition hall managers and the one from me. Since the potential client list was very small, she was able to spend some money on high- grade paper, calligraphy for the envelope addresses, etc.

What was the result? Well, you can actually find that out for yourself. Next time you are at an auto show and find someone at a booth, doing a well above average job, ask them who they work for. My guess is that, having read all this, their answer will not surprise you.

NUGGET

My point here was that anyone can use this formula when applying for a job or when trying to bring in new business for whoever employs you. If you can convince the reader that you speak their language, and that

you are well ahead of their learning curve, you will dramatically widen their comfort zones, vis a vis how they look at you.

By presenting yourself as the equivalent of being an immediate asset for their balance sheet you should become almost irresistible. And remember, they can easily pay you at least 10% more as a "non-employee" and still save money, since they would have no concern with any kind of benefits and there would be no F.I.C.A match to worry about.

Marketing – What it is and Why it's Important

What is marketing? Well, here's my definition – one they will never teach you in business school and, although a bit tongue-in-cheek, it is often quite accurate.

"Advertising is trying to convince somebody to buy something they often do not need, for more money than they can probably afford to spend. Marketing is getting them to buy it more than once."

In the course of speaking on this subject I invariably insult at least a half dozen businesses represented in the room. I never mean anything personal by it but I explain that if I were to stand there, and simply applaud them for what they were doing right, I would be wasting both my time and theirs. So, I would go on to say, I was going to tell them some of the mistakes they are making.

However, as I said earlier, unlike the typical MBA (or Dr. Johnson), I never load them up on theory. Instead, I offer solutions. Some are short term band-aids and others long term (major surgery), but all are designed to turn things around if they were headed in the wrong direction or strengthen something that is already good, but could be much better.

133

In my seminars I repeatedly mention to not be blinded by the idea of "instant success" and understand that patience is sometimes a virtue. (I wish the people in the media understood this because their mantra seems to be that getting it first is more important than getting it right). Ask the people who have been described as having "burst upon the scene" and most of them will tell you that the word "instant" equaled 15 years of hard work and even that may not have been enough. Almost every comedian will tell you that getting "discovered," at "The Improv," came after they'd been playing half-empty rooms, in cities you've never heard of.

(Note: Apropos of almost nothing, years ago there was a Danish classical piano player/comedian (a strange combination indeed) named Victor Borge – one of the two or three funniest people I've ever seen perform. One of the stories he told was about his uncle, who was an inventor.

One day, in his lab, he concocted a soft drink he called "One Up." He didn't like the taste so he created "Two Up." Still not satisfied he came up with "Three Up." When he put that on the market, and it didn't sell very well, he went back to his lab and fiddled around until he had "Four Up." While that was not a big seller he knew he was getting closer and he was quickly able to do some tweaking which resulted in "Five Up," followed by "Six Up." And then he died, without ever knowing how close he had come).

On a somewhat different note I believe that "Luck is the residue of design." Here is how I explain that.

Everyone I have ever known who has been "lucky," including myself, has repeatedly put themselves in a position to have good things happen to them. We understand that there is success and there is education, so we don't fear failure. That is, perhaps, the key reason why we are ready and able to try so often – to get "lucky."

The opposite adage, the one that many believe but which I feel will doom you to a life of disappointment, is "all good things come to those who wait." (not to be confused with patience). The only things that come to those who wait are your bills and maybe the kid from Domino's (although even that requires you to make a phone call). People who sit around, hoping for that $10,000,000 check from Publisher's Clearing House, will get covered in cobwebs, waiting for their doorbell to ring. I have always told friends that if I ever appear to not be pro-active they should take me straight to the hospital, or possibly the morgue.

Just to show that the more things change the more they remain the same, I was faced with a similar situation some 30 years after my first presentation. My son was a sophomore in high school and was in the process of learning that girls were not the enemy or a population to be ignored.

One evening he wandered into my room and said he needed some advice. I slapped myself a couple of times to recover from the shock – this was a first – and asked how I could help.

He explained that there was this girl at school who he really wanted to ask out, but he didn't know what to do.

I pretended to give it some very serious thought then suddenly jumped up and yelled, "I've got it." He face lit up in delight as he waited to hear my solution.

"Justin, here's what you should do," I said. "Ask her."

He immediately became crestfallen as he muttered "Aw dad."

"Look Justin," I responded, "You really want to go out with this girl, right?"

"Sure" he answered.

"Well," I said, would it be fair to say that if you go out with her that can be defined as success and if you don't it can be called failure?"

"I guess so," he agreed.

"OK" I went on. "If you don't ask her then failure is absolutely, 100% guaranteed. If you do ask her you might end up with the same result but at least you've given yourself a chance that she'll say yes. And, if she says no, so what? She really doesn't know who "you" really are, so she can't really be turning "you" down.

I would like to say that, from then on, Justin's social successes replicated those of mine (because I learned to always ask, as explained in the story that follows), several generations earlier, but it was not to be. He decided that rejection was outside his comfort zone and opted not to do what I suggested. In fairness to my son, when I was his age I probably would have made the same "evasive action" choice.

On the other hand, to show you how different things are, in this day and age, two weeks later she asked him out.

Jacqueline Joulette

My advice to Justin was not based on anything I read in a book, and it had not been passed along to me in a father-to-son chat. The fact is, I had experienced what some might categorize as OJT (on-the-job training), that turned out to be an epiphany and was probably more valuable, both short and long-term, than anything I learned in my four years of college.

In my freshman year I was taking the one required math class – for non-science majors (I can't remember its name precisely – it was either called "The Logic of Algebra" or "The Algebra of Logic"). I just wanted to get it out of the way, and move on to courses that better matched my goals.

As you will learn in my bio (actually "autobio" would be more accurate) at the end of the book, I had no trouble with the subject matter. Therefore it came as a surprise when the Professor (and yes, this was back in the day when people of this caliber actually taught freshmen classes) asked me to stick around, after everyone else had left. I racked my brain, trying to figure out what I could have possibly done wrong but, as it turned out, I should not have been worried at all, since his reason was that he had a favor to request.

He asked me (when it's a full professor this really should read, "He told me") if I would tutor a senior in our class. She had already flunked this subject once and, if she couldn't pass it, she wouldn't graduate. The young lady's name was Jacqueline Joulette.

"Jackie" (that was the name she preferred) was captain of the cheerleaders. She was, by far, the best looking girl in school and the person who finished second was Jackie, when she wasn't trying (she also held the number three position – when she wasn't feeling well). People who know me well would be surprised at the thought of me being intimidated, but that's how I felt. Here I was, a 17-year-old freshman, getting to spend two hours every week, with the subject of every male student's dreams (and probably a few females as well).

It turned out that Jackie was a real sweetheart. She was never going to get an A in this class, but an A was not necessary.

After our first tutoring session she suggested we go have a beer. I immediately felt trapped since I was not yet old enough to drink. She obviously picked up on my consternation by saying, "It's on me. It would be very unfair of me to ask my tutor to pay" (as I said, she really was a very sweet young lady, and a perceptive one at that).

We made slow, but measurable progress. In her next test she attained a full letter grade higher than she had previously, by getting a D+. However, within a few weeks she was had pulled several Cs and even got one B-.

Several months later we were sitting around, having another beer (I never did tell my roommates that she was buying for fear that they would consider me mentally unbalanced, if I really thought that was happening). This was the last session before the final and I wanted to keep it short so as not to overload her thinking processes.

There was a big school dance coming up that Saturday and, at some point, I said, "So tell me Jackie, who's the lucky guy taking you to the dance this weekend?" When she told me that she wasn't going I assumed she was going to be out of town. I mentioned that conclusion and she answered, "No, I'll be on campus." Since it was now my turn to talk I asked, "Then why aren't you going?" Her explanation almost knocked me off my now 18-year-old feet. "Because no one has asked me" was her reply.

Before I could say anything else she went on. "Philip, I'm not trying to be boastful here but I know I'm attractive – to the point that everyone thinks I have a date for every occasion. My roommates, who I adore, are not as good looking, and they have dates all the time. They don't believe me when I tell them that they made me jealous. The fact is, I could think of a dozen guys I'd like to go with, but they would have to take the first step (that's how things were done back then).

And then it hit me. I sensed that I had just learned something very, very important.

During that period of time there was not a single function where I didn't show up with a very attractive date. My looks were pretty average, at best, so there seemed to be some kind of disconnect here. During my junior year one of my original roommates pulled me aside and said, "OK, I've been watching you for almost three years and the streak you are on can't be just luck. Since I'm pretty sure it's not your aftershave lotion I want to know your secret." In response I said to him, "Actually there is a secret, but if I let you know what it is you have to promise not to tell anyone, as that would create competition." When he agreed, under the penalty of death, I said, "Pay attention, because it's only two words. I ask."

"Yeah right" he replied. "And I suppose everyone says yes." And that's when he got the real lesson (if he was paying attention). "No, most girls turn me down. At that point I thank them and call someone else."

The fact is that I have an ego that can get inflated to blimp size (that's partially what has me thinking that I could write a book that people will buy). However, in cases like this that "I'm so smart" attitude never comes into play. Now, I will certainly admit that if, after going out on a few dates with someone, they said to me, "Philip, I can't see you any more because, frankly, you bore me to death," that would hurt. But the thought that someone who doesn't really know me at all could have the power to pierce my skin was, is, and always will be inconceivable to me.

And the education I got, while drinking a beer, has served me very well because, in the world of fundraising, if you can't deal with the word "no" you had better find another line of work.

The Best Night/Day of My Life

While the above experience turned out to be a "life lesson" it had one other outcome – what turned out to be the part of best day of my life - although technically I'm including part of one day with an evening from another (that being said, given my unflagging optimism, the best may be yet to come).

I asked the Professor if he could possibly grade Jackie's final exam within a day or two. I was confident that she passed but I knew she was nervous about the results. I'm not sure what would have happened had she failed but she ended up with a "solid C." I asked Dr. Beinert (I can still remember his name) if he would call her and pass along the good news.

The exam had been on a Wednesday and was Jackie's last one (I still had one more the following day). Thursday night she called me (I knew she had heard from the Professor by then). She said (I'm pretty sure this is an exact quote, because these are the type things one remembers), "Philip, thank you. By the way, I forgot to ask you the other day. Who's the lucky girl who will going to the dance on Saturday?" If it's possible to "hear a blush," mine would have echoed.

When I told her that I wasn't planning on attending she said, "Well then why don't you take me?" So much for that rule about girls not asking guys.

I then learned the meaning of the phrase, "brain cramp." In about 10 seconds I had to decide if I would be making an idiot of myself in accepting her invitation and, if that were not the case, did I have the right clothes to wear (at least I didn't have to worry about transportation. I had just turned 18 and knew I could borrow a friend's car).

I felt as if an eternity had gone by (it was only those 10 seconds) before I said something in the affirmative. I can't recall my exact words but they might have been kind of corny - like "I would be honored."

What I knew would be unrequited love for Jackie had already taken root, but it was about to branch out. She said, "One of my roommate's date asked me if I knew what guys would be wearing and I told him that I thought it would be kind of casual – a jacket and tie (that was considered "casual" back then). This gave me the information I needed, without even having to ask.

I should point out that I had to go out and purchase a tie and jacket. Back in those "caveman days" we were required to wear both to every evening meal. I don't know of any freshman who didn't obey the letter of the law but gave no consideration to the spirit. That's why all of us owned only one jacket and only one tie – and there was no dry cleaner anywhere in sight.

The dance was my first experience with "heaven on earth." I can't remember everything that happened because I felt I was floating around. Part of what made it so special is that Jackie did not spend half the evening talking to upper classmen – people who, under other circumstances, would be her element.

She left no question about the fact that I was her date and when she was introducing me to her friends she would say something like, "Philip is my teacher. Without his help I wouldn't be able to graduate."

141

If life had ended, right then and there, I would have had no complaints. My heart was now very firmly in Jackie's hands. And she was about to get a little bit more of it.

While driving her home I got a flat tire, which mortified me (I'm not exactly sure why. I mean it wasn't as if this was intentional on my part). Since this was long before cell phones, I had to walk to a house, about a quarter of a mile away, to call the AAA. When I got back to the car I told Jackie that they would be there in about 30 minutes.

My car was at the top of a hill, with Lake Seneca down below. Jackie looked out the window for a few seconds and said, "Philip, you couldn't have picked a better place for this to happen. It's the best view on campus."

That did it. If this girl had asked me to slay a dragon for her I wouldn't have slayed just one – I would wipe out all their relatives as well.

The half hour we waited turned out to be a fascinating discussion. She told me that she hoped I enjoyed myself as much as she did (now there was an understatement), especially when I was introducing her to my friends – who ended up almost speechless. She pointed out that we would probably be a topic of conversation on campus, for the next few days, and asked if there was anything particular I would like her to say, when she got grilled. I told her that I was delighted with the word teacher.

This was not only the happiest night of my life, to this day I can't think of anything else that might have come close. If you recall the letter I wrote on behalf of the Make-A-Wish Foundation, I spoke about the possibility of getting to live the best day of your life for eternity. In my case my choice would be declared "No contest." It would be the day in the story that follows, and the night of the story you just read.

The exclamation point came at graduation. Normally I would have been long gone by then but a cousin of mine was graduating and I was pretty close to him and his parents. So there I was, sitting in the audience, under a big tent. It was the first week in June and it had snowed the night before (I was in upstate New York). However, by the time the ceremony began the sun was out, the snow was gone, and the weather was perfect.

They gave out diplomas in alphabetical order. Since my cousin's last name was "Johnson" he was right in front of Jackie (Joulette) on line. When he was handed his "sheepskin" he walked off the stage, with Jackie close behind. He came over to where his parents (my aunt and uncle) were standing, with Jackie almost stepping on the back of his shoes. Before anyone could do anything, she threw her arms around me, kissed me (on my lips no less) and said, loud enough for those in the immediate vicinity to hear, "Thank you Philip. I wouldn't be here if it weren't for you."

(Note: I know I could have made this point without relating these events. In my defense I will say this. I'm reasonably sure that anyone reading this has had an experience that, when they recall it, makes them smile (and maybe cry a little bit, knowing it will never happen again). I have always found that given the way I think, it gets even better when I write it down. Once I had done that I decided that no harm could come from including it, other than asking you to read a few more pages).

NUGGET

Seek and ye shall find. You may get lost several times but don't ever let that be the reason for calling off the search.

NUGGET

Put your ego on a back burner. If you don't try you can't possibly succeed. If you do, you might. A slight chance is a heck of a lot better than no chance – unless you are egomaniacal. I know that I have admitted to suffering from this malady, but not when it comes to this subject.

This reminds me of a commercial recently run by one of the phone companies.

A rather nerdy looking guy is having his new phone installed. He said to the guy doing the work, "Last night I gave my new number to three really hot girls. What are the odds that they can't get through to me because they're all trying at the same time?" The installer responded, "About 10,000,000 to one." The nerd though for a second then said, "Great. You're telling me that there's a chance that's what's happening."

Now 10M to one might sound a bit farfetched. Then again, ask anyone who has ever won $100M in a lottery what they think about this "possibility."

While I'm on the Subject – Killing Me Softly

I am including this chapter because I am aware of the fact that I seem to be trying to overwhelm you with my triumphs and I think it important to, every once in a while, relate something that didn't turn out the way I wanted it to. Maybe this was not the worst day of my life, but certainly was the one that broke my heart for the first time – but done so in a way that was touching, to the point of being beautiful. I know this sounds as if I'm describing an oxymoronic situation, but I'll let you judge for yourself.

Her name was (and possibly still is) Roni Katz. My nickname for her? "Kitten." I thought it was cute, refusing to feel that it was obvious and besides, she liked it and what she liked was more important to me than anything.

I was 16. She was 15 – petite, blond, bright and with skin like – OK, since I can't think of any other word or phrase I'll fall back on the tried-and-true one – a baby's bottom.

For most of the time I knew her, it was as a member of our "gang." This was not the Jets or the Sharks – or even close. We were about eight boys and eight girls who enjoyed doing certain things together – bike riding, roller skating and the movies being among them (much better and healthier than texting, tweeting, posting, etc.).

By the time Roni and I went to the movies, all on our own, I had a real case of "puppy love," to the point that I probably should have been dining on Alpo.

After our 3rd M & M date (movie and a malted – for those of you who don't know what a "malted" is, ask your parents) we were sitting on her front porch. It was in October, cold enough that we were bundled up.

A day earlier I decided that I wanted her to be aware about how I felt. So I purchased a pin, about 1" in size, designed in the image of a kitten (of course).

We talked and lightly necked (you might have to ask your parents about that as well) for a few minutes, at which time I took the gift-wrapped box out of my pocket and handed it to her.

She opened it, saw what it was and then pinned in on the lapel of her coat. To this day I cannot believe that

145

the next words I heard were spoken by a 15-year-old, but I was there so I can vouch for the accuracy.

She said, "Philip, the way I feel right now I can't put this next to my heart but I'd like it to be nearby."

It's hard to describe what I felt at the time, other than being totally devastated, but with a bit of an asterisk. In this day and age, if this were a TV sitcom, the comment would be, "I hope we can still be friends." As much as it hurt, I liked the way Roni said it a whole lot better.

Who's Afraid of the Big Bad Wolf? We All Were

The CEO, of the marketing agency I joined back in the late 80's was a "When he was good he was very, very good and when he was bad he was a lot worse than horrid" individual. If he was the good guy he gave you 100% of his attention while the bad guy gave you none, nada, zip - and there was never a hint of anything in between.

He fired me three times, always on a Friday, and the hired me back on the following Monday or Tuesday (I think there was a sadistic streak, somewhere in his personality). Our Creative Director suggested that we create a giant "mood ring" to wrap around the frame of his door, so we would know when to stay away.

Six months later, after my third "fire then rehire" incident, when there 25 people in our conference room, I finally figured out what was going on – why he was the personification of Dr. Jekyll and Mr. Hyde As soon I did I shared it with every one of my co-workers.

When he sat in on a one-hour meeting, he left the room six or seven times (and no, he didn't have a weak bladder) to talk to his stock broker. It was then that I realized that his mood was totally related to whether the Dow Jones average was up or down. After learning that, no one would ever go into his office to ask him something without checking what the stock market was doing. He was so extreme about his "two traits and two traits only" personality that even if I went to see him and said, "Roger, you know so much more about (fill in the blank) than I do so I was wondering if I could tap into your expertise," if the market was down he'd reply with one word – "later."

I went back and double checked. On the three Fridays he fired me the market was down, each time. It was up on one of the following Mondays, but down on the other two. But, on those two occasions it was up on Tuesday. I'm just glad there was not seven or eight down days in a row.

Then there was the day that the market crashed, falling more than 500 points (20%) because, of all things, a weak earnings report from United Airlines. A similar percentage drop today would be more than 2500 points on the Dow Jones average. Knowing we were about to have a volcanic eruption, the likes of which we had never seen before, a very wise person pulled the fire alarm, so the building had to be evacuated.

It was my secretary who thought of what had to be done next. She went up to the Fire Chief and, very sweetly, asked, "Would you suggest that everybody go home (it was a Friday) because the building had to be checked out from top to bottom?" When he asked why she said, "If you don't do that, and we all have to return to our offices, the entire agency might possibly get fired." Thankfully the Chief agreed. When all of us reported back to work on Monday, the waters had calmed as the market was in the process of recovering most of its losses.

NUGGET

As soon as you start a new job, ask your co-workers to fill you in on the personality quirks of the person, or people, you will be reporting to. If you have this information you will me able to maximize your successes and minimize your failures (including the chance of losing your job).

Don't Go There

There are people like me (yes, there really at least a few who fall into that category) who will turn down invitations to join committees, because we know that we will want to run them, especially if we know that the person in charge is very weak when it comes to getting other people in the room involved.

A perfect example of this was an initiative designed to reduce the amount of violence in the Phoenix metropolitan area. A friend of mine asked me to attend and the first sentence from the committee chair blew me away. He said, "The last time we met was three years ago. Those of you who were there (10 out of 52 attendees) will recall we identified 17 priorities." If I was closer to the door I would have left right then. Three years between meetings? 17 "priorities?"

So as not to insult my friend, I stayed and got to hear that they would like to form 12 sub-committees, to meet that same day (despite the fact that almost no one's schedules had that much time available). I was asked to chair one of them but, since I was the Executive Director for a non-profit, I respectfully declined saying that I wouldn't have the time (although if meetings occurred every three years that probably wouldn't have been a problem). However, my response was not "the whole truth and nothing but the truth." I knew, that about 10 minutes after my committee met for the first time, I would want to take over the entire organization, and that was a case where I really didn't have the time.

NUGGET

Get out while the getting is good. If you find yourself in a situation similar to mine, don't stick around because each subsequent meeting you attend will become more and more excruciating. Of course, if it will look good on your resume, attending one once every three years might make it worthwhile.

The Most Powerful Weapon in Your Arsenal (and, although it now costs more than ever, it's still only $.44 cents)

At this point in my lectures (and usually at least a couple of more times) I interject something that, I indicate, will always get noticed, without fail, 100% of the time – not only noticed but truly appreciated. And, as each year goes by, this becomes a more powerful marketing and sales tool, as less and less people do it.

I grew up in a Brooklyn household, in what my son very cutely refers to as "the good old days" (with the emphasis on "old").The rule back then was – "You can't play with it, wear it, listen to it, read it, eat it or spend it until you say thank you for it – and in writing."

When I discuss what I see to be weaknesses in the world of business, the first thing I usually mention is the failure to write thank you notes. I elaborate by citing an example.

Let us say you take seven clients out to dinner at an upscale restaurant. The four bottles of wine you order set you back $400. You should be, to that restaurant, at the head of their most-favorite-customer list. After all, you ordered something with a five-time mark up meaning that your purchase represented a profit of $320. It's as if you had made a gift, of three "Benjamins" and a "Jackson" (I confess – I had to go look in my wallet to recall who is on a $20 bill) to that restaurant owner.

Now, if a friend sends your child a check for $320 as a high school graduation present, or gives you a gift certificate for $320 for your birthday, would you or your child really not send a thank-you card? If so, shame on you. It is the moral and ethically proper thing to do.

Well, it's just as moral and ethical for a company, but 10 times more important. YOU WANT MORE BUSINESS FROM THESE PEOPLE. The best way to maximize the likelihood that will happen is to thank them for what they have already given you.

It doesn't have to be fancy, and it doesn't have to be long. And, you can say the same thing in every note (people don't ever compare them). However, if at all possible it should be handwritten (although if your handwriting is like mine have someone else do it for you) and the envelope should be hand addressed with a real stamp (but not one of the "universal" variety, such as the Liberty Bell).

I will get to the second deadly sin in a second (probably more like five minutes) but let me interject a story here that actually illustrates both points.

When I lived in Manhattan, a friend of mine owned a small restaurant on Second Ave. There were 11 restaurants within two blocks of his establishment.

After much prodding I finally convinced him that there would be a benefit to building up a customer database. In six months it was up to 500 names.

At that point, I told him I was going to demonstrate its value. Late on a Sunday night Phil Vetrano (the restaurant owner) and I sat down with all the paperwork from the weekend, beginning with Friday night. I told him that we were going to pull out the bill for anyone who ordered a bottle of Chardonnay wine. There were a dozen such people, eight of whom were in the database.

I asked Phil how frequently a "good" customer visited him. His answer was about every two months, a pretty reasonable response considering all the competition in the area.

I told Phil that, on Monday, I wanted him to mail the following handwritten note to the eight people he could identify. It was to say:

"Thanks for coming in over the weekend. Your patronage is really important to me and I appreciate it greatly.

I see that you ordered a bottle of Chardonnay. I have just purchased an extraordinary case of this wine. Next time you come in, show this note to the waiter so he'll know which wine you wish to purchase (notice there is nothing being given away). I know you will be pleased."

I asked Phil, taking into consideration that his good customers come in every two months, how long he thought it would take the eighth person receiving this note (in other words, everyone), to return to his establishment. His guess was one month. Mine was three weeks.

We were both far too pessimistic as it took nine days and, if you think it had anything to do with the bottle of wine, you have missed the point.

This was nothing more than a case of ego stroking, of telling someone that you appreciate their business and that you have been paying attention – attention to them.

151

A little aside here – again related to "smart marketing" (there will be more on this subject in a subsequent chapter)

Last year I was at a physical therapist's office. As with all first time visits of this type, I had to fill out some paperwork. The final question was one I had never been asked before but which impressed me no end. It read, "How do you prefer to be addressed?" (Now you understand why I liked Dave Allen, from DHL, so much).

While I'll answer to pretty much anything (including "You idiot" a couple of times, but only because I had been behaving like an idiot) I absolutely prefer Philip. This simple question helped get our relationship off on the right foot. They transferred this one fact to the top of my chart, where the name "Philip" was now written with a Magic Marker, in very large letters, Every single therapist I worked with over the next six weeks (there were four) called me by the name I prefer. What better way to begin any time frame.

This is probably a good time to mention (see the chapter that follows), once again, a cliché that you've already read, and that you will read again – because I think it's that important. I heard this, for the first time in, of all things, a "Head & Shoulders" shampoo commercial, about 30 years ago. I was sure that someone well known, perhaps Will Rogers, had said it first. But, obviously not. After plowing through several pages on Google, the only earlier (but unsubstantiated) reference was another ad, this time for Botany men's suits, in 1966.

You Never Get a 2nd Chance to Make a 1st Impression – Pt. II (or is it III?)

Sounds pretty simple, right? Well it's not. It is very, very complicated and it is very, very important - the first 30 seconds you have with someone will have an importance that is so far out of proportion, to the rest of the time you spend with them, that it is hard to overstate its value. While there will be much said about this in future chapters, especially the ones that talks about receptionists, here's a couple of things worth thinking about.

There are two people waiting to be interviewed for a job. Person A has a shirt hanging out, wrinkled pants and is in need of a haircut. Person B has a shirt that's tucked in, pressed pants and got a haircut that morning.

The interviewer comes out and says he only has time to talk to one person. While person A may be far better qualified and have a much better resume and references, person B will get the interview. It may not be fair, and it may not be right, but it is reality.

I know you've heard that you should not judge a book by its cover but people do that often enough that you'd better accept it as fact.

The second story is one of my favorites. It occurred when I was sitting in my den watching a football game.

(Note: Please forgive me if there was no "first story" or if this is the third one, under whatever umbrella I'm holding at the moment. It's amazing, at least to me, how someone who is so good at math can't count).

My son Justin, 15 years old at the time, wandered in and announced that he had a very important question to ask. He wanted to know why it was so important that girls be good looking.

Now, the easy thing would have been to tell him was that he was wrong. Of course that would have accomplished nothing as he would have simply sought an answer elsewhere or just forgotten about the whole thing.

I told him that I thought I could explain it if he would wait a day.

The following evening I took the yellow pad that was sitting on the table and wrote down two numbers – 740 miles per hour and 186,000 miles per second. I asked Justin if he knew what the numbers represented. I was a bit surprised (and quite pleased) when he recognized both the speed of sound and the speed of light.

I then asked him if he knew the meaning of the phrase "comparing apples to apples." When Justin appeared unsure I explained that to make a comparison you really had to compare similar things. Since the distance (miles) was the same in both phrases it would be necessary to equalize the time by converting either hours to seconds or seconds to hours. Justin decided on the latter. By dividing by 60 twice he concluded that sound traveled about 1/5 of a mile in one second, a heck of a lot slower than light.

I took another blank piece of paper and asked Justin if he knew what his five senses were. It took him a couple of minutes but he did come up with taste, touch, sight, hearing and smell – although I did give him a bit of a hint, as to the last one, by rubbing my nose (it's a good thing that Justin was used to my way of asking questions like this or he would have been long gone by then).

The next request was that he connect the two numbers to two of the senses. Justin figured out, pretty quickly, that sound related to hearing and light to seeing.

I told him to go upstairs and walk back down into the den, pause at the bottom of the staircase and, pretending he didn't know me, stop and just say "Hello." He agreed although at this point he was shaking his head a bit.

When he got to the bottom of the stairs, about 30 feet away from where I was sitting, and said "Hello," I asked him whether I saw him first or heard him first. Justin thought for a second and said, "You saw me first."

"How do you know that?" I asked.

"Because light travels faster than sound."

"Excellent" I said, and went on to explain that our first impressions are always our strongest. Therefore when you see what a girl looks like, it has more influence than the fact that she may be interesting to talk to. It may not be fair but it is the way things work. However, if you know the reason, you may not consider it quite as important as you once did.

Getting Them – and Keeping Them

I never cease to be amazed by the number of businesses that fail to understand who their best customers are and that retaining them is far more important than acquiring new ones.

Here is a perfect example.

Each month I write a check, for $150, to my cable provider. This covers my television, phone and internet service. It doesn't sound like much until, again, you do the math. In the 20 years I've been with them I've sent them $36,000 (adjusted for inflation) in personal checks – yes, $36,000. And what is the cost of servicing me each year, including visits by technicians? I'm going to say $250, with the thought that this is probably on the high side.

People like me are their ATM machines - they get to "withdraw $150" from my checking account every month (and never even have to worry about bank fees) yet not once have I heard anything to encourage me not to switch to "Direct TV" or "The Dish."

I would need to know a few more facts to make a definitive statement – the most important of which is the "lifetime value" of their customers. If I am typical, insofar as annual revenues are concerned, they net $1,550 – and that's year, after year, after year.

I will now address the "cost of acquisition" and "retention."

I'm going to base this on the assumption that an average customer stays with them for three years. This means that, from each new customer, they will net $4,650. So, the question becomes, how much should they (or anyone for that matter) pay, to be given $4,650?

Obviously it's not more than that figure, so now it comes down to how much profit is desired by them. If it's $3,000, they should be willing to spend $1,650 to sign someone up. That's a ridiculously high figure but that doesn't mean it isn't correct. Just look at the amount of money that GEICO or Progressive spends on television advertising. I don't have the actual figures but I suspect that it equates to $500 - $1000 per acquired customer. If it's the former GEICO goes cash positive on my policy in less than one year. It it's the latter it's less than two.

And, once you've "acquired" someone, the more important question must be addressed – how to retain them and make them more valuable to you.

Here's one suggestion:

If their records indicate that their "average" customer stays with them for three years, one of their goals should be changing that "three" to a "four." Since their net income for that extra year is $1550, they should be prepared to spend some "retention dollars."

Tell the customer that, at the end of their 4th year of continuous service, they will receive a 55" plasma high definition television.

Does that expensive? Not really because, in bulk, these can be bought for about $500 apiece. This means that their net profit, for that 4th year, is now $1050. And, if the customer cancels before the end of that year, they receive nothing. So the question here is, would they rather have a net, at the end of three years of $4650, followed by nothing in year four, or $5900 at the end of that fourth year? I guess it must be the former because they've never even hinted a willingness to "go that extra mile."

There Was Something About Mary

A favorite subject of mine, related to the title of this chapter, revolves around one particular job title at a business. In fact, I will tell clients that I can give them sound advice about the individual holding that position, without even meeting them. The job? Receptionist. My advice? If they are not exceptionally good – not just good, or even very good, but exceptionally good, fire them. And if they are outstanding, stop treating it as an entry-level position and give them a raise.

These people have the keys to your front door and they represent you when you are not there. There may be no more important person in your entire organization. They set the tone and they set the mood. They can make people angry or they can make people happy – and not just any people – we're talking about your customers. They are your "face" and your "clothing." Customers will make decisions about your competence based on the way your phone is answered or on what happens when they walk up to your front desk.

(Note: If you think I am overstating something here consider this. How long do you think it would take you to find a highly qualified candidate, to replace an executive making $100,000 per year? Probably less than a week. A great receptionist making $25,000 annually? Probably several months, and that's if you can even find one at all).

And by the way, don't undo all the good that might be accomplished, by having an exceptional person answering your phones, only to backtrack when they are on vacation, sick or at lunch. A "temp" can do you unimaginable harm in just a matter of minutes.

The best solution to this that I've ever heard was the one employed by the agency where I worked for five years. They understood that, eventually, the job of receptionist leads to burnout. When that happened, the person was offered a promotion to assistant account executive (remember, they already knew that this was a highly qualified individual). The caveat was that, on occasion, they would be asked to fill in at the front desk.

The result was that, when I left for Arizona, there were three former receptionists working on the account side of the business. This meant that every time the regular person was away, their place was taken by someone well trained, someone who knew the staff, and someone who was familiar with the clients. The transition was always seamless and the quality of performance was always top-notch. Any required "learning curve" took about 10 minutes.

And, to insure that none of these individuals considered this to be a step backwards, they were offered the choice of $100, or one additional day of paid vacation, for each eight hours they manned ("womaned?") the front desk.

I can put the importance of this into some pretty concrete terms (something I've already written about in "Michelle's Story"). If I walk into a restaurant and the maitre d' says, "Mr. Barnett, how nice to see you again. Your table is ready whenever you would care to sit down" they can get away with some pretty ordinary food and I'm still likely going to enjoy myself. If, on the other hand, the comment is "Have a seat at the bar and we'll call you when your table is ready" they can have an award- winning gourmet chef in the kitchen and the food will still not taste quite right. In this case your emotions are affecting your taste buds. Just think of how that translates to your business.

As I've already mentioned, I use to hold the title of Vice President, Corporate Development. We had offices in Chicago, Baltimore, San Francisco, New York and a corporate headquarters in Fairfield, Connecticut. The receptionist there, Mary, was absolutely extraordinary, especially in light of the fact that she was a 20-year-old whose "formal" education ended with high school. However, she understood her job, and its importance, better than anyone I have ever known before, or since.

On my first day there, Mary came into my office, introduced herself, and then lay down the law - her law. She explained that we both worked for the same company and that I could never lie to her. If my 2 o'clock appointment arrived, and she called me to let me know, and asked me how long before I would be ready, I had to tell her the truth, no matter what the answer. I agreed although I remembered thinking, "What's the big deal?

After a couple of weeks I noticed that, no matter who I was meeting with, they always seemed to be smiling when they walked into my office. When it reached the point of not being able to be chalked up to coincidence, I did a little investigating.

What I learned was that, when Mary buzzed me, and asked me how long I would be, no matter what my answer she would add five minutes to it. This way, when I called her to ask that she send the client my way, it was always sooner than he or she expected. This makes people happy. If it had been the other way around so would their mood have been.

I asked Mary about it and she told me that she had read a line in a book that, for some reason, had made a huge impression. It said,

NUGGET

"Create a level of expectation and then exceed it." This can be said a different way. But the message is still the same – "Under promise and over deliver." It is not complicated but it sure is effective.

I also became aware of the fact that the people in our reception area seemed to forever be in a good mood. By now I was sure that Mary had something to do with it, so I hung around now and then until I learned another one of her major "secrets."

Let me add here that while Mary was reasonably attractive, she was not a flashy dresser and her wedding ring was obvious. She had a pleasant smile but was not flirtatious and was always busy, so the good mood was not based on the fact that she was giving anyone an inordinate amount of time or attention.

Mary had a list of everyone who was expected on any given day. If it was a first time visitor she had a big red star next to their name. When they arrived, she introduced herself and offered the standard, "May I get you some coffee?"

After doing this, she went back to her desk and, on an index card, wrote down "Mr. Jones (Mr. Jones certainly gets around a lot) – six-feet tall, gray hair - takes milk and one Sweet & Low."

The next time he came to the office he was greeted (before he even got to give his name) with "Nice to see you again Mr. Jones. Let me get you some coffee. If I remember correctly that was with milk and one Sweet & Low?"

He could not help but smile. This attractive young lady actually remembered how he took his coffee.

It really is delightful to start every meeting with happy clients. They were told they would have to wait 10 minutes that only turned out to be only five and a receptionist had just done a wonderful job of ego stroking (I use the word ego so much because, whether we admit it or not, everybody has one).

A month or two later I asked Mary where she had acquired this skill. Again her reading had served her well, although this time it was nothing more than an article in Reader's Digest. It was in a dentist's office so it was probably several years old.

It seemed that President Richard Nixon was going to be making a campaign speech in Milwaukee where he would be joined on the podium by the Mayor. On the way to the speech, in the limo, one of Nixon's advance men pulled out a notebook and briefed President on the local officeholder.

When Nixon arrived he said "Nice to see you Mr. Mayor. How is Susan? (His wife). I heard your son Robert just got a college scholarship for football and that your daughter Michelle made the National Honor Society."

He said he was so impressed he felt like he was going to explode with pride. The President of the United States mentioned every member of his family - and by name no less.

The Mayor admitted that, a couple of days later, after he had come down to earth, he figured out that the President had been "briefed" just before arriving. But this didn't diminish it one bit. After all, the President didn't have to listen to that briefing – but he did. Ergo, the mayor must be a pretty important person.

I repeatedly tell senior executives that I hope they understand how simple this is. But because it is simple doesn't mean it isn't effective.

In a world where we are increasingly becoming e-mail addresses with passwords, Social Security numbers and "Dear Customer" letters, we love being recognized as unique individuals.

And here are two additional ways to tell somebody that you think they're "special."

I have a collection of some 25 neckties, each one containing the logo of a different college or university. These were purchased in anticipation of a first meeting with a potential client.

It wasn't hard to learn where the individual had matriculated; even before Google (a call to a secretary usually did the trick). Then it was merely a matter of calling the school's bookstore and giving them a credit card number and a mailing address.

When I walked into the office of a perspective client he would almost immediately notice the tie. The ensuing conversation would always go something like this.

Potential Client: "Did you go to the University of Whatever?"

Me: "No, I didn't."

Potential Client: "Then why are you wearing a University of Whatever tie?"

Me: "Because you did."

I know it sounds corny but people eat this up as it shows that you went out of your way to do something that relates to them.

Ironically, on the same day I was proofreading and editing this portion of the book (for the 7th time), a situation came up that further drives this point home.

I was invited to attend a presentation made at the corporate offices of "AmplifyU," a division of "Girlfriend University." They are a local company whose mission statement involves helping women succeed in the world of entrepreneurs.

I did some research on-line and discovered that, among many other things, a great deal of their graphics employed, not to my surprise, the color pink. So, I visited a very large golf equipment and apparel store, within walking distance of my house, where I bought the only pink shirt they had on display (fortunately it fit me).

A pink golf hat was not quite as easy. But, apropos of what I talk will talk about shortly, instead of walking away and starting from scratch, I asked one of their salespeople if he knew where I could find one. You can imagine my delight when he pointed to a store about

50 yards from where we were standing, a place his wife shopped at all the time In fact, she recently purchased a pink hat there – to wear when participating in the "Race for the Cure." Five minutes later I had exactly what I was looking for (it's a good thing it had an adjustable band because, as I'm sure you've already surmised, I have a very big head).

The next day I walked into their offices, where I met the other 40 attendees. A quick glance around confirmed that I was the only one there who was "pretty in pink."

Will this result in a consulting job for me? I don't know yet but I will guarantee this. Of all the people in attendance, I was the one they will remember the most, if for no other reason than they appreciated the extra effort I had made.

OK, one final "Mary" story (in many ways I've saved the best for last),

In my quest for new business I became aware of the fact that MCI (now operating under the name Verizon) was not happy with one of their agencies and was going to be looking for a new one. Although the size of this particular piece of business ($3,000,000) was not large by New York standards, 60 agencies showed up for the initial briefing.

MCI narrowed it down to 30, then 10, then six and, finally, to three finalists – my agency being one of them. Each agency was given $25,000 to use for our creative executions. I'm pretty sure we all lost money on this phase (our agency spent $50,000) but, fortunately for us, we got the account.

NUGGET

One of the rules I insisted people try to live by is to question success – what are we doing right and how

do we do more of it? This is far preferable to making decisions out of panic when you are saying, "what are we doing wrong and how do we change courses?" That's a much harder question to answer.

With this in mind, I waited six months and then invited their Vice President for Marketing out to lunch. After the usual socializing I asked him, point blank, what it was that caused them to select our agency over our two competitors? Was it creative stuff we'd shown them?

He assured me that this was not the case – that the creative they had been seen was universally excellent. "What was it then?" I asked. The VP's response was, "Philip, every time we called your agency we were spoken to politely. Every message we left was delivered accurately, we were never put on hold for more than 15 seconds, and people returned calls promptly. For heaven's sake Philip, we're a phone company. These things are really important to us."

I went back to our company's headquarters and told this story to my CEO, a no- nonsense individual who scared the life out of most of his employees. When I finished my boss said, "I want everyone from the Manhattan office to join the Connecticut staff in our conference room tomorrow afternoon. And have someone videotape the meeting so we can send it to the other offices."

I let all the appropriate parties know and, the next afternoon, the conference roomed was jammed with 80 people, ranging from Senior Vice Presidents to newly hired secretaries.

Roger turned to me and said, "Tell everyone why we got the MCI account." I repeated the story to the assembled staff. When I finished, he snapped his fingers and, from the back of the room, our two interns appeared, carrying a large blown up check, similar to what you see at golf tournaments. The check, made out in Mary's name, was for $5,000, in effect matching what it took her three months to earn.

I was so impressed that I went into the CEO's office and suggested that we institute a policy that might allow for similar rewards. I was told (not asked) to report back, the next day, with a recommendation.

What I suggested, and what the CEO accepted, word for word, was the following. For every business card I was given by an employee of our agency, where the person whose name was on it was someone who might make use of our services and who would recognize the agency's name when I called, $50 would go to the person who obtained that card. If we got to do a presentation to the potential client the employee would get $500 and, if we were hired, the bonus would become $5,000.

My expectations were that most of the cards would be collected by the secretarial staff when they were out at the singles bars on Friday night. Before blowing off a prospective suitor, they would first do a little agency salesmanship (this may sound a bit sexist, but the fact is, I see a lot more women being bought drinks at a bar, than the other way around).

While this did happen a number of times, the first person to collect was an assistant art director, happily married with three children.

Her next door neighbor was the VP of Marketing for Pitney Bowes, a company we had been trying to get in to see for a couple of years. She had never thought of "talking up" her employer to her neighbor - until now. Once a "reason" was provided, an "incentive" if you will, she became an agency ambassador. She had a card for me the next day; we presented to Pitney Bowes within a week, and were hired before the month was out. We got a great client, she got $5,550, and our entire organization began to think in ways that had never entered their minds before.

I kept track of every piece of business that was acquired (more about that in a minute). Over the next three years the agency ended up with more than $120,000,000 in billings from new clients. At least 15% of that of that – in excess of $18,000,000 - came from leads generated by our own employees, none of who were in the "sales" department. While someone might argue that I was making myself dispensable, the fact is, someone else was responsible for that other $108M (that would be me).

NUGGET

Satisfied employees can often get more business for you than almost anyone else. All you have to do is give them the right ammunition and always remember those five magic words – "Do you have a card?" If they have your card they determine what happens next. If you have theirs you are in control.

Consider the Source

There actually is one more incident, involving Mary, that I think bears mentioning. I'm not sure in this is a good or bad quality, but she was a bit more sensitive than most.

One day I came back from lunch and found her in tears. It seems that she had been verbally acted by one of the administrative assistants. Christine was one of those people who could be as sweet as candy one minute and absolutely vicious the next, and when the latter characteristic reared its ugly head, there was never a logical reason attached.

I had Mary come into my office and sit down. Once she had regained her composure I pointed out to her that, throughout her life, she was going to encounter people whose opinions would be important to her. Their praise would make her glow and their criticism might seem almost hurtful at times.

Conversely there will be those whose praise will be almost meaningless and whose negative comments will be not be worth even listening to.

I then gave her an index card and told her to pin it onto the bulletin board next to her desk. Then, any time she was told something that might upset her, before reacting, she should look at this card and repeat, to herself, the three words written on it. Once she had done so it would be highly unlikely that even one tear would roll down her cheek.

Those three words? **"CONSIDER THE SOURCE."**

Know Who Your Potential Customers Are/Budget Accordingly

Let me now return to the second of my two keys to success (writing thank-you notes was the first).

In doing so, I'm going to pick on a particular industry because they do such a truly terrible job. However, they most certainly do not stand in the corner by themselves, as there are many businesses that would have to take some remedial courses, just to qualify for my Marketing 101 class.

In the course of my lifetime I have probably eaten in 2000 restaurants, ranging from the Four Seasons to a local Burger King. In all of this time, only once (not counting my friend Phil's establishment) has the restaurant attempted to find out who I was, beyond the name on a credit card. That establishment used the information to send me a short thank you note. The result was that I became a regular - because I felt "valued."

And, to add insults to their self-inflicted injuries, only once has a restaurant taken the time to inquire as to what got me to walk through their front door. Was it their newspaper ad? The radio commercial? The flyer left under my windshield wiper? Had I seen their name on a bus shelter? Did a friend tell me?

Think about this. Every three months a typical restaurant evaluates their advertising budget and decides where to spend their money during the next quarter. And what do they base these decisions on? As best I can judge they read tea leaves or flip a coin because they most certainly are not doing it based on information and logic.

Since I mentioned the word "budget" let me spend a couple of minutes on this subject. What I am discussing here will be that part of your marketing plan targeted at acquiring new customers, or keeping the ones you already have – as pointed out earlier, an even more important group.

Some of you remember probably remember reading a book by George Orwell, called "Animal Farm." It included the author's version of the 10 Commandments. The one that still stands out in my mind is "All people are equal, but some are more equal than others."

Now, before anyone takes me to task, I'm not talking about social equality, or equal rights, things I believed in very strongly. Rather I'm referring to customers and potential customers. Here is how I addressed this issue.

In the advertising world there is the phrase "a kill for account." This is one so big, and so important, that you would figuratively kill to obtain it. They represent about one percent of the business that might be available. The second category is major accounts, who representing roughly 10% of the marketplace. The balance, of just under 90%, is considered "over the transom" business. It was work you wouldn't turn down if it walked through your door but you were not going to spend an inordinate amount of time or resources chasing it.

For simplicity sake, let us say that your marketing budget is $100,000 and that there are 1000 potential clients out there. Most businesses would look at that and say, "Well, that's pretty easy. We can budget $100 as the cost of acquiring a new client. That should allow us to do some really interesting things.

This is not the right way of thinking because the first thing you should do is put at least 70% of your marketing dollars into the "Retaining clients" column.

Then, instead of thinking that you can spend $30 on each of those 1000 "possibilities," let me introduce you to "The New Client Budget Triangle." It combines basic geometry, basic math and, of greatest importance, basic marketing logic.

Draw a triangle on a piece of paper. Then draw two horizontal lines, one of them one third of the way up from the bottom of the triangle and the other two thirds of the way up. Your triangle should now be in three sections, with the bottom one much bigger than the top.

In the top section write the numbers 1% = 10, in the middle section put 10% = 100 and in the bottom section write 89% = 890.

Now, divide your marketing budget into three equal parts and put the number that results next to each section. Here is the explanation of what you will find yourself looking at.

- Your top section consists of 1% of the thousand names you began with. This equates to 10 names. You have $10,000 to spend, meaning that $1,000 can be allocated to each name.

- The middle section consists of 10% of the thousand names, which equates to 100 potential clients. You have $10,000 to spend which allows for expending $100 on each.

- The bottom section has 89% of the names – 890 "over the transom" possibilities. Once again you have $10,000 to work with, or $11.24 per name.

For $11.24 you should be able to do three-four, very clever, sequential mailings.

For $100, a couple of creatively outstanding efforts should be no problem.

If the $1000 figure can't get you the attention, of most of the 10 companies at the top of the pyramid, you need to replace your Creative Director and Corporate Development executive.

Since every plan should include some alternatives, here's one. In point of fact, you might be able to disregard everything in this chapter, up until this point, as this may be better (meaning more productive) than anything you and your team can conjure up. It's certainly worth considering since the initial effort, directed at the top two levels, would cost $11,000, instead of $20,000.

I had a friend at an agency, living on the other side of the country, who looked at this drawing and came up with something that was both highly unusual and exceedingly creative. He sent a basic letter of introduction, to those residing in the top two tiers, with an explanation that his budget to "acquire" the reader was $100.

He went on to say that he got overwhelmed with the options at his disposal and that, unable to make a decision, he was enclosing a one-hundred-dollar bill. He suggested that it be donated to the reader's favorite charity. Three of the recipients invited him to come in and make a presentation. He had sent the "Benjamins" to 110 people, spending $11,000. He got one new account with annual billings of just under $2M.

ROI, ROI, ROI.

For anyone not willing to go out on an $11,000 limb, you can try a test of a smaller number. The only problem there is that the size of your mailing may be too small to be statistically reliable. Of course, if you get one new client out of it, you can throw statistics out the window.

I lost touch with my friend but I hope he agreed with me, that it's always nice to be playing with the house's money. In his situation I would take 100 randomly selected names, from the 890 "bottom tier" candidates and send them the same letter, this time accompanied by $50. If that doesn't work you've spent $5,000 of what can be looked at as the new client's money. If it does work you may be sitting on a gold mine. What I would do next is mail to another 200 randomly selected names sending half of them $50 and the other half $100. I might even add a sentence to the letter – "In no way am I trying to 'buy' your business but I won't say the same thing about getting your attention."

(Note: What was going to be the next two chapters were awash in numbers related to the cost of acquisition and when to put a product on the market. Since for many of

you these will not be applicable and/or relevant, I have moved them to the back of the book. The chapter titles are "The Dollars and Sense of It" and "Get Up and Go or Sit Down and Wait." If you think these will be of value you can turn to them right now, and then return here. If you trust my figures the two chapters will add about five minutes to your reading time. Or you can grab your calculator and double check everything. This will add approximately 15 minutes. For a reason that appears in my biographical information, I recommend the former).

Names, Names – Use My Name – And Don't Call Me Sweetie

One of the things I talk about, with great frequency, is the importance of using names and the amount of empowerment it creates (see earlier chapter).

I remember being in a pseudo social/business meeting with someone I knew. As the meeting ended she said to me, "Call me soon sweetie."

The look on my face was similar to one that a lemon might cause. Her parting remark was, to me, the equivalent of scratching a nail across a blackboard. Someone who witnessed this asked me to explain.

"Look" I said, "She and I have known each other for a while but certainly not intimately and certainly not to the point of her using a term of endearment. My name is Philip, that's how I introduce myself, and that's what I prefer being called."

His response was that I shouldn't take it so seriously, that he'd bet she called everyone "Sweetie."

"That's exactly my point," I said. "I'm not everybody, a generic person with a bar code on my forehead. I'm me, an individual who doesn't like be equated with a mass of people, no matter how small."

It's not that I'm setting myself up to be better than anyone but rather that I think of myself as being unique enough to warrant being called by my name.

This leads to a discussion about how best to converse with someone, at least in an initial business discussion.

My suggestion is really quite simple. I always try to take the initiative by saying "Hi, my name is Philip Barnett, and you are?"

If the person answers "Alan Jones" I will then say "Nice to meet you Mr. Jones" and will continue to address him that way until and unless Mr. Jones says something to the effect of "Please call me Alan." On the other hand, if the initial response is "Alan," then Alan is what it will be.

It's pretty simple stuff but very effective and much appreciated. We all have egos and we all like having them stroked. The easiest (and certainly least expensive) way is by the personal recognition that comes from using someone's name, in the way they prefer it being used. Many people will tell you that it doesn't matter how they are addressed but, in almost all cases, it does.

Here is they way the conversation should take place.

Me: "Hello" or "Hi." My name is Philip Barnett.

He: "My name is Alan Jones." Which do you prefer, "Philip, Phil, or Mr. Barnett?"

"He" was not paying enough attention. If he had been he would have known that "Phil" was not a possibility. Otherwise I would have introduced myself as "Phil Barnett."

If the other person simply says "Alan" you can count of the fact that you are on a first-name-only basis. Don't ever ask you if he prefers "Al" or "Alan," since he's already, albeit indirectly, provided you with his preference.

One way to dig a bit deeper is, if he initiates the conversation by saying, "Hi, I'm Alan Jones," you can reply by saying, "Nice to meet you Alan Jones." At that point he would feel almost obligated to tell you what he prefers.

And, always err on the safe side. If you start out with the more formal Mr. or Ms. (far preferable to Miss or Mrs.) the other person will either tell you the name they prefer, or they will say nothing, If it's nothing than keep using Mr. or Ms. until otherwise informed.

You, the reader, may think I'm being over sensitive and, in most cases that may well be true. But, what's not to say that the person I'm talking with doesn't share my belief. Once again, in cases like this it is never wrong to err on the side of safety as this is most certainly not a case of "no risk, no reward." In fact, it could be almost the opposite – if you don't take a risk the likelihood of a reward is greater.

Focus Groups are Not Always a Panacea

While there are occasions where focus groups can serve a purpose, if the questions being asked revolve around purchasing decisions, be very careful how you interpret the results.

I was once sitting in the "client's viewing room" in a suburban mall. On the other side of the two-way mirror was a conference table. Seated around it were 12 shoppers, randomly selected from people who were there that morning, along with a facilitator. The only qualifier was that the participants had to be people who visited the mall at least once a month.

The information being sought related to a new toaster that was about to be put on sale. Several of them were employed to provide those at the table with toasted snacks. When the demonstration was over, one of the units was put into its retail package, which was then passed around, so everyone could see the quality of the graphics.

At this point the facilitator said, "We are considering selling this at $15.95, $17.95 or $19.95. Which price do you think is the most reasonable?"

(Note: This was not my client. I had simply been invited to observe by a friend at the manufacturing company).

As I could have easily predicted, the $17.95 price got 10 out of 12 votes. It's known as "The Goldilocks Response." Not too cheap, not too expensive but just right.

The next question was, "If we put this on sale at $17.95, would you consider buying it?" This time 11 people said yes – the 10 who thought that was the best price, plus the one who had voted for $19.95.

The following week the manufacturer placed displays (each holding a dozen packages) in three stores in the mall – one at each end and one in the middle. After they had been in place for a month, the total number of toasters sold was two – yes two.

I'm not going to pretend to be someone who can read tea leaves, so I certainly had no idea what the results were going to be. But neither did anyone else, including the people on whose behalf the focus group was conducted.

Five weeks after the toasters were made available for purchase, I had lunch with my friend. He asked me if I thought sales would be as bad as seemed to be the case. When I told him that I had no idea, he said "But you were there. You saw and heard the same things I did. The people loved it."

I responded by saying, "Jeff, there are several things you need to understand about what you witnessed. First, and absolute foremost, is the fact that the participants were being asked for their opinions, as evidenced by the use of the word 'consider.' Nobody requested that they confirm their opinions by taking out their wallet or checkbook. People want to be liked and so, with all other things being equal, they will tell the person asking the questions what they think they want to hear.

And, while the second point is less important, it has value. If you want to know how people feel about price points, don't make it a multiple choice question. Just ask them to write down what they think a fair price would be."

NUGGET

Opinions are like belly buttons – everybody has one. "What do you think" may provide you with a wealth of information, but most of it will be useless. Far better is to come up with a polite version of "Put up or shut." Consumers vote one of three ways – with a check, with a credit card or with cash. Never equate opinions with anything meaningful, unless they are supported with purchases.

(Note: In a previous chapter I mentioned an idea I had, and how much time I had put in developing it, including assembling three focus groups, with a dozen people in each one. Of the 36 people participating

33 of them asked if they could buy the product right then and there. Since there was nothing to sell them I let them know that, when it came on the market they would be the first to know, and they would be able to purchase it at a discounted price. The reason this information was so valuable, and encouraging, was because, at no time, did I ask, "Would you buy this?" As I said, responses to that question would be of little value. However, because they wanted to purchase it, even before they were asked if they were interested, the data gathered could, for all intents and purposes, be "taken to the bank" – but not until the product is created. In case anyone is interested, the product will sell for $50 – the participants had been told that – and the manufacturing cost will be less than $1.00. The people doing the actual selling will be physical therapists, who will get to keep $40 per sale, giving them a new profit center. And, to make it even more intriguing, the entire business is in an arena that shows significant growth, year after year, no matter what the shape of the economy. It could be run from an office that's no bigger than 10' X 10'. As pointed out, near the beginning of this book, I never stop selling so any of you who are intrigued by this should contact me).

Get Rid of What is Not Necessary

I recall attending a meeting that got out of control almost before it got started. The company was trying to be all things to all people and, as a result, was wasting an inordinate amount of time, talent, and money. Think back to Playboy Magazine. When they began that's what they were - a magazine. But then they decided to expand – into clubs, books and movies, three areas they knew little or nothing about. I don't have to tell you what happened since you already know. If they had hired a really smart consulting firm, and said to them "fix this," that firm would have told them to immediately get rid of the clubs, the books and the movies.

NUGGET

A "Jack of all trades, master of none" is going to have real difficulty in the employment market, Companies want to hire people who are really, really good at one thing, not someone who can do lots of things, but not be a standout as far as one specific skill is concerned. While there are times that being able to multi-task is a good thing, never get to the point that your employer looks at you as someone who can step in for anyone in an emergency but, when it came time to stay there, you can't fill anyone's shoes.

A company that sells business-to-business should never really consider network television, as so much of the audience has no use for whatever appears on the screen (there are a few that can cross-over from the business to consumer world, such as Staples or Home Depot). Before you spend a lot of energy going after the universe, get a good handle on who you are and what you want. Sometime, this can happen through the process of elimination. Consider this:

A hiker, wandering through the woods one day, came upon a clearing in which stood a magnificent, life size granite sculpture of a horse. The man was an art collector and recognized that he was looking at a masterpiece.

Off to the side stood a little old man, who appeared to be the artist. The collector went over to him and said, "Sir, this is magnificent. There must be a secret to your technique and I hope you'll share it with me."

The old man replied, "Well, I'm getting on in years and I suppose it's time to pass along my knowledge and skill. Therefore I will tell you how I did this.

I found a block of perfect granite, I took my hammer and chisel, and I chipped away everything that didn't look like a horse."

Here's another way of approaching the idea of determining what's really important.

About 30 years ago Alysha, the wife of a close friend, was faced with a broken vacuum cleaner. Rather than take it into a repair shop she decided to try to fix it herself, even though she had no training related to a job such as this.

She sat down on the floor, with the misbehaving cleaner and a bunch of tools. She took the entire unit apart, cleaned every piece, and began to reassemble it. Since she had no directions to follow, there was a lot of trial and error.

Three hours later she had put Humpty Dumpty back together again. The vacuum not only worked perfectly, it seemed to perform better than the day it was bought. But here's the rub:

When completely resembled there were still a half-dozen pieces sitting on the floor, making this a classic case of over-engineering, and wasted money. It relates to the fact that American scientists spent years developing a pen that would work in a zero gravity setting, as exists on the space shuttle. The Russians saved all that research money – they used pencils.

NUGGET

In order for anything to "work," whether that be a product, a plan or an application, there are certain elements that must be present. However, more often than not, there is "overkill," to the point that a good

deal of money, time and effectiveness can be positively impacted by "trimming."

I am well aware of the fact that there are those who feel it important to "explain themselves" (probably several times) just in case the other person doesn't "get it." A perfect example of that is this book. In my defense I would like to think that I'm aware of what I'm doing. As I mentioned earlier, there is a good deal of duplication only because I thought something was so important that it should be reiterated, and then reiterated again (or should that be "re-reiterated?"). But, would I have been better off just saying it once, but using LARGER, CAPITALIZED, BOLD TYPE? I suppose that might work for some, but I am not one of them. My problem would come when I was looking at a point that I had made, three or four different times and I would now be forced to use only once. Had I taken this approach I would still be writing, five years from now.

As I said earlier, Franklin D. Roosevelt once pointed out that it took him about an hour to write a one-hour speech. A 30-minute one took two hours, a 15-minute speech required four hours of writing, etc. It got to the point that a one-minute speech took him almost an entire day. Had I attempted to make this book half as long as it is, it would have taken me at least twice as long to write it.

Some say, "When in doubt, leave it out." I believe "Better safe than sorry." Never ask someone to read between the lines. Interpretation may be necessary in regard to poetry, but not with something like this book. From my perspective, the most negative comment someone might give me would be to say, "What did you mean when you said.....................?"

This reaffirms the difference between me and "Mr. Cheese." Theories can usually be reduced to a sentence or two. **When the intent is to educate (which is what I hope I'm doing here) instead of inspire, more words are needed, and you'll need more than a minute to absorb them. This is easily demonstrated by the number of people who will tell you that they get all the inspiration they need from just 46 words – the condensed version of the "Ten Commandments." To condense these even more I will not be the least bit surprised if Dr. Johnson comes out with a book called, "The 10 Commandments – In Less Than One Minute."**

(Note: Before I am taken to task, probably by many of you, I would never, ever write in such detail as I am doing here, and certainly not with this amount of pseudo duplication. Were I applying for a grant or filling out an application, there are two rules involved. The first one is "ANSWER THE QUESTIONS"- and nothing but the questions. The second rule reads, "See rule #1." However, in this case, there are no questions, so I am free to ramble at will – just as you are free to decide that a "ramblin' man" is not your cup of tea).

The Numbers Should Be the Decision Maker – Not You (your customer's votes count more than yours)

One of the great things about certain aspects of advertising is that its effectiveness can be so easily measured. Take two markets that are essentially the same when it comes to size (population) and demographics. For your test, each market should have only one newspaper (that's very easy to find these days) with similar circulations.

There are a couple of ways to measure things. If it's a mail order ad that's easy (remember, every ad must be coded). If the ad encourages people to purchase your product at "one of these fine stores" you can use the store's orders as your "thermometer."

Among the things you can test are:

- The size of the ad – i.e. ½ page vs. ¼ page.

- The day of the week the ad is run.

- The location of the ad in the newspaper. While this may be beyond your control, you should fight for a right-hand page and, if possible, the upper right-hand corner. Think of what happens when you turn a page. You put your hand in the upper right-hand corner, because you're turning the page from right to left. And, after the page is turned, your eyes first focus on the right-hand page.

- If there is coupon to be cut out insist that it not be backed (on the next or previous page) by another coupon.

- If it's a mail order item you can also test things such as price points, discounts on multiple orders, etc.

(Note: I have not kept on top of current practices but, once upon a time, there was a way to do all of your testing in a single market.

"Back in the day" there were newspapers that offered what was called an "A/B split. For a reason I can't recall, the Louisville Courier-Journal was determined to cover a market that came closest to replicating the rest of the country.

What you could do was give them two versions of your ad, with the only difference being, for example, the selling price. These ads would be typeset so that version A would run in copies one, three, five, etc. and version B would appear in issues two, four, six, etc. This meant that you were getting distribution that was totally random. It also meant that you and your next door neighbor might be looking at two slightly different ads, without ever knowing it (among the other papers that provided this option was the Wall St. Journal). You could easily know (and maybe still can) this was going on because somewhere, on the top of the page, would be the letters A or B.

An interesting sidelight is that the magazine, with the highest per-page ad rate, was also the one with the least expensive one. In the 1970's TV Guide was the #1 (in circulation) magazine in the country and an ad, that ran nationally, reflected that fact. However, they published different versions for every TV market, meaning that there were always 150 variations sitting in people's dens. This afforded the opportunity to pick two basically identical demographics, and test variations of your ad.

Here's a quick quiz. If you could pick any location in TV Guide, where you wanted your ad to be, what would be your choice. OK, time's up. Since at least half the people reading this book have probably never seen a copy of this magazine this question is not really fair, which is why I'm going to provide the answer. It was the page opposite the crossword puzzle. Almost every mail-order ad, back then, included a coupon for you to fill out, so it was an advantage to be paired with a page that necessitated you having a writing instrument in your hand).

Once you are ready to sit down and compare effectiveness, make sure you have the publication's rate sheet in front of you because the ultimate thing to consider is your advertising cost per unit sold.

But be careful in figuring things out, because there is another variable that comes into play – and that's the cost of shipping.

If, ultimately, what you want to compare is retail vs. mail order efficiency, this can be a "make-or-break" difference."

For instance, you have an item that's going to sell for $20.00 (we all know that the actual amount will be either $19.99 or $19.95). The store pays you 50% of the retail price, which equates to $10 per unit. The mail order gets you the full $20.

You ship 100 units to the store and your shipping costs are $100 per shipment equal to $1.00 per unit. This means that you are really getting $900 ($9 per unit).

You sell the same item, at the same price, by mail. But here you add a shipping and handing charge of $5 (actually it would be $4.95). It costs you $1.00 to ship it and $1 to handle/process it. This means that you are really getting $23.

This appears to be a true no-brainer. You sell 100 units to a store and net $900. The same number of mail orders nets you $2300.

But, you're forgetting one thing – the cost of the ad(s) that causes the mail order purchases (these figures are based on the assumption that the retail store(s) will pay for the advertising that features your item. If you have to provide an advertising allowance – i.e. $3 per unit - you can adjust these figures accordingly).

For the sake of this argument (what a silly phrase – I'm not looking to start an argument) let's say that ad costs you $1000, or $10 per unit sold. Although your net is now down to $13 per unit, that's still substantially better than going retail.

But what if the ad costs $1500. The 100 units you sell bring you $2300. However, when you subtract the cost of the ad, you end up with a net of $800 ($8 per unit), and suddenly retail looks like a better option.

Actually it's not even close, as the mail order sales remain far superior. This is certainly a case where "less is more." In fact, it's more than you might think.

When you sell to a store you have one customer. When you sell by mail, in this case, you have 100 customers – and you have their names and addresses. Mailing lists, such as the one you are putting together here, are an asset, both directly (for you), or indirectly (if you "rent" out those names).

"Sharper Image" reached the point where they were making more money from renting out their mailing lists than they were from selling merchandise. Lists such as theirs, with "hot names" (customers who have purchased within the last six months) could easily have been rented for $100 per 1000 names. That means that every time they rented 10,000 names they made $1000 – and this is both a gross and net figure since there were no costs involved.

In fairness, they turned over their names to a list broker, who would take 20%. So, they're now netting $800 but, in addition to having no costs, they had no work to do. And, unlike a piece of property that can only be sold once (like a car), these 10,000 names can be rented ten times in one month, as long as they are not going to businesses competing directly against each other.

Do the math. $8,000 a month equals $96,000 a year. And they didn't have just 100,000 names – they had 3M. If you can't find your calculator I will keep you from having to look for it – the final figure would be $2,880,000 – almost $3M dollars with no expenses, no risk and no work.

So why, one might ask, did they go out of business. It was because they decided to open a chain of retail stores, a business they knew nothing about. The stores bombed and brought down the catalog with them.

Blue Sky Sessions – Getting Great Ideas for Nothing (Other Than the Cost of a Dozen Pizzas and a Half Dozen Six-Packs).

For those of you not familiar with the term "Blue Sky" session it is really easy to explain. It's when you fill a room with people, with the task of addressing only one issue. The only rules are that there is no such thing as a bad idea and everyone in the room is equal.

In the front of the room is an easel, with a giant pad of paper. As ideas are mentioned a "scribe" numbers them and then summarizes the suggestion in a few words. When there are three items on a page, that page is torn off and taped to the wall (I've had several of these generate more than 150 ideas). Going back to the word "empowerment," employees love being part of something where their opinions are considered important.

When all the brains have been drained a halt is called. Pizza and beverages are now served while everyone is given a pad and pen. They are instructed to walk around the room and write down the numbers of the five best ideas they see.

I have facilitated a number of these where the entire "audience" consisted of employees of a company, from the CEO on down. Depending on the nature of the business, there might be as many as three sessions needed, to make sure that everyone gets to participate in one (and only one) of them.

Before we even begin I meet with several of their executives and make a couple of predictions. First, there will be unanimity on several of the suggestions, and more than one person will be heard to say, "I can't believe no one thought of this before."

I go on to say that my guess is that at least two, and probably three, of the "winning" ideas will come from people they might not think of. Again, depending on the nature of the business, these individuals will be receptionists, waiters/busboys, valet parkers and even restroom attendants (they probably know more about customer likes and dislikes than anyone else in the company). After I pointed this out to one client they hired someone for this position. It must have proven valuable because, three years later, he was still there. They had considered simply using a voice activated tape recorder but their attorney told them not to (invasion of privacy issues).

What do all these people have in common (aside from the fact that the good ones are probably underpaid)? They are the ones who have direct contact with your customers and clients. I try to be gentle when I tell those executives that I would be surprised if more than one good idea came from anyone who worked in an office with a door.

There are two barriers that have to be overcome.

The first is that there are people who will be afraid to say anything because they fear being thought of as foolish. I always tell them that the reason there is no such thing as a bad idea is because one suggestion invariably leads to some variation of it. If someone says something that sounds silly, and another person says "What if we took that idea and did this..................?" and the "this" turns out to be a winner, the person who started the chain of events, the one with the silly idea, gets partial credit.

The second occurs when I tell the assemblage that, for this meeting, there are no "bosses" – that everyone in the room is equal. Only about half the people will believe you and, as a result, the other 50% will refrain from joining in.

There is a way to solve this and while it's not totally ethical, there are times the rules need to get slightly bent, in order to attain a goal. And besides, this is one of those "No harm/no foul" scenarios.

I got a crash course in learning about this when I facilitated a session for the Trump Shuttle, shortly after Donald purchased the airline. While the question to be discussed required no explanation (it was, "How to we get more people on our planes?") I could see the "everyone is equal" caveat would never fly (I actually didn't realize this was a pun until after I wrote it).

This was the first time I was absolutely sure that if I didn't "cheat" I would be standing in a silent room – so I "planted" the first suggestion.

When everyone was assembled, I explained the goal and the rules. When I mentioned that there would be no bad ideas and that, in this room all were equal, I got a lot of heads going back and forth – not up and down. This made me feel even better about what was going to happen next.

When I concluded my explanations I said, "Mr. Trump, this is your airline so why don't you kick things off? Give me a way to sell more tickets."

Donald replied, "Why don't we advertise that when you fly on my shuttle you get unlimited alcoholic beverages, at no cost, along with four miniatures to take with you when you deplane?"

The room was dead silent. I looked at Donald and said, "Mr. Trump, I've got to take something back. There is such a thing as a bad idea."

It was then that everyone relaxed and I could read their collective minds – "Boy, if he can say something that absurd what I want to suggest might make sense." At that point hands started being raised, and we were off and running.

When I met with Donald beforehand, to set up my "white lie," I asked him how long he expected to stay – "about 10 minutes" he said. This was a good thing because, in spite of his "scripted" comment, he would still be an intimidating presence.

I can relate a number of stories about Donald but, at this point in time, I will tell you that I really appreciated the fact that he was willing to go along with my little "charade."

(Note: This topic is often confused with "brainstorming" gatherings. In the case of the latter there are far fewer attendees and those present are restricted to people working directly on account. Furthermore they rarely last longer than an hour).

The "Hey Joe" Effect

Whatever it is you do, and however much you may choose to spend, always be aware of the need to create the "Hey Joe" effect if you are mailing to a business. Let me explain.

Magazines such as "Time" and "People" remind advertisers about the fact that if a subscriber finds some really interesting they will "pass it along" to another member of their family and/or a co-worker.

(Note: The first business I owned placed a number of direct response ads in a myriad of magazines. Since each one was coded, when we received an order that code would tell us exactly which magazine and which issue generated it. Our ads in publications such as "Better Homes & Gardens" and "Playboy" would still be bringing in orders four years after the publication date).

Well, this concept is even more critical in direct mail since, no matter what the promises made by the mailing list company, and no matter what it says in that year's reference books, no information is going to be 100% accurate as to the name of the right person, at a potential client, you wish to contact.

Given this fact, you must send out material (on business-to-business solicitations) that is so compelling, so creative or so original that the recipient, who may be the absolute wrong individual you are trying to reach, ends up acting as your personal messenger – that they are so taken with your communication that, quite literally, they hand deliver it to the right person and says to them, "Hey Joe, I've got to show you what I got in the mail today" (this works equally well for people not named Joe).

Rain, Rain Go Away

Some of my failures have been pretty spectacular. I was going to say, as in "crash and burn" but, as you are about to find out, in this case it was too much water, rather than flames, that caused the problem.

The year that Central Park, in NYC, was first closed to vehicular traffic on weekends, a friend and I opened "Lifecycle." We purchased 100 bikes, made arrangements for discounted wine and food from neighboring stores, and thought we were off and running (pedaling to be more accurate). Our grand opening was the Saturday of Memorial Day weekend. It rained.

And it rained the next day and on Memorial Day as well. There are 15 weekends between Memorial Day and Labor Day. Thirty-three Saturdays, Sundays and holidays. It rained on 32 of them. Had Noah been around we would have seen Ark II. It was the wettest summer in NYC history – one, as they say, for the record books.

On that one sunny day we had more than three hundred rentals. Most of them were for less than three hours, so there were a lot of "turnovers" – multiple rentals of the same bikes – not crashes. Unfortunately one day doth not a business maketh so, on the day after Labor Day we sold all our bikes at about $.40 on the dollar and walked away sadder and wiser (who knew there was such a thing, even back then, as weather insurance? Obviously we didn't).

Selling a Product that Doesn't Exist

When you are in the mail order business you can legally sell a product that doesn't exist. This fact caused my first business to disappear, into the night, and resulted in 13 people, plus me, becoming unemployed.

Our company was called "Photo Poster," with an ad headline of "BLOW YOURSELF UP." We took pictures, slides or negatives and enlarged them to 2' X 3' or 3' X 4' posters.

The posters we shipped were in black & white because the machinery that would allow for color enlargements that big was still in its development stage. We placed an order with the manufacturer, with a delivery date six months ahead, when the enlarger and printer would be available for purchase.

The same week we sent in the necessary paper work, our one competitor (much smaller than us) began running ads for color posters. We did a great deal of investigative work and determined that there was no way that he could possibly fulfill orders for that product.

Before sending him a few orders we called his office and asked what the anticipated delivery time would be. The response was "two-three weeks."

A month later, we called and asked when we would receive our color posters. I can accurately quote the answer we got because we recorded it.

"We are so sorry. The enlarger and printer we got did not produce posters that met our quality standards. When they are replaced your order will be given priority status. Or, if you wish, we can send back your photo and money."

Well, the fact is, our competitor did not have the necessary machines and wouldn't, for another six months, assuming he could afford them. So, in effect, he was "financing" his purchase-to-be with the money from unfulfilled orders (the large majority of his customers said that they were willing to wait – not all that surprising since the amount of money involved - $7.95 for the smaller size and $10.95 for the larger size, along with $1.95 for shipping and handling – was not that great).

Beginning with the day he ran his first ad for color posters our orders began to plummet, and things got worse every month.

We tried to file complaints – with the U.S. Post Office (he was, we thought, guilty of mail fraud), and a number of Federal and state agencies. On each occasion we were told that we had no case – because he was not breaking any laws, given that he was returning the money to unhappy customers.

Six months later we were out of business.

It's too bad we weren't in the U.K. Any mail order business there had to prove that they either have inventory or would be able to produce products, immediately upon receiving their first order. A department within their government (I believe it was called the "Fair Trade Agency") were the ones doing the inspecting. Of course that would never happen here as too many people would be yelling, "Get the government out of our lives." At times the philosophy in the U.S. seems to be that we're better off allowing people to lie and deceive, to the detriment of legitimate businesses.

NUGGET

If you are preparing to bring a product to market, use every search engine available (sad to say these were not available in 1969) to see if anyone is planning to employ this kind of scam. If you find that to be true, send them an official "cease and desist" letter. And, if possible, visit their premises and attempt to make a purchase right there and then. If you are unable to, call your Congressman's office. Tell them that you, and all your employees, voted for him (or her) in the last election and that you need their help because a totally unethical business is going to cause you to have to file for bankruptcy.

Those Who Don't Know Shouldn't Do

In 1994 I was elected for the first of three terms as President of the Northern Arizona University Parents' Association (NAUPA). At that time (1993) the group had 400 members who basically served no purpose, other than awarding four $500 scholarships that year. Once I saw how they were "acquired" and what the lines of communication between NAU and NAUPA were, I was surprised that they had many in the fold. I think some parents signed on because they thought they were required to while others believed that their membership would tilt the scales in the favor of their son or daughter, if a professor was wavering between two grades.

The administration told me that I could do what I thought best, but made it clear that they were going to "keep a close eye" on me to make sure I didn't stray too far from the middle of the road.

The first fight came when I insisted that every membership solicitation mailing had to include a return envelope, and that we should test to see if "postage paid" made a difference (it didn't). Their response was that they saw no reason to spend money on a second envelope because, and these are the exact words I heard, "If someone wants to join they should have no problem finding their own envelope." I could see that I was in for a very long year.

NAU has a program, for incoming freshmen (and their parents), called "Previews." These three day/two night sessions are held each weekend in June, plus two in July and one in August. For the most part the parents never get to see their kids during this time. While the students are preparing to pre-register for all their classes, and getting warnings about STDs and "binge" drinking, their parents are trying to figure out why there are 22 meal

195

plan choices and whether or not their offspring are covered on the parents' health insurance policy. And oh yes, they get an STD presentation as well, but from a slightly different perspective – what to do if they find out their child has contracted one (assuming they are willing to share that information and I wouldn't bet on that happening).

I convinced the school to allow me to speak, for 45 minutes, at each Previews session – to explain NAUPA to the parents, and why they should join.

I always began by telling them the same story.

"My son Justin is now a sophomore. The first set of grades arrives when your son or daughter comes home for Christmas vacation. If you pick up the mail, and see an envelope from NAU, you can be pretty sure of what's inside. You will probably do exactly what I did - hold the envelope up to the light, to see if you can read what's enclosed. The school figured this out a long time ago, so there a carbon strip that precludes you from seeing the information you seek. So, unless you open your kid's mail, you will have to wait until they tell you.

I handed the envelope to Justin. He didn't open it until he had gone into his room, and closed the door. When he didn't come out for an hour I knew that the news was not going to be as hoped for. After all, if it was good, he would have been back in the living room in 10 seconds.

It was an hour before he emerged. When I casually said, "So, how did you do?" he looked at me and said, "Why don't I wait to tell you until the day I'm going back to school. After all, why spoil all this time we're going to have together?" Suddenly he had learned how to play the part of the "thoughtful" son. I think he expected an argument and was shocked when all I said was "That makes sense to me" (it really did).

196

Well, on that fateful day he handed me the dreaded piece of paper (at this point I paused for dramatic effect). The number to the left of the decimal point was a zero (gasp from the audience). The number to the right of the decimal point was a two, followed by a zero. Yes, it was a .2 GPA which translated to four Fs and one D. At least he didn't tell me that the problem was that he obviously spent way too much time on one subject."

And then it sunk in – that there was hope for their child. After all, I was standing there telling them this story, which means that a) I hadn't had a major heart attack and b) my son was still in school. So, whatever happened to their student, it couldn't get any worse than this, and I had lived to tell the story.

(Note: In many ways this relates to the "angry customer" I told you about. One way to take a lot of the worry away, from an individual (or group), is to point out that they will never be faced with anything as bad as what you've have had to deal with).

Once again I have probably provided more background than needed. The key point was that I got to speak to each group of parents. As a result of these presentations, an average of 100 parents (per session) joined NAUPA. That brought our total up to 700 – almost double the year before.

However, this is not the gist of the story.

We did a mailing – to every parent who was not a member and got another 400 new members (all the numbers mentioned have been rounded off). I told the school that I wanted to do another solicitation in two weeks. Their reaction was "Why? You will be mailing to the same people and, if they wanted to join, they would have done so at that time."

I had to beg and plead a bit but they finally agreed. The second mailing cost us $1000 and it brought in roughly 300 more parents. The dues were $30 per year so we netted $8,000.

When I started planning for a third attempt the response I got was something like this: "Are you crazy? You've given them two chances and the people who haven't joined don't want to."

This took more of that begging and pleading stuff, this time employing the following example. I asked the school representatives at the meeting (there were four of them) if they ever let a subscription, to a leading magazine like Time, Newsweek or Reader's Digest expire. Two of them had. My question to them was "How many mailings did you get, after the expiration, asking you to "rejoin the flock?" Neither could provide an exact number other than to say "a lot."

I told them that, if it was Time, they got six solicitations. The reason Time mailed that many times is because they knew (from previously conducted tests) that they would lose money on a 7th one.

So, in answer to their question (whether or not I was "crazy"), I told them that I wanted to mail as many times as the mailings made money. They were dubious but let me go ahead. The 3rd mailing brought in about 200 new members, and the 4th one 100. Each time our net, when compared against our costs, got better (percentage wise). The reason was because, with each mailing, we could reduce the number of envelopes mailed by the number of parents who had already enrolled.

At that point I got tired of fighting with them, so we stopped at four. 1000 new members attained through the mail, 200 renewals and 700 more from "Previews" – a total of 1900. The following year, having learned which portions of my speech to emphasize, reducing it from 45 minutes to 30 minutes, and setting up an enrollment table outside the cafeteria, we grew to 2700 members. That year, for the first time in the school's history, the football game, on Parent's Weekend, was standing room only.

In my third year in office the school decided that other NAUPA members should do the "Previews" presentations. I told them that I thought that decision was a mistake (yes, my ego kicked in here but this time it was related to a "greater good") but again, I didn't put up much of a fight. I probably should have because not one of the seven parents who volunteered, after much "persuasion," had ever done a presentation before.

That year our membership fell to 2100, with the entire drop coming from "Previews" sessions.

I "graduated" the same year as Justin. Even if he was still in school I'm pretty sure I would not have sought a 4th term.

At that point the school decided that they would, once again, run NAUPA themselves. I suspect they were afraid that NAUPA would end up with someone like me – someone who would fight them "tooth and nail."

The next year membership dropped to 800. I spoke with a friend who was still a member and asked her how many renewal letters she had received. The response didn't really surprise me – one. She also told me that there were at least 6000 empty seats at the football game. The year our membership peaked, at 2700, we awarded five $5,000 scholarships, 20 $1,000 and 50 $500 scholarships. The year after our Executive Committee left office that number had dropped to 10 – of the $500 variety. The moral of this story is:

NUGGET

The school's Admissions' Department (NAUPA operated under their auspices) expertise was in admissions, not in running a business, and people should do what they do well (that's why the government should bring in some really smart business people to run Medicare and Medicaid). The school seemed to feel that they didn't want to give up control over an organization that used the school's name – even though they knew it worked better when they did – and besides, they never gave up "control" as they could stop anything they really objected to. In a previous chapter I explained why I don't try to change the oil in my car. Well, NAU thought they could do that, and rebuild the transmission as well – without a mechanic in sight.

Gone but Not Forgotten

When US News & World report comes out with their annual "Colleges & Universities" issue, the three Arizona schools (NAU, Arizona State and the University of Arizona) always rank among the lowest when it comes to the percent of alumni making donations. In fact, I seem to recall that there was a year when one of these three reported 5%.

At the risk of being accused that I am pretending to know more than the people running these programs, let me be clear about one thing. I know more than the people running these programs. I will use the college I graduated from as an example of how things should be done.

Last year, 47 years after we graduated, 53% of my class were still making contributions. This is made even more impressive given the fact that at least eight of my former classmates were deceased.

(Note: Just because someone is deceased doesn't mean that they stop giving. In fact their gifts may be far larger than the ones given when they were alive. Here is the simple version of the explanation.

I've been giving the school $100 a year. I would have to do so for 150 straight years to match the $15,000 bequest that's in my will (an amount that I will increase if this book sells enough copies). Any Alumni Association that does not have at least one person dedicated to estate planning, has no idea what they are doing (I told you I'm not opinionated). After all, when people are queried as to why they haven't made a bequest the number one answer, year after year, is that no one ever asked them to. The number two response is that it is thought to be both difficult and expensive. It is neither, as all it requires is one sentence (called a codicil) and no attorney is needed. The third comment is from people who say, "How do I know how much money I will have when I die?" Again, the response is simple – don't leave a dollar amount. Instead make it a percentage of your residual estate).

How were they able to accomplish this? By being aware of the fact that I've already mentioned several times – if you don't know how to get in touch with your "customers" (donors) it's impossible to have any type of relationship with them.

My alma mater started that relationship during the second semester of my senior year. In groups of a dozen we met with members of the school's administration, including the President, who told us how important the support of the Alumni Association was.

At this point everyone in the room was asked for $1. In return we were given cards, indicating that we would officially become members of the Alumni Association, on the day after we graduated. The $1 represented our first year's dues.

The dues "structure" was then explained to us. In our 2nd year we would be asked for $5, in 3rd year it would be $10 and in the 4th year, $25. We were told that the school knew that during the first years after college a number of students would be doing graduate work, while others would probably be on, or near, the bottom rung of the employment ladder.

Of course, the ones who figured out how to "build a better mousetrap" would be in position to give more, and those individuals were encouraged to "up the ante," to the best of their ability.

The key part of this was keeping in touch. We each received at least two first class mailings a year. By putting the words "address correction requested," on the envelope, the Association always had a way of reaching us.

The amount we ended up giving just passed $1M. While that sounds like we got a number of really big gifts, consider this. My graduating class consisted of 250 and 57% (142) keep donating. That works to just over $7050 per member. However, this has been over a 47 year period, making the average annual donation $150. Given the fact that there have been a couple of contributions that exceeded $20,000 and at least two dozen of us whose total contributions have been in the $10,000 range, the "real" average is probably lower (i.e. if 10 donors accounted for $250,000 of that $1M, 132 of us would have given $750,000, equal to $120 per year. I will have a great deal more to say about this in other chapters related to the lifetime value of a custom" (or, as is the case here, a "graduate").

And, to help insure the success of the Alumni Association, every year a person who makes a donation receives a letter from one of the school's current students who has received scholarship money from our organization. This points to the fact that far too few non-profits do – provide updates as to how your money is being spent.

(Note: This may be even more important when it comes to grants. Any non-profit that intends to apply in subsequent years, after the one in which they received funding, should always provide quarterly progress reports, even though they may not be requested. By letting them know of your success stories, brought about by their generosity, your chances of working with them, year after year, are greatly enhanced. Strangely (and this continues to amaze me) there are a number of funders who never ask for these reports meaning that, when looking at a year-two application, they are "flying blind").

There was one other thing done, something I have never heard of since.

A year after graduation a letter was sent to each of our parents. In essence it said," We hope you are pleased with the education your son (daughter) received. We certainly were delighted to have had him (her) as part of our community.

The one thing we are sure you are absolutely delighted about is not having to write any more checks to us – in some cases very large checks. As a result, the balance in your checking or savings account should be substantially higher than it was just a few years ago.

So, we are writing with the hope that you will match that outstanding education, with your new-found wealth, and make a contribution to our "Parents' Alumni Fund." *(Note: in this case, parents were only contacted once as they strongly felt that this type of solicitation should occur only in the year following graduation).*

However, if you still have a child or children in college or planning to attend one, please disregard this request."

I'm not going to go into great detail (among other things I've lost track of what's happened in the years since I left) here but, as the costs related to doing this were so low, the "ROI" was spectacular. I do know that 89 of my classmates' parents made contributions that averaged about $500. That adds up to $44,500. If that average has been maintained, for each graduating class, that Parents' Alumni Fund" would have more than $2.09M in it. I said "would" because money has been spent along the way, primarily for scholarships.

Finally, in regard to those (or any) scholarships, special attention was paid to recipients who had gone on to successful careers. Here the basic message was "Someone helped you. Isn't it time to return the favor?"

And In This Corner, Wrong vs. Right

Let me change directions (again) for a minute or two and discuss the impact an unhappy customer can have on your business or what a truly satisfied client can do to assist you.

There have been several surveys done that indicate out of every 100 people, who might be dissatisfied with a particular product or service, only three of them contact the provider. However, ten of them tell at least 20 other people. Think of that for a minute – 100 people were annoyed at you and suddenly there are 200 more who won't step through your front door.

And sometimes it is worse as someone like me tells not 20 but closer to 200 people, in the course of a year.

Here are examples of both the bad and good sides of this.

When I built my house in Arizona, back in 1993, I decided to put in a pool at the same time. I met with the President of one of the leading pool construction companies in the Valley. We agreed on a design, features and a purchase price of $18,000, to be added to my mortgage. When I left his office I knew that, according to the law, I had 72 hours in which to change my mind. However, I had no reason to think I might want to do so.

That all changed when, two days later, I got a thank you letter. Now, considering my earlier remarks, you might conclude that this would have been considered in a favorable light.

And it was, except for the facts that:

- It was a generic, "Dear Customer" letter. I forgave them that because, after all, it was a thank you letter.

- It was poorly written, with several grammatical errors. I forgave them that because it was, after all, a thank you letter.

- It was printed unevenly and folded in an equally unprofessional manner. I forgave them that because it was, after all, a thank you letter.

- My name and address were printed on a mailing label, applied at an angle, and the postage was from a meter, not a stamp. I forgave them that because, after all, it was a thank you letter.

So, although I can get a bit picky, and think I am certainly more observant than most, I can also be very forgiving.

However, what I could not forgive was the fact that the envelope was addressed to "Philip Barnett or current resident" and that this was done to obtain a lower postage rate that saved them $.04.

After staring at the envelope for a couple of minutes, I picked up the phone, called the President of the company, and canceled the purchase. When he asked why, my explanation was pretty simple. "If saving four cents on a mailing is that important to you, I can't imagine the number of corners you will cut in building my pool. The thought of that makes me so uncomfortable I cannot let you proceed."

Over the next few years I had seven friends or acquaintances tell me they were planning to put in a pool. I shared this story with all of them, "naming names" as I did so. None of them ended up using this company although two of them had them as first on their list.

So, counting my pool, they lost at least three sales, and almost $60,000 in revenue, because they weren't paying attention to perception – a perception that, in the mind of this customer, was equated with a future reality (if the pool manufacturer was smart, and a bit insidious, they should have learned from this experience and waited a day or two longer to send out their "thank you" letter).

To sum this up, think of this adage, which originated in the 14th century.

For want of a nail the shoe was lost.

For want of a shoe the horse was lost.

For want of a horse the rider was lost.

For want of a rider the battle was lost.

For want of a battle the kingdom was lost.

And all for the want of a horseshoe nail.

The "kingdom" that was lost, as a result of my experience, was $60,000 and probably a good deal more. The "nail" was a standard, first class, postage stamp.

Conversely, shortly after I arrived in Phoenix, I had the occasion to meet a date for dinner at one of the better-known upscale restaurants. I got there a few minutes early and spent that time admiring the setting and architecture (designed by one of Frank Lloyd Wright's students).

However, once we sat down to eat, a series of events occurred that turned it into a far less than memorable experience.

Now, had the initial appeal of the place not been so great, I wouldn't have had any second thoughts. I simply would have crossed them off my list and never returned.

However, it had so much going for it that I opted to write a letter to the owners and explain the reasons for my disappointment (as well as what I liked). Two days later I got a call from the owner's daughter who was the general manager. She said, "Mr. Barnett, my parents and I have read your letter and you are absolutely correct in every criticism you made. We would like you and your date from that night to come back and have dinner with us again, on the house. We can do a better job."

We did go back and the restaurant did a much better job. The GM and I became friends and we devised a method to track how much business I was going to bring them, now that I was a satisfied ambassador, rather than an unhappy former customer.

A year later we sat down and went over the figures. Not counting the money I spent there personally (I had become a regular), I had brought their restaurant and small inn $22,000 in revenue. For those of you who understand marketing you may have already figured out that the actual number is probably at least five times that.

Everyone I introduced to their establishment represented a new customer. How many of them came back, brought others and told friends? My conservative estimate is that in the second year they realized well over $100,000 in additional business.

In fact, I'm quite sure that this figure is way too low. It was in that year that a group of golfing friends of mine decided to visit my fair city. I mentioned that this facility had 11 rooms. There were 10 people in their group, but they took every room, with the extra one being their "Let's get together for drinks" location. By doing this they were able to keep potato chips crumbs from being on individual beds. And, they used the bathtub as their cooler. Each day they would purchase a case of beer. The housekeeping staff was instructed to fill the tub with ice cubes and the "brewskis," about an hour before their anticipated return. Those cases of beer cost $18 each. Had they drank that amount at the courses "19th holes" they would have spent more that $150 dollars each day (I've got some pretty smart friends).

I don't know what their bills were at checkout, but this was peak season and the room rates were $250 per night, although they got the multiple bookings and Philip Barnett discounts of 20% - bringing that rate down to $200.

So here's the math. Eleven rooms X seven nights X $200 = $15,400 – and this does not include meals.

Perhaps the most important point here is that, in doing their hotel searches, they never came across the name of this inn so, what got them there was the fact that the location knew how to handle customer service, with the customer having been me.

So, there you have the opposite ends of the spectrum. Four cents in postage costs someone $60,000 and knowing the right way to handle criticism brings in $100,000. Anybody who doesn't believe that the little things not only count, but count a great deal, is likely to fail and, most assuredly, will never come close to maximizing their success.

Giving Your "Product" Away

I once devoted an entire lecture to the fact that you should never be afraid to give away your product, especially if it is a perishable commodity.

Now you're probably thinking that this refers to food that will spoil or rot. No, that's not what I mean but, if you do have such products, please arrange to give them to a food bank.

(Note: This story doesn't real deserve its own chapter, although it does suggest that you make sure your customers have a clear understanding of what you are trying to accomplish. This particular incident was funny, with a "no/harm/no foul" ending. However, as I'm sure you will quickly figure out, there are situations where the results could be much, much more dire.

One of the stores I regularly shop at is called "Sprouts" (it's very similar to "Whole Foods" and "Trader Joe's"). Every week they have a special offer on two of their breads. The products are on a rack that is placed quite close to the store's entrance.

During this particular week they were helping out one of the local homeless shelters. Right next to the bread rack big barrel with a sign attached that read, "Help Feed the Hungry."

Just as I was getting ready to leave this little old woman walked in (she really was little (no more than 5' tall) and she really was old (gray hair and using a walker). She stopped in front of the barrel, read the sign, and proceeded to take one loaf after another, off the bread rack, and place them into the receptacle. I watched her, partially in disbelief, with the rest of me getting ready to burst out laughing.

After "donating" about a dozen loafs, she began to walk away. My first thought was to put the loafs back on the rack. However, it suddenly dawn on me that, if I started to remove them from the barrel, any shopper looking in my direction would think that I was in the process of stealing food from the needy.

Fortunately one of the store managers was standing right behind me. When he stopped laughing he said he would handle it, and gently tell the woman the error of her ways.

The next time I was in the store I noticed that another sentence had been added to the sign. The line read "Please contribute purchased product."

The mistake the store had made, which in this case had no negative outcomes, was to assume that everybody understood the process. As evidenced by this occurrence, that is not always true – and there are a lot of little old ladies, who live in Arizona, who are apt to repeat what I had witnessed).

No, I was talking about is something that, if not sold today, disappears forever – an empty airline seat, hotel room, rental car, etc. And, while I'm not saying to always give these away, or to do it even frequently, I am suggesting that, by judiciously doing so, you can be sowing the seeds for a bountiful harvest.

As is almost always the case, I will provide a real-life example.

Back in 1988 we had, as a client, a hotel in the "business district" of downtown Boston. It was an "all suites" property that was continually overbooked Sunday through Thursday nights and lucky to have 15% occupancy on Friday and Saturday.

Here is what we suggested to their marketing department.

- Identify 100 executives who lived at least 25 miles from the property but not more than 50 miles, and who had never stayed at the hotel. These distances were chosen because we felt it was far enough to make it unlikely that a weekend in town occurred often yet near enough to not make the drive onerous.

- Do a direct mail offer of an absolutely free room night (Friday or Saturday only) for one or two. Put a three-month cut off on the offer while suggesting that the recipient consider the pleasure of having a weekend "in town."

The response rate was 52% - inordinately high perhaps but, then again, it was totally free and it was a very nice hotel.

I asked their three marketing executives to write down, on a piece of paper, and without consulting each other, what they thought the average bill would be at checkout. They must have graduated from the same college because their guesses were almost identical - $58, $62 and $63. My guess was $110.

The actual figure turned out to be $158 (in 1988 dollars). All but one of the acceptances were from couples. All but two of the guests had dinner at the hotel. Forty-five of them had breakfast. Several ordered a pay-per-view movie and others bought things from the mini-bar and in the gift shop. Interestingly, more than 50% ordered a bottle of wine (the most profitable item in their litany of products and services) whereas the norm was less than 15%.

There were two reasons for these changes in behavior. First, the guests felt that they had extra money to spend, given the fact that the room was free. Second, there was an element of guilt involved, to the point that people felt they owed something to the hotel – to thank them for their generosity.

How did I know this? Because, while still married, my wife and I stayed at the Marriott Hotel, on Marco Island in Florida, for five days/four night. This visit was completely free because I was able to cash in enough "Honored Guest" (this is the name of Marriott's loyalty program) points to cover our stay.

Did I just say "free?" When we checked out our bill was almost $900. There were three rounds of golf, a dozen meals and then there was the wine, a $50 bottle every night. I rationalized this by saying (to myself), "I would never order a $50 bottle of wine but, what the heck, our stay here is free." Bill Marriott should have sent me a letter, telling me that I can stay at one of his hotels for "free," any time I wanted to. After all, on a percentage basis, this is their most profitable item, as that $50 bottle of wine costs them $10.

So, as it turned out, these "perishable" rooms were transformed into major profit centers since, at the time, it was estimated that the "cost" (i.e. housekeeping) to have a room filled was $18 per night. It was about $5 for unoccupied rooms since virtually nothing has to be done, on a daily basis, which means that their occupied rooms had a net maintenance cost of $13.

Sounds pretty good, doesn't it? Well, it's was much, much better than good as, within the following 90 days, 31 of the 52 had booked at the hotel again (very often for business associates), for an average of two nights, at reasonably close to full retail price.

Could it get any better than that? You bet it could. One of those 31 booked the hotel for his daughter's $18,000 wedding.

So, for the cost of sending out 100 invitations – less than $50, they realized revenue of more than – well, I think you get the point.

And, we did one other thing with these guests. We invited them to sit on advisory board where their "obligation" was to provide their opinion when asked about various hotel matters. Twenty-three accepted and each received 100 business cards giving them the title of Marketing Advisor. We told them that, if they would distribute these cards, each recipient would be entitled to two free drinks at the bar, and the Marketing Advisor would receive a $10 room credit to use at any time.

Of the 2300 cards printed, 220 were used. Since the hotel captured the names and addresses of the user (it was required to get the free drinks), they were able to track their value.

The cards were used by 180 people who were not in the hotel's database. So, they now had 180 potential new customers.

Next, they tracked them, for the next six months. Twenty-two stayed at the hotel, again for an average of two nights and 40 others had dinner at their main restaurant with an average party size of just over three.

The business cards, which were really intended to stroke the collective egos of those having their names imprinted, cost $460 to print. The amount of business they brought in exceeded $10,000 (which, eventually, turned out to be more than six times that amount). and, just as was originally the case, there were more good things to come. One of the new customers threw an anniversary party for his parents (a $12,000 event) and another chose the hotel for a regional sales conference (worth more than $50,000 to the property).

And why did this all happen? Because the client was not afraid to give away a little bit of their product away. If you are confident that you have a something good, something that can be "used" repeatedly, spending a lot of money on advertising might well turn out to be more expensive than saying, "Here it is. Why don't you give it a try? We think you'll like it."

NUGGET

Sometimes 'tis better to give (your "perishables") than receive, although there are some exceptions, as was the case when people were told to ask for business cards, instead of doling out theirs.

(Note: I am aware that I have mentioned, a lot more than once, situations where things kept getting better and better. While these are all true stories they don't paint the entire picture).

There were a number of instances where success was not the end result. But this is the perfect example of the phrase, "No risk/no reward." The things that didn't work did not require a great deal of money to try (mostly the costs revolved around advertising and mailings – paper, printing, postage, etc.) On the other hand, while there were programs that attained a marginal success rate, there were others, the ones you have been reading about, or that are still yet to come, where the reward was huge.

Here is a perfect example of how things can work out, if you ignore "expert" predictions which, in this case, would have included mine.

The first agency I joined when I moved to Connecticut did the marketing work for a very large mail order business. On one occasion I got to sit in on one of their "product evaluation" sessions.

They repeatedly had items submitted for consideration. At this particular time they had narrowed things down to 10 that would be tested, with an ad budget of $10,000 for each one.

All of us voted as to which one we thought would be the most successful, down to the one we thought would bomb.

They had developed a formula that had been tested enough times – to the point that they felt comfortable in making a prediction. Six of the ten items would not earn back the money spent on ads, two would break even, one would be marginally successful and one would be so strong that it would cover the costs of all ten ads, and then some.

They were almost spot-on as six bombed, two ads were marginally successful and one broke even. What they could not predict was that the "winner" would become a runaway train.

The product was called the "Roto Stripper," (a device that attached to an electric drill), and whose metal flanges, when spinning, remove paint and/or rust). When the ad campaign had run its course, 150,000 orders had been received – and that was just the beginning.

The item was put into the retail market where it sold more than 1.2M units (being featured on "The Tonight Show," where Johnny Carson gave it his unofficial seal of approval, certainly didn't hurt). They had retailers placing reorders a day after receiving a shipment, and paying to have them shipped by air. At one point they were ordering one container load (20,000 units) shipped from China, every day, for 40 days in a row (including ten days when two container loads were ordered).

In fact, while it impacted their profits, some of them came in by air, just to make sure they could keep their major customers happy. The company that did their printing and packaging told them that they had become their biggest customer by a factor of ten and UPS was sending three-four tractor trailers to their distributer's plant, day, after day, after day.

What does this all prove? That the only votes that really count are those cast by the customers, where the "ballots" consist of checks and credit card charges. Why am I so sure of this? Because when the "experts" voted, as to which of the 10 ads would do the best, the "Roto Stripper" finished 9[th.] I think I'll pass on bragging here since I had it dead last on my piece of paper. My reason personifies a horrible mistake in situations like this. My determination was based on nothing other than the fact that I would never purchase it, but all that meant was that one potential sale wouldn't happen.

"But, If You Act Now........."

But please don't confuse this with the ads you see, hear or read, offering you a one-month supply of some "super nutrient," absolutely free. All you have to do is pay the shipping and handling charge of $6.95. The cost of producing those pills is likely no more that $.60. The bottle costs $.15, the package $.20, the postage $.50 and the "handling" (processing) no more than $1.00. So, their costs are $2.45, meaning that their profit, on every one of these products, that they give away free, is $4.50, per order.

If you think I'm kidding, respond to one of these ads. After 30 days call the company and tell them that you're not sure the pill is helping, so you'd like to try it for another month. Ask them if you can get the additional 30 pills for the same $6.95.

If at least 18 out of 20 providers don't agree to do this, I would be shocked. I would also be very surprised if most of them did not offer you a 90-day supply, absolutely free, with shipping and handling charge of $12.95. Their costs on this will be about $3.50, increasing their profit to $9.45. So, in four months they will have given you 120 pills "absolutely free" and profited by $13.95.

The latest rage, being offered on at least a half dozen infomercials, begins with the words, "Here is the absolute best offer on television today. If you order within the next 10 minutes we will give you a second "widget" absolutely free (all you pay is a separate shipping and handling charge). And, when you call, ask about free shipping."

I did call a couple of them and here's what I learned.

- The first widget would cost me $19.95 + $7.95 for shipping and handling. And yes, the second unit was free – all I would have to pay would be a "processing charge" of $5.95. Furthermore, because I'd be getting two units, there would be no shipping charges, meaning that I could subtract $2.00 from the amount due for the first unit. This means that I would pay only $19.95 + $5.95 for the first unit and only $5.95 for the "free" one.

So, let's add everything up. To save you the time the total is $31.95.

Now, I happen to own one of these "widgets" (not purchased as a result of a TV commercial). As best I can judge, the manufacturing cost is about $3.00 ($6.00 for two). Having visited the Post Office I can say for a fact that the shipping charges (for both) would be $1.75. Since I ran a mail order company I can accurately tell you that the total process/handling costs would be no more than $1.00. Toss in $.50 for the shipping container and they will end up with $9.25 in expenses, and a net profit of $22.50.

Oh yes. I didn't "call within the next 10 minutes." I waited another 12 hours. I told the operator that, since I didn't call within the allotted amount of time, I assumed that their special offer would not be available. The person on the other end of the phone said, "I'm not supposed to do this but, in your case, I'm going to make an exception."

This makes me wonder why I'm writing this book, instead of marketing a pill that will cause you to lose weight, increase your sex drive, and make your teeth whiter, all at the same time - and the second unit would be (almost) absolutely free.

Give Customers a Bank Book – With Your Name on It

When American Airlines launched the first Frequent Flyer program the rules of marketing changed forever, at least for those who were astute enough to see what had been accomplished.

In a word it was "equity" – the consumer/customer/client suddenly had certain type of "ownership" in the brand. And ownership translates to loyalty.

Think of any of these plans, whether they be airlines, hotels, credit cards or a myriad of other businesses, as providing the brand free advertising (the card in your wallet and the web site saved on your computer).

And the customer gets the equivalent of a bank book (an account) with the possibility of continual deposits, made by the brand. Why shouldn't the customer be loyal? After all, the customer isn't the one making those deposits into their account – the brand is. How great is that? Great enough that American Airlines saw a significant jump in passengers serviced, passengers who turned out to be a great deal more loyal than was previously the case.

Not only that, the well never runs dry. If you accumulate 40,000 miles, and cash them in for two free coach tickets, what does your next statement look like? I will tell you.

Starting balance	40,000	miles
Two roundtrip coach tickets	-40,000	miles
Temporary balance	0	miles
Special loyalty bonus	5,000	miles
New Balance	5,000	miles

If you had a zero balance that figure would define your loyalty. But now? You're already on your way to a couple of more free tickets.

These programs can exist at any level, from the most sophisticated, computer-driven, models, to those so simple that entering the data into a computer would be a waste of time, money and manpower.

An example of the latter was created for a Toyota dealership I was consulting for back in the late 1980's.

As with most businesses in this category their real profit-center was in their service area. In fact, if you would guarantee that you would have all your servicing done by the dealer, they would sell you the car at cost, and maybe even at a loss. You can check this out for yourself. Call the dealer where you bought your car and ask them how much a "two-year, 36,000 mile" tune-up/servicing would cost - in my case the figure I was quoted was

$575. Then visit the auto servicing location nearest to your house and ask the same question – I did and was quoted $175, for the exact same work. In the latter case I would have my car back in three hours (or less). The dealer would require 24 hours.

What I created for the Toyota dealership was a very simple "punch card" that looked like a Monopoly board, except instead of "properties" the boxes included dollar amounts – specifically $10 or $25. The total value of the card was $250 (the printing cost, for 1000, was $300, while the potential revenue they could generate was more than $200,000 although, admittedly, they would have already had some of that business).

In the middle of the card was a "scratch and win" circle. Once you had $250 of servicing done, evidenced by the fact that all the dollar amounts had been punched out, you would find out what you won. And every card was a guaranteed winner. 98% of them awarded a free oil change, with the other 2% spread among more expensive items, like complete tune-ups. And, there was one card containing the grand prize, a new Toyota.

The key element that made this work was what happened when the customer reached $250. They were not only given a new card, but $50 was immediately punched out. Toyota had made a deposit into the customer's car-care bank.

I moved west before the first full year of the promotion had been completed. However, for the first six months of the year their repeat business, in their service department, was up by 28% over the same period of time in the previous year.

Here's a slight variation. In this case it was a good idea that worked, and then died.

I was retained, by Circle K, to come up with something they could test, insofar as a loyalty program was concerned. I created a punch card, similar to the one I had done for Toyota. Except, in this case, the boxes contained items the store sold – hot dogs, chips, beverages and candy bars (five of each). Once the entire card was punched, the holder was entitled to $2 worth of gas – free (back then this actually meant something as since that $2 bought about two gallons).

Our demographic was teenagers who had just gotten their drivers' license – specifically males. In most states this information is a matter of public record. We opted for Texas, and mailed 5,000 cards to each of four different markets.

When the cards were turned in the driver was given a new one, this time with one of each of the items punched out. Once I saw the results (which were excellent) I stated planning a second mailing to the same 20,000 names, after the ones who had "played the game" were subtracted.

About two weeks before this offer was to go out I asked Circle K for the cards that had been turned in. I needed this much time in order to input the data on the back of the card (the name and address of the cardholder).

Much to my surprise (make that shock), when I got the cards I discovered that no more than 10% of them had this information. It seems that, when Circle K contacted the stores, to advise them of the program, they mailed a two-page description of the plan. The information related to capturing the contact information, before the free gas was given out, was on the second page.

The problem was that Circle K neglected to include the second page. About 10% of their stores figured it out on their own, but not the rest. This made the creation of a data base, of any meaningful size, impossible.

While this created a bump in the road, the response was great enough to warrant starting from scratch, choosing different markets. That is what should have happened – but it didn't. The CEO of Circle K left to go run Blockbuster (not a very wise choice, as it turned out) and his replacement started his tenure by cutting their marketing budget in half, with my program being one of many casualties.

(Note: I've never quite understood why, unless it's illegal, businesses that are public companies, don't give either stock, or stock options, to customers. Here's the most basic of examples. You purchase a car from manufacturer AB. You are offered a rebate of $1500 or $2500 in AB stock. Anyone who opts for the latter now has "equity" in AB and therefore wants them to do well, so the value of their shares will increase. Where do they go first, the next time they want to buy a car? AB would not only be the first place, it is likely that it will be the only one, especially if they are going to get additional stock (I would give them $3000 worth this time, which goes to back to the "lifetime value of a customer" adage). You might even consider giving them an additional $100 in stock for every referral that ends in a sale. Unlike finding a great babysitter, this is something worth sharing, with friends and co-workers).

NUGGET

In all of these programs the message couldn't be simpler. The company is going to give you a special part of themselves. And, not only that, the more you use them, the more they will give you. Finally, if your piggy bank

gets full, after you break it to get out the money (miles, rooms, etc.) they'll give you a brand new one, and it won't be empty. Be the piggy bank distributor and you will prosper.

NUGGET

Anyone who tells you that consumer loyalty can't be bought is a noble individual – they are also wrong. All you have to do is find the tipping point. Let me put it another way.

A man approaches a woman, standing at the bar, in a fancy hotel. He buys her a drink then says to her, "Would you come up to my room with me for $10,000?" While he's not all that great looking, he's talking about a lot of money so she says "Sure." He then asks, "How about for $10?" She gets an outraged look on her face and, through gritted teeth says, "What do you think I am, some kind of prostitute?" His answer is, "I think we've pretty much established that. Now we're just negotiating the price."

Advertising - What Were They Thinking? Or Were They Thinking at All?

In question and answer sessions that follow my talks, I am almost always asked my opinion about advertising. My response is that I won't dwell on this because I feel it is vastly overrated and far too much money is spent in this arena. However, I never hesitate to tell listeners what I believed to be the best TV ad campaign of my lifetime.

It was only two words; it named the product and, using a sense of humor, repeatedly demonstrated the many situations where the product could be used. The two words? "Got Milk?"

One of their spots showed a man, locked in a room filled with nothing but dry cereal. All the audio said was "Got Milk?" My favorite ad, of the six spots they ran, showed a man, with his mouth stuffed with cake. He gets a call from a contest he entered. The voice on the other end said, "For $10,000 can you name the first president of the United State?" Crumbs began spewing out of his mouth but he was still unable to talk. His caller said, "Well, it seems as if our contestant hung up. It was either that or he didn't know the answer because all I heard was 'Gorg Wersontoon." The next two words? "Got Milk?

As for the best ad I've ever written? Well, it's obviously a pretty subjective question but here's my response, first with some background.

In many ways I am very old fashioned. In my humble opinion (OK, not so humble) I believe that people should be proud of what they do and not be afraid to exhibit that pride in their advertising. I also believe in playing up one's strengths and, with all things being equal, not being afraid to exhibit a sense of humor.

My CPA had complained that everyone thought of her as a "bean counter." She hated the phrase and asked for some help as to how to best present herself, with the hope of getting new business. What I suggested was exactly the opposite of what she expected. I told her to **make fun of the things people make fun of.**

I had her photographed in turn-of-the-century accounting garb – visor, garters on the sleeves, etc. She was standing next to an old fashioned roll-top desk, on top of which sat a giant jar of jelly beans.

The copy read as follows:

Question: **WHY HIRE A BEAN COUNTER?**

Answer: **Because** the government insists that you file reports related to your bean count.

Because most people don't want to count their own beans.

Because even those who don't mind the counting can't keep track of the official bean counting rules, which seem to change every year.

Question: **WHY HIRE ACCOUNTING WORLD TO BE YOUR BEAN**

COUNTER?

Answer: **Because** Accounting World clients get to keep more of their beans.

Because, far more often than not, Accounting World clients have more beans on 12/31 than they did on 1/1.

So, whether it be one bean in savings, or two in the stock market, they remain your beans – in your piggy bank or in your brokerage account. Remember, anyone can have their beans and then eat them. However, only with expert advise and planning can you eat your beans yet still have even more of them when you're done.

When you reach the point that dealing with your beans becomes something you don't want to have to think about, call Accounting World at 800-888-1040.

NUGGET

When you are in a business that people make fun of, or that is the butt of jokes, instead of fighting the image

that people have, go along with it, to the point that you are funnier than they are. But, in the process of doing so, make sure you include the benefits you provide.

(Note: For some reason, most of the good ads I've written have been for friends, with no money changing hands. Maybe it's the fact that I was operating under no pressure, to meet deadlines or justify my fees, that made it easier.

A BLT on Toast w/Mayo
(but hold the B, the L, the T and the toast)

(Note: Some of you may recognize this title as a variation of Jack Nicholson's scene in "Five Easy Pieces," except he was trying to get an order of toast).

I've given you an example of my long-form ad so, to balance things off, here is the story of its polar opposite – only 11 words. For those of you who find it difficult to believe, that I could write something this short, read on (in fact that's what I'm hoping all of you will do, if for no other reason than I've made you curious). My favorite one-sentence ad was handed over, free of charge, to a relative of a relative – someone trying to make an impression in her first week of work.

She had just started in the advertising department at the Mayo Clinic's facility in Scottsdale, AZ (my home town). Over lunch she mentioned that they were having a perception problem in that people seem to think of them as the "last resort," as in "Things got so bad I finally went to the Mayo Clinic."

She went on to tell me that they had a number of primary care physicians so, in effect, the Clinic could be your family doctor. The question at hand was how best to get that message across.

I gave her one sentence. Her boss loved it. Her boss's boss loved it. The hospital's Executive Board loved it. Unfortunately, the only ones who didn't love it were the decision makers at the "home office," in Rochester, MN. They thought it was too frivolous for a hospital of great repute. The line was *"The recipe for good health should always include a little Mayo."*

To this day (almost 20 years later) I think the good folks back in the "Land of a Thousand Lakes" needed to lighten up a bit, especially if they wanted to convince people that going to the Mayo Clinic did not always mean that it was a matter of life and death.

Obviously, as far as the second of my ads went, there was no way to measure its effectiveness – since it never ran. As for the CPA, the evidence was circumstantial, since she had never run an ad before. However, they could do some year-to-year comparisons.

In the previous year, in the months of June – August (the slowest time in that business) they had signed on two new clients. In those same three months, a year later, after the ad ran (in May), they picked up six new accounts. I'll leave any decisions about the ads' effectiveness to whoever wishes to pass judgment.

On the Other Hand We Have...............

As far as bad advertising, there are so many examples that I find it hard to know where to begin. So, I'll pick on one of our local companies. What was America West Airlines (now US Air) thinking? They ran a very expensive-to-create series of TV ads featuring a rock and roll group that appeared as if they just got out of prison. Each character looked and acted worse than the next. They were, almost in their own words, losers. Do potential passengers really want to be associated with losers? And do they really want to find themselves trapped next to one of these people on a plane – for several hours?

With all that being said I, as well as the awards committees, often forget about the bottom line. For years viewers voted an ad by Anacin (it showed a hammer, repeatedly hitting a head, as the representation of a "pounding" headache) as the most annoying one on television. Obviously "annoying" didn't equate with sales since the more often they ran the ad the more their revenues from this brand went up. One pundit suggested that the real intent of the ad was to give the viewer a "pounding" headache. It may have been delivering a subliminal message – that the only way to be able to put up with our commercials is to buy our product (remember, back then, there was no such thing as a remote and certainly no way to fast-forward through a commercial).

At the opposite end of the spectrum was a radio campaign – a series of ads for Piels Beer. They featured Carl Reiner and Mel Brooks and, during the time they were on the air, won half dozen "best in show" awards. However, midway through the last cycle of radio spots the company declared bankruptcy.

I also call out those companies who seemed to feel that their TV ads are so compelling viewers never turn their head or leave the room. If I ever do a television ad that does not name the product, both in vision and voice, it's time to change careers.

(Note: A while back I received a call from an outraged friend of mine. The strange thing was that her complaint was something I had thought of months ago.

229

However, as it didn't impact me directly, I put it on the backburner (I have a special stove that has a dozen of them).

The ad she heard was for a discount store that said they sold things "at a fraction of department store prices." She had seen a dress, in Macy's, where it was selling for $99.99. She called the discounter to see if they stocked that particular piece of apparel, in her size. When she was told that they did she decided to drive over there (about 15 miles from where she lived) because she really loved the design and color.

When she located the dress she was shocked to discover that its price was $97.99. She asked to see a manager who told her that she didn't see what the problem was since $97.99 is "a fraction" of $99.99. I wish Andy Rooney was still alive because he would have loved calling the store on the carpet.

And, the fact is that the dress would have ended up being more expensive because that 30-mile roundtrip cost her $6.00 in gas, not to mention wasting an hour of her time.

If she ever asks me to picket the store with her I will be happy to be there. I will make sure we do so on the store's property – which is illegal. Were they to threaten to call the police we wouldn't move. But I would call friends I have at two of our local stations, affiliated with national networks, and invite them to send one of their mobile units to where we were standing. However, before doing so, I would make sure this chain was not advertising on their stations since, sad to say, money almost always triumphs over morality).

This final story is being added because, if nothing else, it is funny enough to make me smile.

There is a store, in NYC which, for the last 20 years, has had a sign in its front window that reads, "LOST OUR LEASE – EVERYTHING ON SALE." If anyone inquires about this they are told, "The sign is absolutely true. Several years ago I went looking for my lease. The last time I saw the document it was in my desk drawer, but it's not there now, so I think it's fair to say that I lost it."

One last ("last" comes after "final," but before "absolutely last/final") word on advertising, at least for the moment.

I spent a couple of years working in the world of infomercials or, as I once heard them called, "hyperbole on steroids." What follows should be considered a work in progress as each week seems to bring forth a heretofore unknown phrase. I include this paragraph with the hope that each reader thinks of something they might be able to add. If you do please contact me and say, "But wait, there's more."

"Get ready to take down this toll-free number. It's the fishing invention of the century. The incredible weight loss program all America is talking about. Lose 30 pounds in a month, 20 pounds in a week, eight pounds in 48 hours. The inches will melt away. A special TV offer for folks 55 and over. A treasury of the most beautiful music ever recorded. It's rod, reel, line, bobber, the whole thing. Makes hundreds of julienne fries in just seconds. Eliminates ugly facial hair. Takes 10 strokes off your score. Adds 40 yards to your drives. Seals, protects and beautifies. Fades horrid age spots. Cleans from inside your home. Guaranteed not to split, crack or peel. Requires no medical exam. If not satisfied your money cheerfully refunded. Double your money back. Keeps tarnish from coming back. You get the original hits by the original artists. Designed by leading orthopedic surgeons. Used by the astronauts. Built to last a lifetime.

Made of amazing space-age plastic with the look and feel of genuine leather. Four easy payments and we'll pay the first one. Layered in 14-carat gold. Optional heat and massage unit. You can't be turned down. Handy credit card organizer. Flip-up foot rest. Studded with real dimonelles. Room for hundreds of your favorite recipes. Cuts tomatoes paper-thin. Matching goldtone chain. Free walnut-finish display stand you'll be proud to own. Runs on ordinary household current. Not available in stores. Goes with any décor. Never needs waxing. And boy, does it catch fish! Your hands never touch water. Your friend will wonder how you did it. Operators are standing by. You may already have won. You'll wonder how you got along without us. Look for our announcement in Sunday's paper. There's never been anything like it. Inflates in less than a minute. All your favorite teams. Makes mountains of cole slaw. Goes where ordinary brushes cannot. Pays for itself with just one use. How much would you expect to pay? Costs just pennies a day. Yes, that's less than $.71 cents per month, regardless of your age or medical status. And we won't bill you until next February. Money back if not delighted. Can you think of a better gift for Junior or Dad at just $19.95? That's right, just $9.95. At this price we're practically giving them away. Compare at twice the price. Thousands sold at $49.95. Not 99.00 or even $79.00 but only $39.95. So you don't forget call before midnight tonight. Accept no substitutes. Beware of imitations. As seen on TV. Free calculator with your paid subscription. Cancel at any time. You've heard about the magic of Wok cooking. Free placement service for qualified graduates. Cooks an entire meal at one time. No obligation. The book is yours to keep. No salesman will call. While supplies last. Offer will not be repeated this year. Remember, the call is free. Void where prohibited. (And here comes my absolute favorite) Send us back the unused portion of your product and we'll send you back

the unused portion of your money. BUT WAIT, THERE'S MORE!!!

While what you've just read is the world of infomercials, reduced to one lengthy paragraph that could serve as the basis of almost every televised drug ad you see today. Recently I saw a 60-second spot that included 28 possible side effects, including death. Since I can live with my condition I think I'll keep my medicine chest looking like Mother Hubbard's cupboard. By the way is there any drug, other than nausea medications, that does not have nausea as a potential side effect?

Marketing Yourself - Off and On the Job

Seemingly this chapter is really not related to the subject matter of this book. Having said that there is, once again, a lesson to be learned here – don't fear your own creativity. And besides, any time you apply for a job or try to get a new client you are "marketing yourself."

I remember sitting in my office one day when my administrative assistant, who was recently divorced, began complaining about the problems related to getting back into the dating game again, especially because she hated the bar scene.

I offered a broad suggestion and then a specific one.

I told Suzanne to consider doing some volunteer work – either for a charity whose cause she supported or, perhaps, for a political candidate. I pointed out that there are several advantages to using these as venues for meeting people – you will share certain interests, the other person is unlikely to be in financial difficulty (or they wouldn't have the time to volunteer) and, of greatest importance, the fact that they are not there to meet people makes meeting them that much easier.

People in bars tend to be either overly defensive or too aggressive. The result is this artificial barrier that makes it difficult to get to know someone. Everyone is so busy trying to impress (or act nonchalant) that reality never gets through the front door.

On the other hand, people tend not to show up (to help stuff envelopes, paint a building, or hand out food) expecting to be hit on. Without meaning to be crude, it is that very fact that makes the "hitting" easier (for either sex). People's guards are down and their real self tends to be on display.

The specific idea I gave Suzanne was this:

"Suzanne, next week there's a Chamber of Commerce 'Business After Hours' mixer being held. It's a networking event that provides a wonderful social opportunity.

Let me tell you what you will find when you get there. There will be about 400 attendees, half men and half women. Of the 200 men, 100 will be married and 100 will be single. Of the 100 who are single, a third will be too old for you and a third will be too young. Of the 33 who are left a third will be too short and a third will be too heavy (for some reason men are almost never considered to be too tall or too thin). This leaves 11 reasonably qualified people. You know they're employed (pretty much a prerequisite for attending) and you don't even have to ask them their name (it's on their badge).

Not only that, you know where they work (it's on the badge as well) which allows for a very easy opening of a conversation. If it says Motorola, ask them if they know your friend who works there and if it says JKL Manufacturing, inquire as to what JKL does. Once you've got a conversation going (the hardest part), nature can take its course. And, if you suddenly find yourself bored, there's always that person you really have to talk to, who's on the other side of the room."

I went on to point out that while the Chamber of Commerce never mentions this in their literature, they are an outstanding singles club, as are a multitude of networking organizations.

It was a little strange, considering how much of an extrovert I am, but I share Suzanne's distaste for bars, especially as a means of meeting people. I never quite figured out how to initiate a conversation without sounding foolish (i.e. "Come here often?" or "What's your sign?" – I think I'm dating myself here).

In fact, I have had only had one real success story to talk about.

A friend and I were meeting a mutual acquaintance, who was visiting from out of town. The three of us were standing a few feet behind a bar where every seat was taken. Among the people seated there were three women whose backs were to us. However, because the area behind the bottles was a mirror, it was easy to see what everyone looked like (remember, light travels faster than sound, which may not have all that important here since it was so noisy that I couldn't hear the conversation going on at the bar).

I was quickly smitten (I'm not sure I have ever used the word before) by the middle one of the three and decided that I had to figure out some way of meeting her.

The conversation between my friends went on for a few more minutes although I was not really listening, as my attention was focused elsewhere.

Suddenly I said (to myself), "I've got it, or at least I think I do. There's a dollar bill on the floor under her bar stool and, if it's not hers, I think I may have an opening."

I took a few steps, picked up the dollar bill and tapped the young lady on the shoulder. The conversation then went like this:

Me: "Excuse me, but I found this dollar bill under your chair and thought you might have dropped it."

She: "No, it's not mine" (had she claimed it as her own I would have been dead in the water).

Me: "Well, then I'm faced with a bit of a dilemma. I found the dollar but it was under your chair. That kind of makes it our dollar but I don't think either one of us can do much with fifty cents. So, I have a suggestion. Why don't I use the dollar to purchase a lottery ticket? Then, when we win a million dollars, we'll have something worthwhile to split."

She: (laughing) "That sounds like a great idea."

Me: "Good, now who should I call to tell them they're rich?"

At that point "she" gave "me" her name and phone number.

I waited two days and then called "She". I said, "There's good news and there's bad news. The good news is that we won the lottery. The bad news is that we only had three correct numbers and so we get $5.00. Since sharing that won't let either one of us retire, how about if I use that as a down payment on taking you out to dinner?"

She agreed and it turned out to be one of the longest relationships I was involved in since being divorced.

It took a couple of years before I realized that, if I wanted to be devious, given that all is fair in love and war, I could just palm a dollar bill and then pretend to find it, under the chair of the person I wish to meet. (If they claimed it for their own I would exit gracefully, complete with the knowledge that this was not a person I really wanted to meet).

I can't report on the subsequent success of this "tactic" since I have yet to find the appropriate time and place to employ it.

I will take this opportunity to provide you with my all-time favorite "pick-up" technique, as told to me by a good friend.

She was in the supermarket and, out of the corner of her eye she saw, in her words, a real "hunk." The first thing she did was "parallel shop." This allowed her to make sure he wasn't wearing a wedding ring and that there were no diapers in his shopping cart. Once she decided he was "fair game," she approached him, in the produce section and said, "I'm sorry but I could not help coming over to tell you how much you look like my fifth husband." When he responded with, "How many times have you been married?" she replied "four." This might have worked if his girlfriend didn't walk over, just as he started laughing. For some reason, when he told her about the exchange, she failed to see the humor in it (if I were offering advice I would have told him that to be in a relationship, with someone who lacked a sense of humor, did not bode well).

(Note: It seems that every time I bring up a subject I think of one more thing I want to mention – in this case it is words that aren't, when you come right down to it, words. I am including this because it peripherally relates to one of the above stories as it represents that other "long relationship." You will be pleased to know that, when it comes to this subject, there will no more 'drop-ins' since two is all there have been.

My friend Michelle, who you've already read about, was supposed to run an errand for me. When I got home she told me that she thought she had screwed things up, because she "misunderheard" me. That has become one of my favorites as it combines two explanations (hearing and comprehension) into one word and, as you can tell, I believe in brevity (I'm still searching for that sarcasm font).

This leads me to what I mentioned in the first paragraph of this note.

For the six months prior to moving to Arizona I was dating Joanne, a single mom with a three-year-old son. I'm not suggesting that he was hyper but he had been banned from the local McDonald's.

Joanne and I had a Saturday night dinner date and I called her, the day before, to confirm the time I was going to be picking her up. Once that was accomplished here's how the conversation went.

Joanne: "Philip, I don't need to know where we're going but I'd appreciate it if you'd let me know what the proper attire will be."

Philip: "It's pretty fancy so I don't think you can be over-dressed."

Joanne: "Then I think I'll wear that little black dress you like so much."

Philip: "That will be fine, but I give you fair warning. When I arrive at your house I might spend at least 30 minutes kissing your neck."

Joanne: "Why Philip, is this day before play?"

I would like to think that she had never said this before, but rather had made it up, on the spot. She was certainly bright and quick enough to have done so. But, on the chance that the comment was a "rerun" I didn't ask.

This is because, in many situations, you shouldn't ask a question where one of the possible answers would prove to be disappointing. As Jack Nicholson said to Tom Cruise, there are times where "You can't handle the truth").

NUGGET

There are situations where you can be clever, devious or both! The situation doesn't always call for it, and you never want to be inappropriate. However, there are a number of occasions, as in the "girl at the bar" story, where there is no downside risk and plenty of upside potential. My guess is that you are a lot more creative than you think – most people are.

The Power of Empowerment

Earlier in the book I talked about the value of empowerment, when it comes to providing an unhappy customer the possibility of coming up with their own solution.

This temporary turning-over-of-power has so many more applications. The basic premise behind all of them is to have the other person feel as if they have choices, where all of their options result in what you wanted to accomplish.

When I lived back in Connecticut, my wife and I were having dinner at a co-worker's house. He and his wife had a two-year-old son who was the clone of the Energizer Bunny.

When it was time for him to go to bed, his Dad said, "OK Brian, it's your choice tonight. Do you want me to carry you upstairs on my shoulders or do you want to go up by yourself?" Which ever choice Brian made, he was going to bed.

Appropriate Reactions

One day I walked through my front door, after a truly miserable day at work, only to trip over my son's jacket, lying on the floor, just where it always seemed to be. I went somewhat ballistic and yelled at him - to get downstairs and hang up the jacket.

A couple of days later the polar opposite occurred – a couple of new clients, a great lunch, etc. When I tripped over the same coat I simply picked it up and put it on a hangar.

The problem here is that neither reaction was correct and that my son was being overly punished (me yelling) or indirectly rewarded (me doing the chore) based on things that he had nothing to do with. What I should have done, in both cases, was simply ask him, in a reasonably calm voice, to please come downstairs and hang up his coat.

However, as I have said before (at least I think I have), I had no real training in parenting and was constantly trying to figure out a set of rules for something that had no apparent rulebook. In fact, as successful as I was in marketing, only once can I brag about coming up with an effective way of "communicating" with my son.

It seemed that I was at the end of the rope with Justin. I had already grounded him for life (twice) and was incredibly frustrated at being unable to come up with something that would have an impact on his behavior. He was a typical 14-year-old at the time, convinced that he was a lot smarter than his father.

I applied as much of the right side of my brain as I could and, after 10 minutes of intense thought, came up with a plan. I went into the garage, got a hammer and chisel and took them to the door of Justin's room. I then used the tools to knock out the pins holding the hinges. I removed his door and told him that he could have it back only after 48 hours of civilized behavior. It was the only angelic period of Justin's teenage years. To a person that age privacy is critical so being, for all intents and purposes, left naked, can really turn someone around.

A friend of mine liked the idea so much that she insisted that she was going to invent Velcro hinges so she could remove her daughter's door at will.

Although it's probably not necessary to point this out, you probably can see how this applies in the world of business. If you overreact or do the opposite, you will have a client wondering what they did to warrant that kind of treatment.

NUGGET

Once again, don't be afraid to be creative. Things that are done the same way all the time quickly wear out their welcome as you get tuned out. And take care that you never allow unrelated events to affect how you deal with your children, clients or customers. They have nothing to do with your bad mood, or your problems, so figure out how to check them at the door (unless someone has removed it).

Simpler is Almost Always Better

All of us occasionally try to complicate things. For some reason we believe that the more we say or write, the likelihood of getting our point across increases (I know, this book suggests that "hypocrisy" is probably my middle name) In point of fact, more often than not, it causes a good deal of confusion and then wastes a lot of time, as you attempt to clarify things. In fairness to myself, the reason I employ the "more" (rather than "less") approach is because I want to really emphasize the things I believe to be the most important.

NUGGET

Occam's razor – This is the principle that says, when faced with competing hypotheses that are equal in other respects, select the one that makes the fewest new assumptions. In other words, the simplest solution is often the best one. As for the reason for the name, I have no idea. I did go to Wikipedia to check the spelling (which can also be Ockham) but started to fall asleep before I got through two paragraphs explaining the history of the phrase.

You Have Two Ears and One Mouth and They Should Be Used in that Proportion

When I was in the non-profit world I filed dozens of grant applications. Very early on in the process, after failing to be a finalist, I called someone in the granting organization to see if I could learn where I went astray (this is always recommended). Doing something wrong, the same way twice, and expecting different results, will often result in unemployment.

Having learned this, every time I was looking to receive a grant of $10,000 or more (which meant almost all of the time), I would make an appointment to meet with the person who would be evaluating the applications. I would begin by saying, "I'm certainly not here to ask that you answer your own questions. However, I want to make sure I understand all of them."

I would then go on to ask that they explain certain segments, even if I thought I knew what they were looking for. And I would take copious notes. Sometimes I would ask permission to record our meeting (no one ever objected) with the explanation that this would save me the time spent trying to read my own handwriting.

(Note: Being able to record something like this offers another huge advantage. It allows you to hear everything that is said, which is impossible if you have to spend time writing. And, you can easily confirm what you thought you heard by listening to the recording. There is one other thing I found helpful. I would look at my watch to see exactly when the conversation began. The only writing I would do was to put down the exact time I deemed something to be of above average importance was said. This way I could easily find it during the playback stage of the process.

This, in turn, gave me the freedom to concentrate on things such as tone and nuance.

Among the things I've learned is that most people love hearing the sound of their own voice (which is not the same as hearing what your voice sounds like), reading their own words and having their own opinions confirmed. And I didn't have to worry about hearing the words "You again?" as I never tried this twice with the same grantor (unless the questions on their application had changed).

Here is where I'm going to brag a bit (I'm sure that there are several of you who are thinking about going back to the beginning of the book to see if this the 5th – or even 50th time I am patting myself on the back)

When I was running the Child Crisis Center, I submitted 30 grant applications. All were related to the "Kids' Campus" we intended to build.

I visited 26 of the potential funders, and we ended up getting money from 24 of them. What was especially nice was that two foundations gave us more money than I asked for.

Point and Counterpoint - Before You Start Writing

One of the earlier nuggets suggested that, before you start writing anything, such as a grant application, you read the questions – all of them. Then, after making a copy of the application, next to each question, put a number of bullet points that you intend to include in your answer - but don't start writing yet.

Read the questions again, look at your bullet points and ask yourself "While my bullet points are interesting and informative, DO THEY ANSWER THE QUESTION?" Far too often people (and I have certainly been guilty of this and, in fact, may be doing it here) fall in love with their own words. **They are determined to make their point, even if that point is pointless as it doesn't address the point of the question.**

Once again, and I can never say this too often, make sure that, when you are reading a question, you understand the meaning of what they wrote, not your interpretation. If there is any doubt, call and ask questions (a face-to-face meeting, although preferable, is not always possible). The fact that you do this should not work against you in any way. But, if you hear something like "figure it out for yourself," throw that application away and spend your time working on something more likely to succeed.

If a teacher asks, "What did Shakespeare mean when he wrote 'To be, or not to be, that is the question,' at some point, if you can't figure it out, he or she should tell you – after all, he (or she) is the teacher and you are the student. A granting organization is the equivalent of a teacher in that they ask questions. However, if they are unwilling to answer legitimate ones from applicant's (students) you don't want to try to participate in their grant process because, should you get a grant (which is unlikely, if they exhibit this kind of attitude), they will drive you crazy, from day one.

I have served on six "Peer Review Panels" for the U.S. Department of Education. We were asked to evaluate applications for grants to cover after school physical fitness programs. Each year 100 grants are awarded. This money is distributed over a three-year period, with the average award being $300,000 ($100,000 per year), although some have for as much as $500,000.

The applications have six sections, with different point values assigned to each. The points add up to 100 and, to become a finalist, the applicant must receive a score of 90 or higher. Each document is "scored" by three individuals. If our scores are too far apart (more than 10 points) we work with a facilitator who helps us argue our points to our fellow panel members. We each move a little here, and bend a little there, until we get within that ten point differential.

One reason we were often a bit too far apart is because of something the Department allows that I continually object to – but I have yet to convince anyone in authority that they are being unfair. Specifically it relates to the fact that a candidate has to be awarded an appropriate score, even if the information provided is not where it should be. Their attitude seems to be, "When we tell you it's time for dinner, we just want to make sure you come inside. If you choose to eat in the attic, that's fine – as long as you're in the house." I can just see the look on my mother's face if I had even suggested that I didn't believe it necessary for me to sit down at the table, with the rest of the family.

But hey, it's the government. One of the rules calls for 12-pt. type – but if someone used 10-pt., when filling out the application, there is no penalty, even though it gives the rule- breaker a significant advantage.

This is a very long introduction to the point I want to make or, to be more accurate, make again.

Each panel gets 15 applications to score so, in total, I have read 90 of them.

The number of scores over 90? Two.

The number of scores under 25? Seventeen.

The number of scores under 10? Seven.

The number of scores under 5? Two.

How could this be? When you take SAT tests you get 200 points just for entering your name on the score sheet.

While there have been a myriad of reasons that account for these horrendous performances the one that probably accounted for 80% of the deducted points related to the fact that the applicant DIDN'T ANSWER THE QUESTION!

If a question says, "Explain how gang activity affects programs that exist currently. Begin by stating what percentage of students have been identified as being gang members."

There is only one way to answer, at least if you are serious about getting a grant.

"According to our Police Department, 13% of middle school students are believed to be gang members. That percentage increases to 31% for those in high school. This gang activity has had many negative affects on our existing programs, the most serious being what happens when we can't provide adequate transportation home. And, we have had a great deal of theft, of equipment, because of not having enough supervision."

That's it. That's all that should be written. You will notice that several words that appear in the question also can be found in the response (gang activity, exist, affects, percentage and gang members). Also note that it doesn't mention money (how much is needed, how it will be spent, and when it is required).

An inordinate number of applicants never even come close to providing anything similar to what I just recommended. Others want to throw the kitchen sink into their answer. They might mention that they intend to use the money to upgrade their kitchen or purchase new beds. The problem there is that the question never asked for this information. Or they feel it important to give the percentage of children in the "free school lunch" program. Once again, that fact has nothing to do with what is being sought.

What can make matters even worse is if this is the first question, because any answer, that includes things not asked, will get you off on the wrong foot. Remember, once again, that you never get a 2nd chance to make a 1st impression.

One of your goals should be to create a situation where you will be given the benefit of the doubt and you can do this by making sure your first answer is perfect. Otherwise you will be creating doubt, which will influence how everything else you write is judged.

Think of this in terms of placing an order. If the provider does whatever they were expected to do, the chances that you will order again will be enhanced. If they slip up on their 10th shipment you will probably be willing to cut them some slack. However, if that error occurs right out of the box, you will be fighting your own bad reputation, from that point on.

NUGGET

In one of the Bush/Gore debates, prior to the 2000 election, the candidates were told that, in this particular format, there would be no opening statement. After the first question asked of both of them, they proceeded to totally ignore it so that they might give – yes, you guessed it - their standard opening statement. I wish the moderator had stopped both of them and said "PLEASE ANSWER THE QUESTION" (this is what makes these debates a total waste of time unless, of course, someone says something dumb enough to allow the media to burn them on the editorial and Op-Ed stakes). Unfortunately applicants have no one to yell at them. That's why, on the top of each page of the application, you should put a Post-it note that reads, in very large letters, "ANSWER THE QUESTION!!!!!"

In cases like this it is not pandering to "tell someone what they want to hear." You may not like the questions but, to be quite blunt, they have no interest in your opinions. They want their questions answered.

One of the many things I don't understand is why applicants don't contact a previous winner (the names are a matter of public record) and ask for assistance. You would not be competing with them since, for this program, you can receive a grant only once in a ten-year period. In fact, if they are in the same geographic

area as you are, they should want to assist you –
remember, "A rising tide lifts all boats."

When I was running the West Valley Child Crisis Center
(WVCCC) I wanted to apply for a capital campaign
grant from The Kresge Foundation (the family that started
K-Mart). I knew that the college I had graduated from
had been successful in this regard, so I called their
Development Director and asked if she had any advice.

She said, "Philip, their application is pretty straight
forward, but there are a couple of things you should
know. They consider themselves to be 'The Kresge
Foundation,' not the "Kresge Foundation." It may seem
trivial but they like to see the "T" in "The" capitalized
(reaffirming that names can be important). And, there is
question that asks you to tell them what percentage of
your Board of Directors has contributed to your capital
campaign fund. There is only one correct answer – 100%.
If it's less than that their attitude will be, why should we
support you when there are members of your board who
don't?"

I'm not saying that knowing these two things, in
advance, tipped the scale in our favor but they certainly
didn't hurt.

Let me tell you how absurd things can get at times. A
couple of days before I was going to fly to Michigan, to
make a presentation to them, our capital campaign fund
still had not received a contribution from two of our board
members – in spite of the fact that they had been told
how critical it was, and that it didn't matter how much
they gave (because that question was not asked on their
application – see story above). So, the morning of my
flight, I wrote out two $10 checks, with the notation that
these represented contributions from those recalcitrant
individuals. On the way to the airport I deposited them

into our fund, meaning that I did not feel terribly guilty when my answer to their question was, "100%."

NIMBY – Not In My Back Yard

In the non-profit world your own geographic area is probably the last place to look for assistance, since everyone is knocking on the same doors. Without meaning to sound rude, if I have found the secret to getting money from the locally-based RST Company, and I'm at the monthly meeting of AFP (Association of Fundraising Professionals), the last person I'm going to share my idea with is anyone else in the room (my competition).

This is the most important reason to attend national conventions – not to hear keynote speeches that you've probably heard before and not to attend workshops where you may know more than the presenter. You should spend as much of your time as possible tracking down people who run successful programs in other parts of the country and start off by saying, "I could really use your help. I'm guessing you agree that good ideas don't stop at the border and that, given how successful you've been, you've had to have had more than your share. Who do think I should be targeting?" First, people love being complemented and second, they like showing off how smart they are.

A couple of weeks after 9/11 I was at a sparsely attended convention in Anaheim (a lot of people weren't ready to get back on an airplane yet). No more than 30 minutes after sitting down for lunch, on the first day, there began a rather animated conversation about raising money. It will come as no surprise to learn that I did the most talking – this time in the form of questions, otherwise known as "brain tapping."

During dessert the woman on my left handed me a cocktail napkin (I still have it, 10 years later) with a name and phone number on it. She told me this company was their biggest donor and she heard that they still had some money left in their "contributions budget," that had to be spent before the end of the calendar year. The reason she felt comfortable letting me know this was because this company had just made one-time-only, three-year, seven-figure commitment to them.

That same day, while still in California, I called the number she had given me (too many people look at something like this as being a "manana without the urgency" task). I spoke with her contact who faxed me, at my hotel, their grant application. I made a copy of it and used the time made available, during my plane ride home, to create my first draft. A week before Christmas I had a check for $118,000.

Shown the Door - Again

In regards to the non-profit I'm talking about here, I was allowed to sign any expense check for less than $1000 (larger ones required a co-signature from one of the Board's officers). However, I could be questioned about any expense at all. I never saw any problem with this (admittedly I'd only been their Executive Director for three months) until the President of the Board asked me about the $30 that had been spent to send flowers to someone in Minnesota – the person who had connected me to the grantor.

I explained why I had done this and then had it proven to me, once again, that there are people who wouldn't recognize "class," even if it bit them on their posterior portion. He looked at me and said, "I don't understand why you had to send her anything. I mean we already had the check. Now, if you were trying to get information out of her, the flowers might have made sense but, spending money, after the fact, seems pointless."

The Vice-President of the Board gave me a "calm down" gesture and said Alan, "Why don't you and I discuss this after the meeting." I decided to be quiet and not throw caution to the wind, as I am prone to do. However, I actually drew blood from having bit my tongue.

The next morning Alicia stopped by my office. She began by saying, "Philip, I know, I know, trust me, I know." She then went on to add "Alan's term as President is up in three months, and he's term limited insofar as being able to serve on the Board again. So let's both agree that we'd never let one of our kids marry one of his, and sit tight for a few more months. Think of it as a kidney stone – this too shall pass."

This is nowhere close to being a "happily ever after" story. The grant I applied for stated that the funds would be used for six different programs. At the first Board meeting, after the check arrived, I suggested to the Board that we get started on these projects. When nothing happened, I reminded them again. After six weeks I changed my tone a bit and said "We have to start spending this money since the funder wants quarterly updates."

The next day I was fired, via a letter, delivered by a messenger. It seemed that Alan "controlled" three of the four positions on the Executive Committee (two of them owned businesses that sold products to Alan's company). Their three votes determined everything that got done, including hiring and firing. The gist of the letter said that I obviously was not comfortable with the policy regarding my relationship with the Board because, if I was, I never would have demanded (I actually never used that word) that the Board do something. In other words I was fired for insubordination by insisting that the grant money be used.

Alicia stopped by my house that evening. She kept apologizing and told me that she "fought the fight" until she lost her voice.

I never did find out what happened. The "revenge" part of me hoped that the grantor asked for their money back. However, this was overruled by knowing that funds were to be used to set up mentoring programs for "at risk" kids. Then again, if the money was just sitting in a checking account, they might as well request that it be returned.

I contemplated writing to the grantor, telling them what had happened, and suggesting that they "retrieve" their money and give it to another worthwhile non-profit. However, a lawyer friend of mine cautioned that I not do that because it could put me in a tenuous legal situation.

The last chapter of the "sordid" affair?" Six months later the organization was dissolved and I still don't what happened to the money.

NUGGET

No matter how good you think you might be at things related to an application process, you won't know for sure until you have a check in your hand. What you can be sure of is that several checks were deposited by grant winners a year ago. Track down one of the recipients, buy them lunch and tap into their brains. If they provide help, go ahead and send those flowers as I'm sure you've got a much greater sense of proper behavior than Alan did.

NUGGET

Politics are everywhere (it would be nice if Washington, DC was not one of them). Whether it's a job you are holding, or an account/sale you are trying to get, be aware of "the lay of the land." Find out who has the real power and which people are "under the thumb" of that individual.

This leads to one of the few situations where I am not prepared, and unwilling, to make a recommendation. Unless you are extremely fortunate you are going to eventually find yourself in a conflict – where principle will be up against pragmatism. There is something you feel strongly about, the facts are all on your side but, if you bring it up, you stand a good chance of losing your job.

There was a time, depending on your age, I would have said to stand up for what you believe in – there are always going to be places looking for people with high moral character. However, that was then and this is now. Earlier I mentioned that there is a section of my brain that is pragmatically wired. In this economy that section would kick in.

This means that you might have to bite both your tongue and a bullet, at least for a while. The person you report to, who is at the root of all the issues you disagree about, may leave, "dead or alive."

This is another example of doing what I say, rather than emulating what I've done. I have been fired three times, and all for the same reason – my refusal to "go along to get along." Did it feel good to stand up for myself? It most certainly did – for a week or two. That's when my mortgage payment became due.

Follow Their Careers

(Note: Although this is probably out of place, it just came to mind and putting it here is a lot easier than spending 10 minutes, hemming and hawing, before deciding on its final resting place, which might be the wrong one at that).

So, here is one more thing to point out, under the headline "Keeping Track of People."

When I was at the agency, one of our favorite accounts was a client who couldn't praise our work enough. In fact, they submitted a number of our ads to the "Addy" committee" (think Emmy/Oscar/Tony Awards for the advertising industry, the world of "Mad Men") and we won several times.

About six months before following Horace Greeley's advice, when I headed towards the other side of the country, I told a couple of our account executives that their client's VP of Advertising was leaving for a slightly better position at another company. They were not at all happy to hear this. Since he had been our "best friend" on the account, they were concerned about future business for us.

I told them that instead of being down, they should be elated. The client was going to continue to retain us because they loved what we were doing for them and their sales were continuing to climb.

As for the VP, what this meant was that we now had a friend at the company he was joining.

When it comes to getting new accounts this is what is meant by the term, "low hanging fruit" – the easiest to harvest. I called the now "here-he-is-again" Mr. Jones, just to congratulate him. However, before I could get a word out my mouth he said, "You must be psychic. I was just ready to call you. How soon can we meet so I can fill you in on what I need?"

This fruit was so easy to pick that I never had to stretch or even reach. It was, and remains, the only time in my career when I landed a new account with saying a word.

And it's not only the "top guns" you should keep track of. One of my co-workers got to know an administrative assistant who made a career move. She had been the liaison between our agency and her boss, so she was well aware of the quality of our work and was more than happy to recommend us to her new employer, once we asked for that favor. Of course we would not have been able to do that if we had not kept track of her.

Even better is when one of your employees decides to change teams, in this case moving from the seller's (agency) side, to the buyer's (client) side of the picture. Unless he or she departed on bad terms, they should be more than willing to help facilitate a meeting at their new "home."

NUGGET

Here's my advice for anyone in the "new business" business. Get the names of every key executive at every existing client, including their assistants. Read the list enough times so as to have the names "ring an alert bell" when you hear or see them. If you learn that they have moved to a different company, contact him or her immediately (the same day you learn of a move isn't a day to soon). It has been suggested that you should not try to reach someone during their first few days at their new position. I agree with that sentiment but remind you

that, by the time you learn about the fact that they've moved, they've probably been in their new job for at least a week. Remember, people like to do business with people they like, people they trust and people who they can rely on to produce quality work.

A Selling Technique I'll Bet You Never Thought Of

If you have a business that is selling a product or service and that receives phone calls, from people wishing to place orders, you have the opportunity to do some free advertising to an audience that will be paying attention.

There are countless surveys that indicate that people find it acceptable to be put on hold, as long as the time does not exceed 52 seconds. I know that sounds like a strange number but it is the average of several tests. To be on the safe side, don't keep anyone waiting for more than 30-40 seconds.

Knowing this, try putting people on hold, even when you don't have to, in order to do a little uninterrupted selling. But make sure your phone is answered by real live voice (people prefer that by a margin so great that it's not even worth mentioning).

(Note: The situation about to be described is not one the agency would normally undertake. However, there are not many businesses owned by your CEO's nephew).

The test that we did was for his take-out/deliver pizza restaurant. The person answering the phone was instructed to say the following:

"Hi, this is Angela at Antonio's Pizzeria. I'm just finishing up taking an order. I'm going to put you on hold but I promise to be back in less than a minute."(a perfect example of "under promise/over deliver").

The customer then got to hear 30-40 seconds of "suggestions" (bread sticks, desserts, salads, etc.).

Before initiating the test we had Antonio (his actual name was Sidney, but that moniker did not have quite the same amount of "old country" charm as something that sounded Italian) accumulate a month's worth of statistics, specifically to determine the exact size of an order when the person was put on hold and got to listen to music, or not put on hold at all. The average dollar amount was $11.63.

After putting in a CD messaging system (which cost about $840 per year - $70 per month - for the hardware and four different sets of software), the number jumped to $12.88. Not all that impressive? Think again.

Antonio's averaged 25 calls per day so they were now making an additional $31.25 per day, $937.50 per month or $11,406.25 per year, all for an investment of $880. When one talks about ROI (Return on Investment), it doesn't get much better than this. The reason I said doesn't get "much" better is because nothing will ever surpass turning $.20 into $200,000.

Giving Credit – When Credit Isn't Due

Any of you who have ever been in sales have, I am sure, found yourself in situations where "no sales" was probably a better description of the division you headed. No matter how good somebody might be in so far as creating revenue, there will be times that your employees can't seem to do anything right – and that can cause both frustration and depression.

Here is something I've done twice, and both times it has worked perfectly.

When I was running a manufacturing business I was in charge of "Major Accounts." While they represented no more than 10% of our clients, they provided at least 40% of our business.

There was a large order that had just been placed. Because my best salesperson was in the doldrums, I asked my client for a favor. I said, "Beverly, who always leads this company in sales, has hit a real dry spell and her morale is not what it should be. So, here's what I'd like you to do. I'm going to tell Beverly that I don't have the time to get in touch with you so would she please make the call. I will add the fact that I think this could be a big order so she should use her most persuasive sales techniques."

Later that afternoon, Beverly came flying (I'd swear her feet weren't touching the ground) into my office. Her face was beaming and her voice was so excited that I had to tell her to slow down. What she said, very proudly, was that she had just made a sale that was larger than her combined efforts, for the entire month. Suffice it to say, Beverly was back on track, a fact reflected by her record going forward.

The other time I employed this approach was when I was running a non-profit. Fund raising may be the most difficult business to be in. If the word "no" deflates your ego you had better find another line of work, because you'll get that response at least 90% of the time.

As was the case before, I had made a fairly substantial "sale" – a contribution of $50,000. And, as was the case before, the head of our fundraising arm had run into a long series of brick walls.

I explained the situation to the donor - what I was hoping to accomplish – and he readily agreed to my script. To make a long story short (which I almost never do), I suggested that Emily call him, because I thought he was equivocating and I believed that she might be able to "close the sale." This time it took less than an hour before Emily was standing in front of my desk yelling, "You won't believe what just happened" (up until then the largest gift that Emily had been able to attain was $10,000). Emily was back.

I know that elsewhere I mention this – but it's worth repeating. It is amazing what you can accomplish if you do not care who gets the credit.

An Excellent Source of Information

Many years ago I became aware of a forum that can be uniquely effective in getting information on, or to, any publicly held company. It will only cost you a few dollars and, very often, you'll get a free meal out of it.

All you have to do is buy one share of stock and you are entitled to attend the annual shareholder's meeting, where you are permitted to ask questions.

Consider this scenario. You have a product/service you are trying to sell to the UVW Company (I'm trying to work my way through the alphabet). You know you have the best price or, perhaps, a technology that represents a "step up." Your problem is getting through the seemingly endless list of assistant purchasing agents.

Go to the annual meeting, raise your hand, and say something like this:

"Mr. Chairman, I am a shareholder of the UVW Company so I have a very strong interest in seeing your economic picture be as bright as possible. I now find myself in a position to do something about it and would like your advice as to how to proceed.

My company has a piece of proprietary software that we are very confident will dramatically reduce your expenses. We'd like to contact the appropriate person in your organization so that they might test it and confirm what we believe to be true. Who do you suggest we get in touch with?"

You will either get an answer, right then and there, or you will be contacted very shortly. With your request now being a matter of public record, you can be assured that you will get a personal response, one way or the other. The two times I employed this methodology it worked – at least insofar as getting contacted. One conversation was not productive while the other one got me faster deliveries on some chemicals my company used. Amazingly the supplier was shipping product to New York City, from a facility in Ohio, in spite of the fact that they had a warehouse, just on the other side of the river, in New Jersey.

However had this somehow have managed to fall through one of the company's cracks, to the point that I had not received a satisfactory response, I would have gone back a year later and started out by saying, "I'm very concerned that the UVW Company either mislead me or patronized me when I was told that they would have someone get in touch with me. If you'd like you can check the minutes from last year" (I would never do this unless I had an alternate supplier). I would then ask my question again. Should that have occurred I can almost guarantee that someone will talk to me, before I left the room. People say "Don't mess with Texas." My response, to anyone who suggests that this true, is to tell them that dealing with determined New Yorkers will get even messier.

And here is one more suggestion. If your "Google," "Yahoo" and "Ask Jeeves" search engines can't help you, call your Congressman. Their aides are there to assist constituents and if that's how you identify yourself you will be amazed at how quickly they can track something down for you or point you in the right direction.

About 10 years ago my land-line phone system stopped working. I used my cell phone to call my service provider, where I was told that they were aware of the problem and that I should have my service back within two weeks. "Two weeks?" I said. "Most of the people living in my community are senior citizens who don't own cell phones. What if one of them has to call 911?" The answer I got was, "Perhaps you weren't listening. I said it will take up to two weeks."

Since his supervisor wasn't there I called my Congressman's office. I related the story to one of his aides, who said that they'd get back to me, on my cell phone, within the hour.

Forty-five minutes later I got the promised call. The aide said that he had called the Corporation Commission, who determines the rates for utilities, including phone companies. When the Corporation Commission calls and says "Jump" their response is "How high and when can I come down?"

The result was that our community's phone service was back working two hours later.

NUGGET

While calling someone like the Better Business Bureau may make you feel better, you rarely get any help. It's the people who control purses strings that have the real power.

When the Numbers Don't Add Up

- Isn't it ironic that when an advertising agency lands a new account it is described as a $20M piece of business whereas the now former agency calls it a $5M loss?

- My employer, back in Connecticut, was the largest independent direct response agency in the country, for three years running. Then, out of the blue, we were passed by someone none of us had ever heard of. It took a little bit of digging around before we found out what happened. Their figures included postage spent on behalf of their clients. This is verboten as those dollars are simply "passed through," from the client, through the agency and eventually, to the Post Office. Had we employed their policy (or lack thereof) we would have been five times their size, just from one of our clients (Citibank) who we mailed 20M envelopes for, six times per year.

Listening to Yourself

One of the hardest things to do is have a real awareness of what you sound like. You never hear your own voice when you speak, so it's very easy to have clichés slip into your speech patterns.

I think most of us are aware of the multiple "like y' know" phrase that a teenager can use 15 times in less than one minute, but even those of us who consider ourselves pretty good communicators can fall prey to sloppy dialogue.

Here's an easy way how to learn what you are saying so that you can avoid these pitfalls.

Get a small recording device that can be attached to your phone. Periodically (once every three – six months), when you know you're going to be talking to a friend, for a fairly lengthy amount of time, record the call (to be on the safe side you should tell them what you're doing – and why) and listen to it the next day.

What you want to pay attention to is you – and only regarding speaking "style" (as opposed to "content"). Aside from the fact that you will feel, as most people do, that you don't like the sound of your own voice very much, you will find this to be very educational.

I discovered was that three words/phrases had worked their way in to my personal vernacular. I had a tendency to occasionally begin a sentence with the word "frankly" (which implies that I hadn't been frank up until that point) or the phrase, "Well, to tell you the truth/To be perfectly honest" (which sort of suggests that I had been lying until then, otherwise why the need to suddenly point out that I was now telling the truth or being honest?).

To this day I occasionally find something I am not pleased with. I look at this the same way as having my car tuned up, except it's far less expensive – as in free.

I am not as concerned (as many seem to be) with the word "uh." Most of the time, at least with me, I use it when my mouth is trying to catch up with my brain, but I'm not ready to "yield the mike" (let someone else start talking). I think of this as the "hold-on-a-second" uh.

I admit to having a couple of other pet peeves, primarily because it is not teenagers doing these things. The next time you hear some type of interview, count how often the person responding begins their answer with the word "well," I'm betting that you find it occurs more than 80% of the time.

The second one involves everyone who ever wins an Oscar, Tony, Emmy, Grammy, etc.

What they invariably say is, "I'd like to thank my parents. I'd like to thank my agent, and I'd like to thank my spouse, without whose support this award would not have been possible. What's with the "I'd like to thank" first words. Of course you'd like to thank them, because that's what you're in the process of doing. If they just got rid of those four words, said at least 100 times per event, the shows might actually end on time.

(Note: There is one word that causes me to cringe – "Whatever." That's because it translates to "Who cares what you think?").

Advertising Can Help – Especially When it Doesn't Cost Anything

A few years ago I was standing at a Chamber of Commerce "Business after Hours" networking event (these were held monthly). A friend of mine, who I hadn't seen for a while, wandered over. When I asked what was going on in her life, she responded that she was between jobs and looking for work.

Most people attending events like this wear a badge that provides their name and where they work. Some people only put their down their name, as had Katherine.

I picked up a felt tipped and, under Katherine's name, wrote, in big letters, "Seeking Gainful Employment."

Over the next two hours Katherine was given 11 business cards. During the next week, three of those resulted in interviews. Within two weeks, one of those interviews became a job (her new employer told her that he appreciated her creative, "in-your-face" approach). As this book is being written, Katherine is still there, has gotten three promotions and is now making more money, a lot more money, than she ever had before.

NUGGET

It almost always pays to advertise, especially when you don't have to pay anything at all. A badge at an event is nothing more than a miniature billboard, so why not take advantage of the free space, especially when you are in an environment chock full of potential employers.

Back By Popular Demand - The Story of Violet

Based on a lot of solid input from people I admire and respect, and the way I was raised, thank you notes have always been as much a part of my life as brushing my teeth. To repeat something I said earlier, my parents told me that I couldn't wear it, listen to it, play with it, eat it or spend it until I said thank you for it (I usually wrote these notes a day or two after I received the gift – unless it was something I didn't like, in which case it reached the point that I had to be reminded).

I had a close friend, who was required to follow the same rules. However, she was a lot cleverer than me. A few days before her birthday, and a few days before Christmas, she would write out a dozen thank you notes, leaving a blank spot where she could enter what the gift was. All that was left to do, on "receiving day," was to fill in that blank, put "Dear Uncle Joe and Aunt Josephine" at the top, and address the envelope.

I believe her all time record was the year she had all her notes in the mailbox within 20 minutes after opening her last gift. She knew, as I've already mentioned, that people never compare cards like this. We did share the same 1ˢᵗ amendment to the rule – we could do the wearing, listening, playing, eating or spending as soon we showed our parents the cards.

The first Christmas she did this her brother and sister were not the least bit happy. She staved off a revolt by showing them her "trick," which they began "performing" the following year.

I want to remind anyone in the business world, whether you are involved with a for-profit or non-profit organization, that handwritten thank you notes are "the key to the gates of sales and fundraising heaven." This time I will make my point by telling you about Violet, a case where $63 morphed into at least $324,000, and possibly a good deal more.

Violet, a retired widow, called our Crisis Center one day and asked if she and a friend could visit and bring our children some home-baked cookies. While we didn't publish our street addresses (for security reasons) we were always delighted to accommodate requests such as this.

I gave the two ladies a rather extensive tour (it turned out we were the third shelter they had visited over the past few months) and answered lots of questions. The next day I wrote a lengthy thank-you letter and had a half-dozen of our kids make cards from colored paper, glue, cotton balls, sparkles, etc. (it's fascinating to see how a six-year-old draws herself, eating a cookie). We mailed these to Violet, in individual envelopes, each one hand-addressed by the "artist."

About a month later I got a call from Violet. The conversation went something like this:

Violet: "Mr. Barnett, I've gotten the first of two checks, representing the dissolution of my late husband's pension fund, and I really don't want to pay the taxes that will result. I'd like to contribute each of them to your organization. The problem is that I'm 86 years old and I don't drive any more."

Me: "That's incredibly generous of you Violet. You can certainly mail it to us."

Violet: "I don't trust the Post Office."

Me: "Well then Violet, I'd be pleased to come pick it up (Violet lived 20 miles west of our facility and I lived 15 miles in the other direction). If you don't mind me asking Violet, how much is the check for?"

Violet: "This one is for $12,000 and the next one will be the same."

Me: "I'm getting in my car as we speak."

(Note: Shame on me. I should have immediately told Violet that I would drive to her house. So much of philanthropy is related to relationships and these do not exist if the Post Office is allowed to intervene).

I ran into the play area and had a couple of the kids make a giant thank-you card to take with me. On the way there I stopped to buy some flowers (violets of course).

Violet lived in a very small, but immaculate, house in a retirement community. We chatted for about an hour and she handed me a $12,000 check.

Three months later I got another call from Violet. She said that she had the other check for us but, since she knew she lived far away from us, she was now prepared to mail this one. I told her not to do that, that I really would love to see her again and that I'd be happy to make the drive. She said that would be OK but not to bring anything for her. I agreed and suggested that I take her to lunch. Her response was that she didn't eat very much to which I answered "No problem, you'll be my cheap date." She thought that to be funny and we agreed on a date and time.

I picked her up and we drove to a local restaurant – this was in Sun City so, aside from the waiters and waitresses, I was about 30 years younger than everyone else in the room. I got to take most of her lunch home with me, along with another $12,000 check (the check only stayed "at home" until the following day).

In addition, Violet felt the need to apologize for the fact that her first "standard" contribution to us had been for only $100. Very gently I reminded her that the $24,000 was a contribution.

I tried to tell her that apologies weren't necessary, but that didn't stop her from continuing. She said, "Philip, I don't live a very extravagant life although, once a year, I try to go on a vacation, to somewhere I've never been before. I budget my money very carefully and have found that I need about $42,000 each year. $1500 a month, about 45% of that, comes from Social Security so I want to see if you can figure out how much I'm worth."

Since I've always been pretty good with numbers (you will learn more about this later), it took me only about a minute to come up with my estimate. I said, "Violet, I'm guessing that it's somewhere in the neighborhood of $600,000 (nice neighborhood)."

She was very impressed that, for all intents and purposes, I had gotten the number exactly right. She explained, "When my husband passed away he left me that amount in municipal bonds. They pay an average interest of 4%, which is tax free. So that is where I get the $24,000 each year that supplements my Social Security."

When I got back to work, I asked all of our 15 children to make cards for Violet. They were mailed the next morning.

Two weeks later Violet called to let me know that she had rewritten her will to make our organization the major beneficiary (she had no children).

Let's see - $20 in flowers, $10 for gas, another $20 for lunch, about $3 in art & crafts supplies and $10 in postage. An "investment" of $63 for what will probably turn out to be something in the neighborhood of $324,000 (another nice neighborhood). And, it could even be even more.

I eventually learned that the first two shelters Violet had visited had sent her generic "Dear Donor" letters.

NUGGET

There's a lesson to be learned here, one that I hope is obvious, given the number of times I've mentioned it. If you don't say "thank you," in a personalized way, you can lose lots and lots of money, although you'll probably never know how much, which means you may never change your policy. Now that I've told you the importance of this, if the shoe fits you should alter that policy accordingly – not after the next Board meeting, not next week and not tomorrow. You should put down this book and do it right now.

Here is one other example.

The Crisis Center owned two vans. One day one of them had a fan belt break. I arranged to have it taken to the place where I had my car serviced (you've already read something about them - "It's sometimes better to receive than give" - and there will be more a bit later - "A Case History" – because they did good work and I was sure they would give us the lowest price possible (which they did).

Later that day I asked each of our kids to create thank you cards featuring cars and trucks (they were much better at this than they were with kids eating cookies). The following week I got a call from the service facility. The manager told me he had received the cards and taped them to the wall, next to letters from customers. Immediately after doing this he began to get comments from people in his waiting room (each card began with the words "Thank you for fixing our van").

He said that for as long as he got cards like these he would service both of our vans at no charge – and that would include parts, labor and even towing if necessary.

This is another great case of ROI. The art supplies and postage (all the cards were sent in the same envelope) couldn't have cost more than a few dollars. What we got in return was thousands of dollars worth of service. Over the next two years it may have added up to $10,000 ($2500 per van, per year) as both vehicles were quite old. In fact it got to the point that one of my employees suggested that we name one of them "Flattery" because "Flattery will get you nowhere."

NUGGET

I'm sure it didn't hurt that I had been a customer of theirs for more than 10 years as well as having referred several friends. This was a case of my "loyalty" being rewarded, albeit not with air miles or hotel room credits.

One Hand Washing the Other

I never cease to be amazed that more people don't take the path of least resistance when it comes to one part of their fundraising program. Every non-profit I've ever been involved with has at least one event a year that involves an auction – usually both live and silent ones.

When I first meet with a prize-gathering committee they invariably are at a loss as to how to go about their task. I can usually handle that quite easily by telling them what I do.

Any restaurant I eat at frequently gets asked for a "dinner for two" certificate. Every golf course I play at regularly gets asked for a free foursome. Not only do most of them agree, they often end up donating more than I requested.

Several years ago, PGA golfer Tom Lehman, a friend and a true salt-of-the-earth individual, offered two tickets to the British Open, where he would be the defending champion. These were going to be the grand prize in a raffle to assist the JGA (Junior Golf Association).

I called Marriott, explained what I was trying to put together and asked if they would provide a one-week's-stay. They said they'd get back to me (I'm sure they used that time to check out how good a customer I had been) and, the following day, they told me they'd be happy to (and I didn't even have to use any of my "Honored Guest" points).

Next was British Airways. They had recently announced that they were inaugurating non-stop service between Phoenix and London. I called their Marketing Director and told him that, in return for two tickets, they would be listed in all our ads and brochures, as a lead sponsor, thereby getting a ton of free publicity for a new "product." They agreed as well.

Much to my surprise British Air made these Business Class seats and Marriott gave the winners a suite (I suspect that these gestures were due, in part, to the fact that they didn't have a plethora of bookings/reservations for the week in question). Finally I was able to get Hertz to provide a car for seven days, simply by telling them that their name would be featured, right next to British Air and Marriott.

Let's see. The airline tickets were worth about $10,000, the suite about $3,000 and the car rental roughly $700. As for the tickets to the tournament itself they were, to quote a well known ad, "priceless."

The second prize was a "Party Suite," seating 75 people, at a Diamondbacks game – probably a result of the fact that I was a season ticket holder and, as I've already mentioned, knew Jerry Colangelo, the team owner.

The rest of the prizes, mostly obtained by my committee, included lots of golf foursomes (some with celebrities), lots of dinners and an assortment of golf equipment and apparel. All in all, we ended up with 117 prizes. Since we promised to sell no more than 1000 tickets (at $100 each), the odds of winning were better than one in ten.

Our revenue for the raffle turned out to be $99,800 (two checks bounced) and our costs, for the prizes, was $0.00. Actually we raised $10,000 more because, ironically, the winner of the Grand Prize had no interest in golf. At his own suggestion we auctioned off the package with the highest bid being that ten grand.

All you have to do is recall the previous chapters that talked about the value of asking. Now, I will say that not every golf course, or restaurant, said "yes," but more than 75% of them did, because the people doing the asking were loyal customers.

Here is another variation on this "modus operandi" (way of doing business).

My former wife was an exceptionally good golfer (I think I beat her once, in 17 years of marriage – it's a good thing my golf scores and ego were mutually exclusive). She belonged to the Women's Club at our local course. Their one big event each year was the awards banquet. As with most festivities such as this there are a number of committees formed – food and beverage, invitations, etc. The one committee no one ever wanted to head up was prizes. My wife, at that time, was a flight attendant. At the meeting where the committee assignments were made, she was away on a trip so, naturally, she was elected to head up the prize committee.

When she learned about this she was not the least bit happy, primarily because she had never done anything like this before and had no idea how to proceed, When she asked for my help I agreed to provide it, under one condition, that I be allowed to speak for about one minute at the banquet – a condition she promised she would make happen.

We were living in Southport, CT at the time, a very small town in a very wealthy county. Over the course of several years I had gotten to know virtually every business within a five mile radius of where we lived – the restaurants, the boutiques, the liquor stores, etc.

I called on each of them, explained why I was there and asked them for a donated gift of some kind. My promise was that, if after three months they felt as if they had made a mistake, I would reimburse them the wholesale cost of their contribution. I knew I was crawling way out on a limb here but I also was aware that I was going to be successful, because I would be doing something I had a real expertise at.

When I got my one minute, at the very beginning of the luncheon, I stood up in front of the group I said, "Ladies, on the table in front of each one of you is a list of the businesses that provided the prizes you are about to award. It is imperative, and I mean imperative, that you patronize these establishments and, when you do, tell them that the reason you are there is to thank them for their support. If you do that, the person in charge of obtaining the prizes next year will have a very easy job, to the point that many of you will probably ask to be that committee's chair."

In less than a week I knew that smooth sailing lay ahead. The owner of the store where I bought my wine had donated a gift box, containing three bottles of reasonably expensive product. He called me and asked that he be immediately signed up for the luncheon the following year, and that he would be contributing four such gifts. Was he just being magnanimous? No. He was being smart since, the day before he called me, one of the members of the Women's Club had stopped in and asked him to provide all of the beverages for her husband's 50th birthday party – a $5,000 order.

The amount of money spent on this project? $0.00.Once again, my loyalty resulted in a true win/win situation.

By the following year businesses that had participated were falling all over themselves to sign up as future prize donors/sponsors. In fact, the largest women's clothing store in the area contributed a $1000 wardrobe. Very wisely the women decided to divide this into four prizes, since one of their most important tournaments involved foursomes, and this way every member of the winning team would get the identical prize.

Finally, let me mention that I'll wager that anyone reading this book could go out and get 25 prizes in less than a week. I've mentioned some obvious ones already, but how about supermarkets, a free tax-return preparation (one of their members was married to a CPA) and a local salon. Then there's free movie tickets – something theatres are always will to contribute because they know how much the recipients will spend at their concession stand.

By now I think you get my point.

But there is one thing to avoid – "conditional prizes" – i.e. one free meal when you purchase one selling at the same, or a higher price. These are almost meaningless as such offers appear in the local newspapers, almost every day.

Protecting Your Brand From "Hijackers"

You will shortly read about the #1 listing on the "Really Dumb Remark" hit parade. This one was not quite as bad – but close. At the time, because I got involved, it almost turned into a really big story that the media would have devoured.

As I've mentioned, my former wife was an excellent golfer. While living in Connecticut I decided, as a birthday present, I would buy her a slot in the "Michelob Pro-Am," a tournament in support of our local hospital.

I sent in the $250 which was returned to me the following week. I called the Anheuser-Busch distributor, who was putting on the tournament, to find out what was going on and was told that the event was for men only (although their promotional material never mentioned that). When I asked why he told me that men don't like playing with women who might be better than they are.

276

When I got over being incredulous I called the Michelob brand manager, in St. Louis, who I happened to know (although I would have done the same thing even if I hadn't). When I explained what was going on he told me that the parent company had nothing to do with it, as the event was being put on by the local distributor.

I'm not sure if I have ever put on my lecturer's hat faster. I said "Robert, the tournament has your brand's name on it, not JKL Distributor." He responded by telling me that, in situations like this, they had no control over what gets done.

I answered back, telling him, "Robert, you are a friend of mine but you are incredibly naïve, and I'm going to prove it to you. I'm going to call the local chapter of NOW (National Association of Women), an extremely activist group, and ask them to picket the event – which I can almost guarantee they will. Then I will get in touch will all of the distributor's major accounts and tell them that they can also expect to be picketed. My next call will be to the local media, as well as USA Today and the New York Times, who will love to cover a story like this. After doing that I'm going back to NOW and ask them to run a full-page ad, in our local paper, headlined "Don't Drink Michelob – and Here's Why." Since they've done things like this before, please tell me if you don't think this will affect your brand."

Robert asked if he could call me back in an hour. It took less than that amount of time for me to be on a conference call with Robert and the owner of the distributorship. Both of them were tripping over themselves in apologizing and promising that the event would be open to women, starting the following year. I told them while that was all well and good, I didn't think it came close to erasing the problem. When I was asked what would, I first asked them a question, "How much does the JLK Distributor contribute to the fundraising effort and how much does Anheuser-Busch contribute?" The answers I got were $10,000 and $0.

After learning that I told them that if the distributor increased their contribution to $25,000 and if Michelob matched it I would "call off the dogs" (I had a real soft spot in my heart for the hospital that was benefitting from this event because, several years earlier, they had literally saved my son's life). It took them less than a minute to both agree to my "terms."

I realize that this has been another one of my personal stories but, I hope, that each one of them makes a point that is helpful. In this case there are two of them. First, always be careful that someone doesn't "hijack" your brand. It may be your most important asset so it must be protected. One other way this can happen is if you are in the supermarket business and you allow your leased big trucks to go unwashed, as there are people who will think, "dirty truck = dirty store."

The second lesson here is that one person really can make a difference. If you are persistent, and can make a good enough case for your "mission," smart businesses will respond. Oh, and by the way, over the course of the entire scenario I just described my only expense was one long-distance call to St. Louis.

NUGGET

I'm sure there will be those who, after reading the previous chapters, will accuse me of bragging – and they will be right. However, I'm not looking for kudos or applause. What I hope to accomplish is convincing people that one person, with enough drive and energy, can accomplish a great deal. The greatest reward I

could get from this is to learn that some of you get kudos and applause, when you earn it.

Actually there is one other thing. When people ask you to tell them your secret for success you can tell them, "It all began when I read this book about crocks, cheese, macaroni and photographers."

A Marketing Case History (Dear Client – There's good news and there's bad news).

Since this entire book is grounded in practical approaches to real situations, I thought it might be of beneficial if I included an entire case history.

The story of ABC Auto is especially appropriate as it deals with an area that virtually everyone has been exposed to. We all drive cars and we all have some familiarity with having them serviced.

ABC was where I had taken my cars for 11 years. For most of this time they had been a single location facility but had recently expanded dramatically, to the point that they had nine service locations and two body shops.

Part of the problems they were experiencing related to growing pains but others went a lot deeper than that – all the way to their corporate culture.

I was asked to be a mystery shopper, by visiting each facility. These in-person visits were to get an oil change from the service facilities and to get an estimate on repairing some major dents from the body shops. To paint a more complete picture, visits were also made to a pair of competitors, including their body shops.

To say that this turned out to be enlightening would be an understatement. By the time I finished, I had prepared a 60-page report and done three presentations – to upper management and two groups of store managers.

The sub-title of this chapter says that there was good and bad news. In this case the bad news was that the client had lots and lots of problems. The good news was that it presented an equal number of opportunities for improvement. I will provide a condensed version of the entire scenario, because I think there are many lessons to be learned here.

Mr. George Peters
ABC Automotive Company
8000 Central Ave.
Phoenix, AZ 85001

Dear Mr. Peters.

I have completed my in-person assessments of each your 11 facilities. I also visited two of your competitors. The written reports on all of these experiences are attached.

This summary is designed to tell you what happened when I stopped in, attempting to get an oil change, after confirming that I needed one.

I visited all nine service ABC locations. I explained that I wasn't sure if I needed an oil change since my son was supposed to have had it done the week before but, when I asked him for a receipt, so that I could reimburse him, he told me that he lost it. Besides, I added, there was no reminder sticker on the upper left hand corner of the windshield (I removed the one that was there).

Two days before I started calling on your facilities I had the oil changed. Four of your locations told me that everything was fine. Two of them said that things were "marginal" and, if I was going to wait, it shouldn't be for more than another 1,000 miles. And three places said it should be done right away. Suffice it to say, you've got a big problem here.

Summary:

- When I walked up to the counter, not a single ABC employee, at any of your 11 locations, introduced themselves by name. And, not a single person asked me my name (until it was time to fill out the paperwork to have the oil change done). The provider/customer relationship should be as personal as possible and this is impossible if no one knows who they are talking to.

- On only one occasion (and that was after I had been waiting for almost 30 minutes) was I asked if I had previously had work done by ABC. YOU NEVER GET A SECOND CHANCE TO MAKE A FIRST IMPRESSION and you don't know if you are "making a first impression" unless you find out if this is a first time customer.

- New customers should be given special treatment (it's the only way to maximize the likelihood that they become regulars). Remember, ALL CUSTOMERS ARE EQUAL, BUT SOME ARE MORE EQUAL THAN OTHERS.

- Only four of the nine locations were able to take me (at 7:30 A.M.) without an appointment. While I understand that it's good to be busy, I also know that you should be doing everything possible to not turn away business, ESPECIALLY IF IT'S A FIRST TIME CUSTOMER. I can tell you that none of the five places that couldn't wait on me immediately did anything to make me want to come back. As I mention in one of my reports, the ideal thing to have said was "If you leave your car, we'll drive you to where you need to go (if it's in the neighborhood) and then pick you up when your car is ready."

- I BELIEVE IT IS CRITICAL THAT YOUR COMPUTERS BE LINKED TOGETHER SO THAT ALL LOCATIONS CAN ACCESS A CUSTOMER'S HISTORY.

- There was obviously a real lack of consistency (your locations should, as much as possible, be mirror images of each other – customers are more comfortable if there is familiarity). And, as I've mentioned, on three occasions a facility tried to sell me a service that I did not need, having had it done only a couple of days earlier.

- I do not understand your offer of a "premium" oil change. It was not offered at every location and, when it was, I was told it involved a better grade of oil. This is a terrible idea because the customer will think that, if they don't agree to it, they will be getting something inferior. Car wash places, for example, are different in that each price "bump" provides something additional (i.e. hand waxing). If they followed your pattern I would be asked if I wanted the "premium" brand of detergent.

- On balance, your facilities are "barely OK." (An average of 3, on a scale of 1 – 10, with 10 being the highest).Wastepaper baskets were almost never empty, including first thing in the morning, in most cases there was no reading material and the television reception was poor. Also, there should always be a sugar substitute offered when there is coffee. Female customers (and lots of men, including me) appreciate that.

- THERE WAS NO INCENTIVE OFFERED TO GET ME TO COME BACK. I felt that I was considered a "one-time-only" customer and that no one had an interest in turning me into a regular.

- NO ONE ASKED ME FOR AN E-MAIL ADDRESS. I believe that you have an enormous marketing opportunity here. However, you are going to have to do some data collecting. Primarily, what you need to know is the customer's name, e-mail address, and how many miles they drive per week or month.

For example, if you know that someone drives 300 miles a week they should need an oil change roughly every 12 weeks. You can e-mail them, two weeks in advance, and remind them. You can even allow them to make an appointment by responding to the e-mail. Likewise you know when they will be in need of a major servicing.

- There was no consistency in telling me things that were wrong with my car (including whether or not I needed an oil change). The first location I went told me that everything was fine, the second place said I had leak in a shock and that I should consider new transmission fluid and the third told me to consider a new fuel filter and new wiper blades and that the front strut bumpers needed repairing (I had no idea what these were so I suggest you consider putting up some large charts, similar to the anatomy ones that doctors use, that show all the "inner workings" of the car and what the function is for each one). Five people told me that everything checked out fine while another employee said that two of the tires were bad.

- In the cases where I could not be taken right away, no one attempted to suggest another ABC facility. For example, when the Phoenix location could not help me at once, they should have called the Scottsdale location (six miles away) to see if they might. This suggests that your facilities may consider themselves to be in competition with each other.

- Although my car needed some bodywork, no one mentioned that ABC also owns two facilities that could handle that.

- Not all of the front desk personnel were professionally dressed.

As far as your two body shops were concerned, their quotes were $100 apart and I was told that the work would require four business days. The two competitors of yours that I visited, had prices at least $50 lower than your lowest price and they would have been able to get my car back to me within three business days. They count Saturday as a business day whereas you don't.

Overall, I never felt "courted." The places that couldn't take me certainly did nothing that would make me want to go there again and the places that were able to accommodate me did nothing to make me want to come back. I could not help but feel that I was being looked at as a one-time, $19.95, customer.

In order for you to change things I believe things have to change, beginning with the moment the customer walks in the front door. An ABC employee should introduce himself or herself by name and determine who they are talking to. They should immediately begin addressing that person by name (Mr. X or Ms. Y). They should let the customer know that they (the ABC employee) will personally be handling or supervising the work to be done. The customer should immediately be given a card with the employee's name on it. The reason for this is that, very often, when a customer is waiting, they forget who it was they were talking to. Having a card, from the very beginning, provides the customer with a reference, which allows them to address your employee by name.

If a walk-in cannot be accommodated immediately, everything possible should be done to get their business.

You should know how long procedures are going to take. If it's 45 minutes, tell the customer one-hour. CREATE A LEVEL OF EXPECTATION AND THEN EXCEED IT.

There should be benefits related to being an ABC customer – incentives for coming back and for referring new business. If every visit is looked at as a "one off" you end up spending far too much money on advertising. Take most of the dollars you spend trying to get people to come through the front door for the first time and use them to get people to become "regulars" – retention programs. YOUR BEST CUSTOMER IS YOUR CUSTOMER.

NUGGET

People and businesses tend to do to business with people and companies that make them feel special.

NUGGET

"Mystery shop" your business on a regular basis. How is the phone answered? What is the attitude of the receptionist? Does the sales staff understand the balance between being pushy and complacent? You should have a check list of six – twelve things to confirm (i.e. the cleanliness of the restrooms), and you should perform these "check-ups" at least twice a year.

Furthermore, on at least one visit each year, tell your shopper to be "tough" by making unreasonable demands, complaining about pricing, etc. It's easy to take care of someone who keeps saying "No problem." It's another thing to deal with people who come in with a chip on their shoulder – and there will be lots of chips, on lots of shoulders.

Read the Paper (and Take Notes)

There are a number of ways of finding new business. Sometimes it's almost as easy as shooting fish in a barrel. I got Donald Trump as a client, when he was in the process of launching the Trump Shuttle airline, by simply calling him that morning (he was far, far easier to reach than I imagined at the time) and saying, "Now that you own a brand new company, you must need an advertising agency." We got hired the next day, while everyone else was waiting to hear some kind of official announcement or RFP (Request for Proposal). In this case, my judgment was that Donald Trump would never do things the way everyone else did and that his personality was such as to approve of a "let's get it done right now" approach.

Donald actually hired three agencies on the same day, one to handle his general advertising, one to be responsible for his direct mail campaigns (that was us) and a public relations firm (although I'm not sure why he would need one since Donald was determined to personally handle anything that related directly to the public).

NUGGET

I can't swear that this is true, because I've never been in a position to put the two pieces together. That being said, it sounded logical that you can determine the speed at which people will make business decisions by the length of time it takes them to decide what they will order for lunch or dinner.

The other related incident took a bit longer to develop but was even more gratifying.

I had done a "cold call" mailing (I'm not really sure what to call this as "Cold mail mailing" sounds ridiculous) to

400 potential clients. It was a very creative piece that got a several responses and, ultimately, two new clients. However, it was a rejection, a turn down, a "no thank you," that I'm going to tell you about.

It came from the VP of Marketing for a large cruise line based in Miami. Ms. Raferty wrote that, while she was very taken by the caliber of our creative, the fact was that she already had an advertising agency she was pleased with.

I was very impressed on two counts. First, she was complimenting our work and second, she believed in rewarding good work with loyalty. I'm not sure I would want a client who jumped ship, no pun intended, just because they got a clever mailing. If they were willing to ditch someone that easily, down the road they would surely do the same to us, probably well before we recovered our investment in them.

So I filed her note away and really didn't think much about it, at for at least six months.

Then, one day while reading the "People on the Move" section in the Wall St. Journal, I saw mention of the fact that Ms. Raferty was moving to Hyatt International in Chicago, to head up a brand new division.

In point of fact, she was already there, although she did not even have a secretary to screen her calls. Thus, I was able to get to her directly.

(Note: If you are having trouble reaching a busy executive who is overly "protected" by assistants, try calling at seven in the morning, six at night or, even better, on non-major holidays such as President's Day. I, as do many busy executives, often use days like this to catch up on work in a quieter-than-normal environment and, if our phone rings, we will instinctively pick it up ourselves).

OK, back to Ms. Raferty. I refreshed her memory as to who I was (she remembered the mailing) and then mentioned that since she was heading a new division, I presumed it was impossible that she could have an agency she was satisfied with.

Her response was exactly what I wanted to hear. She said, "Philip, I need an agency immediately."

She knew I was calling from Connecticut so my next remark nearly floored her. I told her I would have one of our top Art Directors and our Vice President, Creative Services in her office within an hour. While she was still trying to figure that out, I assured her that we did not have a company supersonic jet but we did have a major office in Chicago, about three miles away from where she was sitting.

While I had to have someone skip lunch, and had another person juggle an afternoon worth of meetings, two of our top people were in her reception room, portfolios in hand, within 45 minutes.

She hired us, on the spot, before anyone else even knew of the opportunity. Why? Because I followed the careers of people who have a favorable impression of our abilities but who did not need them when I initially contacted them.

Say Goodnight Gracie

Back when television actually had shows that were truly funny the "George Burns and Gracie Allen Show" would always end with the same two lines:

George: "Say goodnight Gracie."

Gracie: "Goodnight Gracie."

What made the show so enjoyable was the fact that Gracie Allen did not know the meaning of the word context. She simply took everything literally, often with hilarious results.

The idea of "what did I say vs. what did they hear" repeatedly has ramifications in our everyday lives, whether personal or business. Let me give you some examples that will bring this point home.

Jim Lavenson, a truly wonderful gentleman, who once ran the famed Plaza Hotel in New York City, told me this very apropos story.

"If you wanted a second drink in the Plaza's famous Oak Bar, you got it with a simple technique — tripping the waiter, and then pinning him to the floor. You had to ask him. You'd think, wouldn't you, that it would be easy to change that pattern of behavior by the Oak Room waiters. After all, they make additional tips on additional drinks. Simple sales training. Right? Right!

I had our general manager for the Oak Room, along with the maitre d', learn my new policy. It was inspirational. When the guest's glass is down to being one-third full, the waiter was to come up to the table and ask the guest if he or she would like a second drink. Complicated? No. Workable? Absolutely. It couldn't miss, I thought.

About a month after establishing this revolutionary policy I joined the General Manager for a drink. I noticed that, at a nearby table, there were four men all with empty glasses. No waiter was near them. After watching for fifteen minutes my ulcer gave out. The manager called over the maitre d' and asked what happened to the second-drink program. The maitre d' called over to the captain, pointed out the other table and said, 'Whatever happened to Mr. Lavenson's second drink program?' The captain called over the waiter, who broke out into a huge smile as he explained that the men at the next table already had their second drinks.

The point I'm emphasizing might more easily understood by a story I recently read.

WHAT CAUSES ARTHRITIS?

A drunken man, who smelled like beer, sat down on a subway next to a priest.

The man's tie was stained, his face was plastered with red lipstick and a half-empty bottle of gin was sticking out of his torn coat pocket.

He opened his newspaper and began reading. After a few minutes he turned to the priest and asked,

"Say Father, what causes arthritis?"

The priest replied, "My Son, it's caused by loose living, being with cheap, wicked women, too much alcohol, contempt for your fellow man, sleeping around with prostitutes and the lack of a bath."

The drunk muttered in response, "Well, I'll be damned," then returned to his paper.

The priest, thinking about what he had said, nudged the man and apologized.

"I'm very sorry. I didn't mean to come on so strong. How long have you had arthritis?"

The drunk answered, "I don't have it, Father. I was just reading here that the Pope does."

MORAL: Make sure you understand the question before answering it.

NUGGET

This has been said before, as in the above joke and it will be mentioned again and again, and again and again - what did I say vs. what did they hear. The reason I throw this at the reader (that's you) so often is because it requires an ability that contradicts normal behavior patterns. Because of egos, manifested in the fact that we think we have the perfect solution, strategy, tactic and plan, we tend to spend more time thinking about we're going to say next than we do paying attention to the person talking to us. We spend far too much time talking "to" others than we do talking "with" them

Here are two more examples, this time involving my son.

When he was quite young I would drive him to pre-school every morning. Along the way I always stopped to pick up a newspaper. When I got out of the car I'd say to him, "Justin, I'll be back in a second." After several months of this, one morning he looked at me and asked, "Daddy, how come you're never back in a first?"

Think about this for a minute. When children learn a language they are not taught context, or nuance. A word has only one meaning. He had absorbed "first" as being the initial word in a sequence of first, second, third, etc. The class had not gotten into telling time yet (second, minute and hour).

Going backwards in time, the second story occurred when Justin was about two. My ex-wife and a girlfriend were going to go out to lunch and planned to take him along. It was going to be his first time in a restaurant and they spent much of the morning preparing him for the event – "Justin, we're going out to lunch later," "Justin, we're going to have lunch in a restaurant," "Justin, you're really going to enjoy lunch," etc.

They decided to go to an IHOP. After being seated the waitress came over to take their orders. She wrote down what the adults wanted then leaned over the table and very sweetly said, "And what would you like little boy?" Justin looked up at her, paused for a second and then, at the top of his lungs, screamed out, "LUNCH!"

NUGGET

With adults, as well as children, there are words and phrases that can have more than one meaning. So, try to make sure that the ones you use are fully understood. There is nothing wrong with repeating something, in a slightly different way, to make sure you get your point across, as long as you don't bore them to death (I hope that's not the case here although probably not since, if I had, you would have given up several chapters earlier).

Media Alert

Early in my career I spent a couple of years writing press releases. It didn't take long for me to conclude that they were almost never read and that you would have to come pretty close to announcing the start of WW III before getting anyone's attention.

I longed for the day when I had my own business so that I could shake things up a bit. All it took was about 25 years until the situation was finally right.

I had formed a partnership with a Geordie Hormel, of the Hormel meat family and owner of the Wrigley Mansion

Club. He was at the time, and remains (even though he has passed away), the strangest person I had ever known and so far out in left field that he wasn't really even in the ballpark (see chapter to come). Getting him to agree with my plan to do what follows took about twenty seconds - as easy as asking.

Here is what the two releases said:

MARKETING 101 RELEASES CORPORATE MISSION STATEMENT

Marketing 101, Ltd, the recently formed consulting firm, has issued its corporate mission statement, it was announced today by Philip Barnett and Geordie Hormel, co-founders of the agency.

"We intend to tell our clients things that are correct, not expedient" stated Mr. Barnett.

"Right on" added Mr. Hormel.

We intend to emphasize the need for clear, concise communications" Mr. Barnett continued.

"Write on" added Mr. Hormel.

"We believe we have the ability to properly market anything, from soup to nuts, from birthdays to funerals." Barnett went on.

"Rite on" added Mr. Hormel.

"In fact," Mr. Barnett concluded, "we'll not only re-invent the wheel, if necessary we just might re-invent the airplane."

"Wright on" added Mr. Hormel.

MARKETING 101 LTD., ANNOUNCES SEARCH FOR ROCKET SURGEON AND BRAIN SCIENTIST TO COMPLETE STAFF

Marketing 101, Ltd. is looking to round out its staff by hiring a rocket surgeon and brain scientist it was announced today by Philip Barnett, President of the consulting firm.

Mr. Barnett stated, "While we constantly preach the simple approach and tell our clients that you don't have to be a rocket surgeon (unless your rocket needs to be cut up, and put back together) to follow our line of thinking, or a brain scientist (unless you have MRI scans to be evaluated) to understand our recommendations, the fact is you never know, so why not plan for the future?"

Mr. Hormel, co-founder of the firm, although unavailable for comment, commented, "It sounds like a good idea to me."

These releases were mailed to a dozen newspapers and magazines. Nine must have thrown them away. Two called and asked for a clarification. The other newspaper also called, this time to tell us how much they appreciated the fact that ours was just not another sleep-inducing series of announcements. In fact, they were planning on printing one release that week and the other during the following one.

In point of fact, I didn't expect to have anything happen at all. The first release was the result of a discussion I was part of, related to how many different ways a word could be spelled, and all the totally different meanings each spelling could have. The second was composed shortly after I heard someone on television say, "Hey, it's not brain surgery we're talking about." I said to myself, "It's always not brain surgery. This doesn't bode well for anyone in medical school, studying to be a brain surgeon."

I got four calls as a result of the stories that ran. Three of them didn't understand that these were meant to be tongue-in-cheek. The one that got it hired us to be their Public Relations firm. To say that they saw themselves as irreverent would be a huge understatement.

I will give Geordie credit for one thing. His third wife was as sharp as a tack. When they bought the Wrigley Mansion Club they opened a very fancy restaurant there. The Biltmore Property Owners' Association threatened to sue them, saying that their bylaws precluded this from being done, since it would be open to the public.

Her response was to immediately announce that the facility was being converted to a private club, to be used only by members. The dues were $1 which covered a ten-year period. The Association gave up when one of their members, a well known attorney, told them that if they went to court there was no way they could win, since "ex post facto" (after-the-fact) laws are not legal.

The Real Learning Comes Outside the Classroom (But Only If You Ask Questions)

One of my reoccurring mantras is that you should learn far more out in the real world than you do in the classroom. Notice the use of the word "should" in the previous sentence.

The reason this doesn't happen, with far greater frequency, relates to mindset. We walk into a school expecting to be taught. We have notebooks and pencils, there are teachers and textbooks, assignments and exams. Everyone, especially our parents, keep reminding us that we are there to learn.

Then we move to that "real world." We are now working and school is behind us. Teachers, notes, books, exams and parents are yesterday's news as we concentrate on getting a job, earning a paycheck and paying our bills.

However, the fact is that our education is just beginning but only if we remain open minded, and curious enough to recognize that we don't know everything, just because we graduated.

When should your "continuing education" begin? Today couldn't be soon enough.

It can start when you apply for a job.

The chances are that you won't be offered a position by every firm you apply to. Rather than simply chalk it up to bad luck, why not try to find out why.

Call the company and ask for the Director of Human Resources. Explain that you had been turned down for a job with their company and would like, if possible, to learn something from the experience. Inquire if there was any particular reason why you were not successful, if there was anything lacking on your application or resume.

Now, more often than not you will be told that it was simply a case of someone being more qualified. However, you can occasionally pick up some invaluable pieces of information. For example, one of your references may not be speaking as glowingly about you as you might have thought. Or you neglected to provide enough information about your computer skills. Or they were looking for someone who had done more in the area of community service.

Take all this data and incorporate in into your next application. Your chances of success will be increased.

And, once you are working, don't ever stop learning. The more questions you ask the smarter you will become and promotions will be that much easier to obtain.

NUGGET

If they were to say that you are too old, too fat, that you're the wrong sex or have the wrong skin color, call a lawyer because you've got one heck of a law suit. I would even go so far as to suggest you record all the calls made where the intent is to learn why you weren't hired.

Dumber Than Dumb

When I owned my first business the young man who ran my mailroom was married to a woman (let me toss in this thought – at what age does a girl become a woman?) who worked for the Federal government, in their Equal Employment Opportunity division.

She was very good at her job, to the point that she became known by people in the private sector. One of them invited her to interview for a new position at their company. That person would be responsible for "compliance" - seeing to it that the business did not violate any regulations. Since she knew the inside and outside of every one of the rules, she would be a perfect hire. However, as you are about to find out, they apparently had not even bothered to scan that "rulebook."

The interview reached the point where the HR Director asked her what she expected her salary to be. She was making $20,000 at the time and had decided that she would not switch jobs for less than $22,000.

When she gave that figure to the interviewer, his response may have been the dumbest in the sum total of responses, in the history of our planet. He said, and this is an exact quote, "Mrs. Ryan, I'm going to be frank with you. I could probably pay that salary if you were a man but you're obviously not. When I couple that with the fact that you are married the best I can do is $18,000."

As that point she stood up and stated that she had to leave. When he inquired as to why she explained that she had to go back to her office so she could immediately launch an investigation of his company.

I challenge any and all readers to come up with something stupider. The only think I can think of was if she was a single mom, African American amputee, at which point he probably would have told her that she would have to pay them, if she wanted to work there.

Regressive Analysis

Here's a reason to investigate things that don't work out as you wish.

One of our former clients was a major credit card company. Each year a certain number of cardholders would choose not to renew their memberships.

We took a random sampling of these names and either called or wrote them to determine what it was that caused them to leave the fold – was it related to annual fees, interest rates, benefits, etc.? This information proved invaluable in structuring future renewal offers.

Likewise it was important to learn what it was that attracted new customers. Again, a random sample was queried as to what it was that they found most appealing about the "product."

In both cases incentives were often employed. Active customers were offered a $5-$10 credit on their card for filling out a questionnaire. Naturally this was not as easy with cancellations but, because the lifetime value of the customer was so important, a bit more money could be spent. One of their more successful promotions was to offer a $25 credit and the waiver of the next annual fee for former customers who would answer the questions and re-enlist.

However, the fact of the matter is, figuring out what you're doing wrong may be impossible or, if discovered, might be too expensive, or unproductive, to change. What you should be asking is, more often than not, "What are we doing right and how do we do more of it?" If you build on your successes instead of trying to over-analyze your failures, you will do yourself far more good.

NUGGET

You don't have to spend a great deal of money to get enough data to be considered meaningful. 100 customers can tell you a whole lot more than a room full of lecturing professors (while 100 people may normally not be a large enough figure to allow one to produce reliable predictions, in this case it should provide you some useful information).

Cutting Your Nose to Spite Your Face

The person I just referred to, the individual who ran my mail room, came to me one day with a suggestion. He had figured out a change in procedure that could save 10 seconds on every order shipped. That might not sound like a lot until you consider the fact that we were sending out 500 packages a day, so this meant more than 83 minutes would not be necessary.

I have always encouraged employees to come up with ideas like this, but I also know that they all should not immediately be implemented – as was the case here.

The next day I asked John to switch jobs with someone, so that he could be involved in order processing, not shipping. It only took him an hour to figure out that the 10 seconds saved would add 30 seconds to the pre-production phase, resulting in a net loss of almost 166 minutes. However, it was important that John learn this, on his own. Otherwise he would taken my "come to me with suggestions" mantra as being nothing more than lip service.

I learned about the value of this type of approach from "People's Express," a now defunct discount airline, based in Washington, DC.

Aside from the jobs that required a license (pilots and mechanics), or special safety training (stewardesses – that's what they were called back then), every employee got to work at every job. This ended up dramatically increasing, in a positive way, those categories ranked by the passengers. I think I only need one example to have you understand why.

Everyone who worked in the baggage department, loading and unloading suitcases, got to spend a couple of days behind the "Customer Service – Lost Luggage" desk. In doing so they learned how incredibly angry someone can get when they learn that their golf clubs were sent to Santa Fe instead of Santa Barbara. When their two days were up they couldn't wait to get back to their old job, where there performance measurably improved. Interestingly enough, the people they had switched with, felt the same way as the program was put in place in January, when the baggage handlers, working out-of-doors, were continually fighting potential frostbite.

NUGGET

More often than not employees will not get a chance to see the entire "forest" – the view from 10,000 feet as it were. However, by being introduced to the "trees" that surround them, they can learn to appreciate how they interact and impact each other.

Knowing You Will Fail – But Going Ahead Anyhow

Most people are familiar with the phrase "shoot for the moon." Well, I'm here to tell you that sometimes you should try, even though you know you don't have enough fuel to get there. Here are two stories that explain why.

In the National Football League there is something called "The Rooney Rule." It states that any time a team is looking to hire a new head coach they are required to interview at least one minority candidate. While occasionally it has had the desired effect, far more often than not these interviews are just window dressing. The team knows exactly who they plan to hire so the interviews of African Americans and Hispanics is simply being done to obey the letter of the law (these are the only minorities that apply here – at least until China decides to add football to their sports' academy curriculum).

Not too long ago I heard a highly rated assistant coach, a "candidate" for a top job, interviewed after someone else was awarded the position. The radio host asked the rejected applicant if he resented being put through a pointless process that involved not much more than pandering.

His answer was not what I expected to hear. He said not only didn't it bother him, he planned to do it again. When asked why he answered, "I fully expect to be hired for one of these jobs in the future. But, while I might have a ton of on-the-field credentials, I need to know more about what it's like to sit in a conference room with a handful of executives. I want to know the questions I can expect and I want to see their reactions to my responses. As far as I'm concerned these are dress rehearsals – and they usually picked up the tab for lunch."

(Note: A year after this interview took place this assistant coach was hired for the job at the top of the ladder. He credited much of his success to the fact that he felt very comfortable throughout the entire process).

The second case involved the agency I worked for. NBC was looking to see who would handle the advertising for the next Olympics. This would involve roughly $200M in billings.

We knew we had no way of landing the account as our total annual billings at the time barely exceeded that amount. We were simply too small.

However, we wanted to learn what it was like making a presentation to a television network so that one day, when we were truly qualified to handle the business, we would know what to expect before we walked in the door.

We actually did a pretty good job (and learned a lot). I also found out just how creative our Creative Director could be.

As the finishing touch to the half hour we were given, we planned to present them with a cake that included their logo, the Olympics logo, and our logo. It was an ice cream cake and we were told to take it out of the freezer about 45 minutes before serving.

That's what we did – which turned out to not be a very good idea, as our meeting was postponed for an hour and no one thought to put it back where it was very cold.

You have to picture what the top of this cake looked like. The Olympic logo was "a piece of cake" (sorry, this is another irresistible comment) to translate to icing, as was ours. However, as you probably know, NBC has its famous peacock – eight colors. It cost us $200 just to have that decoration done.

When we were ready for our big moment one of our staff members walked into the room carrying a box. With a mental drum roll the top was taken off. What happened next?

One hour and forty-five minutes was far too much for this cake to handle – the top now looked like a watercolor, created by a four-year-old. Our Creative Director, being quick on his feet (which he was actually standing on) said, "We just want you to know that there are things you should be careful about. This will be the Winter Olympics and, without careful planning, things can melt. You might want to make sure that whichever agency you choose, if it's not us, is aware of that" (fortunately our logo was part of the "meltdown" so the cake was never looked at as an example of the type of work we did).

NUGGET

Put yourself in learning scenarios, even if you know you will not succeed, at that point in time. And, unless you

have a great Creative Director, before you walk into the room, make a list of everything that could possibly go wrong, and what you will do in response (actually this step should always be taken before you walk through anyone's door).

Trust – But Verify

When I was getting ready to start my first business, I had a budget of $1000 (this was a long time ago). I had to wait two weeks before my office space would be available so I decided to use that time in order to be able to hit the ground running, right out of the starting blocks (two clichés in one sentence). Among other things I wanted was to get my printing done – letterhead, business cards, etc. I called the phone company to make an appointment for them to install their equipment. While I was on the phone I asked if they could provide the phone number I was going to be assigned. It took them about 10 seconds to give it to me. With that piece of information I gave my printer the go-ahead.

Come opening day, I looked at our phones and saw that the number was different than what I had been told. After my pulse returned to normal I asked how this could have possibly have happened. Their response was to inquire if I had anything in writing, regarding their earlier "assurance." I didn't so 30% of my budget was now scrap paper (that's not quite fair as the envelopes were still usable). This was the first time I understood the meaning of the phrase "Trust, but verify." AND ALWAYS GET IT IN WRITING.

This is especially true if you are dealing with a monopoly, which AT&T was back then. When that occurs you can't give your business to someone else – because there is no other option. Leverage can be a powerful weapon but the lack of it can leave you defenseless.

I don't mean to suggest that you become paranoid. Instead I am telling you – in certain situations become paranoid.

Planning for a Disaster

I am an authority as to the previous nugget – forgetting the "Five P's" (Prior Planning Prevents Poor Performance").

A colleague and I flew up to Rochester, NY to make a presentation at the corporate headquarters of Eastman Kodak. This was long before the days of PowerPoint, (overhead transparencies then, and still, head the list called "The Worst Ways to Communicate") so we decided to impress them by using the top-of-the-line slide projector in the industry – the one they manufactured.

We were ushered into a very impressive conference room where we asked one of the four executives in attendance to lower the screen (at least we did one thing right – calling ahead to insure that they were equipped for our presentation). We put the slide carousel onto the projector and flipped the "on/off" switch. – and nothing happened. No problem we thought, that's why there's a spare bulb. But the extra bulb was not there – because the last person who used the projector failed to replace it after having found it necessary to use the spare.

Naturally we were embarrassed – very embarrassed (suggesting that they hold the slides up to the light, and then pass them around, did not seem like a good idea). However, we knew we were in the best place to ask for help. After all, we were at the home office of our potential client, looking for a bulb to fit a projector that they manufactured.

Unfortunately not a single one of their executives had the faintest idea how to locate a bulb, anywhere on their entire campus (somewhere, in all of this, there has to be a joke. "How many Kodak executives does it take to find a slide projector's light bulb?" I've figured out the question but still don't know the answer – but it has to be more than four).

We did have a printed "leave behind," which we distributed to everyone in the room, but it was not the same.

From the beginning we knew it was a long shot, as far as getting this piece of business, although we had been given a shot, nonetheless. Suffice it to say, Eastman Kodak did not become a client of ours. Heck, if I was them I wouldn't have hired us either.

The next day we had a new office policy, regarding anything removed from one of our storage rooms. The person taking it out had to sign a checklist, confirming that all necessary elements (including replacement bulbs) were at hand, item by individual item. And, when they brought things back they had to repeat the process. Should something have been "used up" (i.e. a spare bulb) it was their responsibility to replace it.

This didn't help with Kodak but we did learn a valuable lesson. The next person to use the projector had heard our horror story so he had his own spare bulbs – a half dozen of them.

NUGGET

At the beginning of this book I related a story where I told a CEO that if I could get through to him, imagine how effective I would be in reaching new customers, on his behalf. That story, and the Kodak debacle, goes back

to that adage that you only have one shot at that first impression. What I did with the CEO resulted in being invited to take the next step towards developing an agency/client relationship. What we did with Kodak caused them to say, "We don't think another step will be necessary."

If it Sounds to Good to be True - Another Kind of Disaster

I am sure that most of you are familiar with the admonition that "If it sounds too good to be true it probably is." This adage is almost always employed in conjunction with some kind of "con" (just think about Bernie Madoff). These "Have I got a deal for you" offers will invariably deplete your savings account.

However, there is another facet that no one every talks about.

A little less than a year ago I came up with an idea (which remains in the "idea" stage) for a product/service. It was based on more than 500 hours of personal experience. A friend of mine (now a former friend), after hearing about it, was effusive in his belief that this would be a sure-fire success. To back this up, he called me a week later, to tell me that he had shown it to a private investor who was prepared to put up the entire $400,000 that was needed. Suffice it to say I was on cloud nine because, even if I cut the most conservative sales and profit projections in half, the numbers were still very impressive.

For the next six months I kept hearing that the money would be available "any day." Each reason for the delay was different, and all of them sounded reasonable.

I eventually learned that I was simply being told what my former friend thought I wanted to hear (he was right), and that this "investor," as best I can tell, either didn't exist or didn't have the money,

Was I "Madoffed?" Not really, since I never spent a penny. However, I did put in several 60-hour weeks, writing and refining the 50-page business plan, conducting focus groups and interviewing potential customers/clients.

This experienced made me a bit more cynical while, at the same time, becoming almost totally exhausted, both physically and emotionally. What I still can't figure out was the purpose of this entire charade, especially as it was being enacted by a friend-at-the-time.

Having told my story, if this has perked the interest of any reader out there, let me know (pbarnett6@cox.net). I'll bet you'll end up telling me that those conservative projections are far, far too low, and that might even be true of my most optimistic numbers.

NUGGET

The reason I included this previous story is to point out that there are many ways to be conned, and money is not always the worst of them. You can earn more money but you can never reacquire wasted time.

(Note: There are times when people won't trust the fact that something defies logic, and ends up being almost too good to be true – except it is that good.)

The supermarket where I shop occasionally run a special on milk – sometimes on half gallons and other times on gallons. A few weeks ago a gallon was selling at $2.46 while a half gallon's price was $.88. I was standing behind a customer who had purchased two gallon containers. It took me almost five minutes to explain to him that he would save money if he purchased four half gallons instead.

I had to overcome his insistence that there must be some kind of a trick to this. A part of my explanation included the concept of "loss leaders," where a store such as this will always have a few items, such as milk, that they are selling at a loss, just to get you into the store. I finished by telling him that, if the store didn't know that the average milk purchase would buy a basketful of regularly priced items, they would never do this. I ended up saving his place in line, while he went to make the swap.

The other example I will share involves a mistake, one that can happen with surprising frequency.

Because it is such a "big ticket" item I am very thorough when it comes to pricing out airline fares. There have been several times where I have discovered that two one-way tickets cost less than one round – on the same flights.

A now deceased friend of mine gave me a simple explanation. These days fares change with such frequency (sometimes daily) than an airline literally can't keep up with itself, with the result being these types of bargains.

The moral of this story is nothing more than "Check first – buy second").

What We've Got is a Failure to Communicate

There are six adages I "repeat repeatedly" (as I just did) throughout this book, and this is one of them -- "What did I say/write vs. what did you hear/read."

This can be easily illustrated by a story told about J. Edgar Hoover.

It seems that the former F.B.I. Director was a stickler for neatness, especially on written reports filed by agents. He received a particularly sloppy memo from a Regional Director and fired it back with a handwritten note that said, "Pay more attention to the borders." The recipient immediately assigned 100 additional agents to guard the borders between the United States, Canada and Mexico.

The problem, of course, is that by not confirming what is meant you can head off in a direction that has nothing to do with what is being discussed.

To emphasize this point I will, as always, relate a story, again from my agency days. But, before doing that I'm going to fill you in on a variation of how information can get totally discombobulated, in less than a minute.

When I was a senior in high school I took a class in journalism. About 10 minutes after sitting down, on the first day, the front door to the classroom opened and some kid came bursting through it, closely followed by another kid, swinging a tennis racquet at the first entrant's head.

Once they had exited the back door, and before anything could be said, the teacher told us to take out a piece of blank paper, along with a pen or pencil, and answer the following questions (they were already written on a blackboard that had been covered by a sheet).

- How tall was each boy?

- What were each of them wearing - both the items and their colors?

- What was the color of each of their hair?

- What was the style of each of their hair?

- What, if anything, was said?

These 11 questions were used to define first impressions from eye witnesses. The best anyone did was to get eight correct.

So, be wary of eye witness accounts, especially when the first reaction of the viewer is shock. What you just read is a case of "What did we see vs. what actually happened."

OK, back to my story.

I remember sitting in on a meeting our agency had with a new client. The account executive came away from it with what he thought were the things the client hoped to have an ad campaign accomplish. He transmitted this information to the creative people who proceeded to produce a package of absolutely stunning ads.

Four weeks later they went back to the client to present everything and were shocked to hear them say, "That looks like an award winning campaign, but not for us. Those ads have nothing to do with the problems we are trying to solve."

Not only was a month of work wasted, we were made to look pretty foolish, which is what we deserved. What should have happened was, during that one-month period, there should have been a number of "reality checks" between the account executive and a representative from the client. And, with absolute certainty, I can tell you that at least one person from the creative side of the agency should have been at the initial meeting – otherwise they are not getting things from the horse's mouth.

(Note: Perhaps some of you can recall a game called "Whisper," played when we were young). For those of you unfamiliar with this word, here's how it worked.

You form a circle of ten people. One of you turns to the person on your right (or left) and whispers a short paragraph (two or three sentences) into their ear. They listen and then turn to the person on their right (or left) and repeat what you whispered. By the time things get back to you, the words will have, at best, a faint resemblance to what you said. To really drive home the point I'm making, after whispering to the one seated on your right (left), do the same thing, using identical verbiage, to the individual on your left (right). The results will be almost comical. But, if you do this, try very hard not to be "the man (woman) in the middle," as this is the person whose ears get whispered into, at exactly the same time).

Remember, if you simply assume that your trains are on the same track you are likely to end up at two totally different destinations with each of you wondering what happened to the other party.

You don't have to give away your creativity in advance of being finished but you should always confirm that the messages you plan to deliver are what the client expects.

Part and parcel of this is understanding how another person is "programmed" to learn. If you know this, getting on the same train becomes so much easier. I've read several books related to learning theories but it was the one on "Accelerated Learning" that really hit home. It was there that I discovered that individuals tend to have one predominant learning style – we are visual, we are auditory or we are kinesthetic.

How do you know which you are? Well, there are several long answers but the short explanation is to check on the type of reaction you have to various statements or situations. If, instinctively, you respond by saying, "I see what you mean" you are likely to be a visual learner. If your answer is, "I hear what you're saying" you do best when being talked to. And, if you come back with, "I feel I understand what you're talking about" you are probably a kinesthetic (hands on) learner.

You've probably heard stories of a child who appeared to be anything but bright and then suddenly "blossomed" in the third grade. What happened, more likely than not, is that he or she simply had a teacher who was communicating in the "style" that the child was mentally prepared to absorb.

There is one other thing to consider, something I learned about only recently.

If you are on the "seller" side of the equation it can be very helpful to listen to the "speech patterns" of the person you are talking to. If they use very long sentences, and talk for extended periods of time, you should try to keep yours as short as possible. They want to "be in control" of the dialogue so, if you ramble on for too long a time (as I often do), they will begin to get restless – and if that's their reaction they will start to tune you out.

On the other hand, if their words sound almost like bullet points, yours should as well, as they are likely in a hurry (as you can see, shorter is almost always better although it is possible that, up until now, you weren't aware of why). One thing you should always do, before entering any type of face-to-face encounter, is determine how much time is available for you. Once you know that, figure out how much of that time you actually need to get your points across, or make your sales pitch. My guess is that it will end up being less than 1/3 of the time allotted, which means you can cede the floor for a majority of meeting.

And always make sure you get to your key statements as early as possible (they can always be repeated). The last thing in the world you want to happen is for time to run out, or the meeting suddenly coming to an abrupt and unexpected end, with you sitting there, with your "ammunition" still in your attaché case.

Finally, be cognizant of the other person's vocabulary. If it doesn't ever include words that suggest a higher degree of intellect, don't show off by throwing your "smarts" at them. Just because someone has reach a pre-eminent position doesn't mean they read the New York Times or Wall St. Journal every day. If their comments mimic the language normally found in the Daily News, so should yours. Nobody wants to be put in a position of feeling inferior and/or not understanding what you're saying.

NUGGET

Remember what was said earlier. You have two ears and one mouth and they should be used in that proportion. Your only goal is to make a sale or get a job. If you speak for five minutes, and that is the result, you've won. If you are allowed to do most of the talking but walk out with no order, or still unemployed, you have lost - even if you got to say every single thing you wanted to.

One other "tidbit" of advice. Pay attention to the photos and plaques on someone's wall and/or desk. It's always nice to know (for future use), if your potential employer plays golf, or has a daughter who rides horses. If nothing else, this will allow for some relaxed preliminary conversation the next time you meet (i.e. "I see you played Pebble Beach. I'd love to do that one day. Was it as good as its reputation?" – remember, people love expressing their opinions). But never bring this up at an initial get together (unless they do) because it will be seen, more often than not, as an attempt to be ingratiating.

It Should Never Take More Than Two Phone Calls

(Note: Most of this chapter is taken from a speech I made, long before the phrase "search engine" became part of our everyday vocabulary. However, even with all the information that Google and Wikipedia, among others, can provide, good old-fashioned "digging deep" never goes out of fashion).

The #1 reason people don't succeed in getting what they're looking for is simply because they give up too quickly. Instead of trusting their own instincts, they simply quit, at least for the moment.

Here's an example.

You want to learn the name of the longest river in Montana. You really don't have the faintest idea of who to ask so you take an educated guess. You call the Governor's office and ask your question. The person at the other ends says that they don't know and here's where the mistake is made.

Most people say "thank you," hang up and then try to decide what to do next. If, instead, you were simply to say, "Who do you suggest I call?" you will invariably be pointed in the right direction. Montana probably has a Department of the Interior, or Water Resources, or Land Management – someone who will have the data at their fingertips.

315

So, trust your first guess, not for it to be correct but for it to provide the key that will open the right door.

"No" Isn't a Stop Sign - Just an Opportunity to Change Directions

I am constantly telling anyone who will listen that the word "no" is accepted far too often as being definitive. I suggest that what it is, more often than not, is the equivalent of finding the front door to the house locked. Yes, most people walk away but those who figure out that there are other entrances invariably find themselves on the inside, looking out.

Here is but one story that contains two examples.

The company I was working for decided, at the very last minute, that they wanted to exhibit at a major trade fair in Hanover, West Germany (before the Berlin Wall was torn down). The plan was to take a booth, for the nine-day run of the show, and have me staff it.

The first problem occurred when it was discovered that the U.S. section of the exhibition hall had been sold out for more than six months.

While most people would have adopted a "wait until next year" attitude, I asked for a list of the American companies that would be exhibiting. I called the one located closest to my office and asked if they might be interested in sharing the cost of their booth. They agreed immediately (they had try to obtain a smaller booth but none were available) and the first roadblock had been overcome.

The second fly in the ointment came when I tried to get a hotel room. The nearest availability was at a location in a town that was a ninety-minute train ride away. This would have meant a three-hour commute every day.

Not to be deterred, I called the Chamber of Commerce in Hanover and asked if local residents ever rented out houses or apartments when major trade shows were held. Yes, I was told, and I was given a list of available properties. A few questions and answers later and I had arranged for a one-bedroom apartment, 10 minutes from the fairgrounds. The "rent" was less than 50% the cost of the hotel room and included breakfast, prepared by the apartment owner (who had moved in with his brother) every morning.

And so, because I refused to accept negative responses, I was able to get something even better than expected at half of what others paid. And, to make this story even more rewarding, it was at this show that I met the company from Finland who turned out to be our best customer (see the DHL letter that appears earlier in this book).

The Most Important Thing to Manage – Your Time

When I was a freshman in college, on the first day of school, the Dean of Students appeared before all 300 of us. He said, "Gentlemen, the book I am holding in my hand will be your bible for the next four years. It is called a Day Timer. You will get one and, if you are smart, you will write down everything in it – your class schedules, your test schedules, when you are expected at work, your parents' birthdays – everything.

No matter how smart you think you are, no matter how much you learned in high school or prep school, I can guarantee that you do not have enough, if any, experience in managing your time.

You are going all going to be taking five courses of three hours each. That's 15 hours a week that you will know where to be and when to be there. After that you are on your own – with no parents or proctors to remind you to hit the books or that a term paper is due. If you don't figure out how to productively spend the other 104 hours every week, assuming you sleep seven hours a night, the likelihood is that you will not be back for your sophomore year."

I had a funny experience that illustrates the relevance of this better than anything I could conjure up.

Earlier on I mentioned the "Previews" sessions at NAU. During the breaks between presentations I would get to chat with smaller groups, on a much more casual basis. In one of those get-togethers (four parents with two sons) I was talking to the guys about what Orientation Week would be like. I let them know that there were probably going to be a hundred activities to partake in, with only 25% of them being required.

Among the ones that weren't was a two-hour block of instruction called "Time Management." I urged them to attend because it would provide a wealth of information that would make their lives much easier and far more productive.

A couple of months later I was on campus for Parents' Weekend. I ran into them and asked how they liked the course I had recommended. They looked at me, rather sheepishly, and admitted that they hadn't attended it. When I asked why they told me that they forgot to write down the day and time it was being held. As they say in court – "Asked and answered."

Of all the things I was taught in college this was certainly one of the most valuable – and remains so to this day. Time is a finite item that cannot be recovered or expanded upon – the hour I wasted yesterday cannot be withdrawn from a time vault and although I know I'm going to have a lot of work to do tomorrow, I can't purchase a couple of extra hours.

There is one other point I would like to make about how effective time management can make one's life a good deal easier – perhaps less stressful is more accurate.

If you consider all the team sports that exist, the one position that is the most stressful is a hockey goalie. He has to be attentive for a bit more than one half hour for each period, during which he never gets to sit down – and he almost always plays the whole game. The fact that his team may be on offense matters little as that condition can change in a matter of seconds.

Many years ago I heard an interview with Tony Esposito, one of the outstanding goalies of his generation. The reporter asked him how he was able to concentrate for such an extended period of time. Tony explained that it was impossible, that what he did was divide the game into 12 five-minute periods. His goal was to shut out the opposition for five minutes. after which that game ended, and the next game began. This also made it much easier to put a goal scored against him in the past – after all, it happened in an earlier played game.

The next time you are faced with a similar condition consider using the same approach. For instance, if it's an hour-long exam, don't look at having to pay attention to everything for all 60 minutes. If the exam has six parts, you only have to pay attention to one part for 10 min. and you needn't think of anything else. Of course, you have an advantage that no goalie ever has. If you finish early you can go back and correct mistakes.

NUGGET

By scheduling wisely you will not only accomplish more, you will end up with more free time. In fact you should schedule that free time – that way you won't feel the least bit guilty if you spend a couple of hours doing anything you'd like, including nothing.

Breaking News – They Must Think We are Idiots

The reason I am inserting this here simply because I just saw/heard these two ads, during the network news.

The first was from a car company discussing how important "forward thinking" and innovation are. They said that without these traits "the world would still be flat." Really? There was actually a time when it was flat? Did someone insert some air hoses and pump it up, as with a tire or a balloon? It's amazing how disrespectful an advertiser can be, in regards to their audience. I suppose their excuse might be that they didn't think that the viewers would be "tuned in" to an ad but, if that's the case, why run the ad in the first place.

The other was for a "medical device" that promised to eliminate pain. The obnoxious-sounding voice-over announcer said, "You can pay up to $2,000 for this product but ours sells for less than a fraction of that price." "Less than a fraction?" Isn't less than a fraction a fraction?

I have never figured out if the copywriters needed to go back to school or that they believed nobody really listens while hearing.

Lifetime Value of a Customer (Numero Dos, or Maybe Tres)

The importance of understanding this cannot be over emphasized. You can be sure the cable TV providers, insurance companies and cell service providers understand. They don't look at you as a $50 - $150 a month customer. You're a $600 - $1800 a year/$3,000 - $9,000 over five years customer. That's why they are willing to spend so much on the cost of acquisition.

Take a look at your business, whether it be a restaurant, an office supply store or an auto service facility. How many times a year does a good customer come in, for one reason or another?

Ten is probably a reasonable answer (even for the car servicing business as most families have at least two cars).

If the customer spends $50 each time, and a third of that is gross profit, you can certainly spend a hundred dollars to acquire them, if you follow a number of things suggested earlier in this book,

Know Where the Business Comes From – the Value of Direct Response

Several years ago there was a Diet Pepsi TV ad campaign featuring Ray Charles and the line, "You got the right one baby, uh huh."

Shortly after Labor Day the Wall Street Journal was interviewing the Diet Pepsi brand manager and asked if he could attribute the sales bump, over the past couple of months, to the message Mr. Charles was delivering. His answer was, "Well, it was either that or the fact that the temperatures this summer were five degrees higher than normal."

In other words he really didn't know, which leads one to wonder whether anyone can really be comfortable in the fact that "image" advertising is working. There is one exception. Years ago the New Yorker ran a cartoon showing a Russian couple watching a TV ad for an automobile. When it concluded, with the words, "Don't wait, act right now," the couple got up and ran out the front door of their house, in order to get to the dealership as quickly as possible. I'll bet that there are several advertisers who wish we were a dictatorship, so that they would be able to "dictate" to their listening/viewing audiences.

This goes a long way towards explaining why I am such a huge fan of direct response advertising – something with a code that can be measured, most often with "precise precision."

Here is an example that demonstrates the value.

There was a restaurant, in Connecticut, owned by some friends of mine. It was decorated in a unique and off-beat style and featured cuisine that people either really liked, or really didn't. When patrons were asked if they would come back a second time, the answers would invariably be, "Absolutely" or "Absolutely not" – there was no middle ground.

They had done a mailing to 5000 households and were convinced that it was a flop as their response rate was 2% - 100 couples (all numbers have been rounded off). Since the mailing cost them $5,000 and the average bill for a couple was $120, of which one-third was gross profit, they had a profit of $4000, against that $5000 dollar expense. And so, they surmised, this direct mail stuff was not such a great idea.

However, I pointed out to them that, because they knew who their customers were, they could do some meaningful follow-up research and learn a good deal more than the raw returns might indicate.

Here is what they discovered (once again the figures have been rounded off):

50 of those 100 couples never returned but 10 became "regulars," to the point of patronizing this establishment six more times a year. 10 others visited four more times, 10 ate there three additional times, 10 others twice more and the final 10 only once. Thus the 100 visits turned out to be 200 a year. With $40 gross profit per visit they now had $8,000 against the $5,000 expense.

As is so often the case it resulted in a lot more than that. Industry statistics suggest that, over the next four years those 200 visits will drop by 50% each year so that there will be 100, followed by 50, 25, 12, 6 and 3 (they did stay in business that long). This adds up to another 196, an additional $7,840 in gross profit. So now they have $15,840 against that $5,000 expense.

And, it probably doesn't stop there. Historical data indicates that 20% of the couples who subsequently visit a restaurant bring guests and several tell other people about it. And, finally, if the mailing were of a larger size, the costs would have been reduced.

By the time everything was added up, they were roughly getting a six-time return on their investment, rather than losing money as they had originally thought. However, without being able to track things precisely none of this would have been known.

All this goes back to an earlier admonition – know who your customers are, find out what got them into your facility and then learn as much about them as possible.

In this scenario try to find out something from those who you will never see again (ask that employees to point out people who seemed displeased). I told my friends to, if they could offer an after-dinner drink so that they could speak with some of these individuals before they left the premises.

The Q & A sessions began with this comment. "We know that our establishment is not 'middle of the road,' and that's by design. The last thing we wanted was a situation where our patrons said we were 'OK,' and when asked if they would return all said 'Maybe.'

We're pretty sure that you think we never got to the level of even being OK but we'd still like to ask you a few questions. And these will not be about things like the décor or menu, because we are very happy with what we're doing. However, while those may not have been your cup of tea, there may be a few things you found wanting that we are positioned to do something about."

They didn't get all that many useful suggestions but there was one that they instituted immediately. By an astute juggling of their waiters and waitresses, if there were four people at a table, when they were served each course, they would all get their food at the exact same time. It required some pretty difficult choreography but almost every one of their patrons commented positively about it – and a well known, and highly respected, restaurant critic made special mention of this in his review – 3 ½ stars (out of four) regarding the food and four stars for the quality of the service.

Tennyson Was Right – Failure (Losing) is Not a Disgrace

One of the most misunderstood lines of poetry ever written is from a work entitled, "In Memoriam, A.H.H."

by Alfred Lloyd Tennyson. It is almost always quoted in some type of romantic context although the author had something totally different in mind.

A.H.H. was Tennyson's close friend who had died and this work was a tribute to their friendship and an explanation of Tennyson's viewpoints about life.

Tennyson was a heterosexual so, when he said, "Tis better to have loved and lost than never to have loved at all" he was referring to the benefits derived from making the effort. The real translation of this line is that it's better to try, succeed, only to fail rather than not to have tried in the first place (in which case you can't possibly succeed).

The problem is, at least in this country, we teach children, almost from day one, that failure is a disgrace, something to be avoided at any cost. Schools therefore teach students to pass, rather than learn, and we become afraid to venture even a foot away from the white line that runs down the middle of the road.

NUGGET

I don't believe in failure, unless it's making the same mistake over and over again. I believe in success and education. Learn from what goes wrong and it has enormous value. Don't try in the first place and your knowledge will increase by nothing.

"Druthers"

I'm not sure I have ever met a single person who, occasionally, does not need a kick in the butt. The first thing we often think of, when the alarm clock goes off is, "Why do I have to go to work today?" Well, here's one thought. On your night table keep a piece of paper that reads:

The other things I might be doing today.

- Keeping my root canal appointment.

- Telling my neighbor that our dog won't dig up their flower bed again.

- Explaining to my son (daughter) that telling his (her) teacher that they are an idiot is not a good idea.

- Trying to figure out how to complete four fifteen-minute tasks in less than half an hour.

- Deciding which of the things I plan to make for dinner my family will hate least.

- Stepping on the scale.

- Figuring out the best way to get from here to there, when I don't know where "there" is.

- Changing the oil in my car.

- Calling the AAA because my car seems to have no oil in it.

- Adding up my anticipated expenses for the month.

- Adding up my anticipated income for the month.

- Trying to figure out why the expenses are always greater than the income.

- Returning my accountant's call (he never has good news).

Wow! I can't wait to get to work.

Windfalls, Luck and Intuition

The beginning of the first Gulf War, in 1991, was broadcast live, on CNN. In that particular timeslot CNN had been averaging 300,000 viewers. This figure jumped to 30,000,000 within an hour after the war began.

CNN decided to cancel all advertising with the exception of one company. Time-Life Books was their biggest advertiser, and there was some concern that they would be offended. Besides, CNN figured, viewers could use a break of a couple of minutes, every hour (this was before DVRs or "pause" buttons).

Time-Life was paying at a rate based on the "standard at the time" viewership, but they got 100 times what was anticipated. Since rates could not be changed, after the fact, this was the equivalent of "buy one, get 99 free." As might be expected, it was, by far, the biggest revenue night Time-Life had ever experienced (and probably still is).

There are those who suggest that much of success relates to timing, while others emphasize location. In my mind it is often a combination of both – being in the right place at the right time. In the case just cited, had the war broken out in the morning, Time-Life would have had no benefit, since they ran all their ads later in the day. If the station covering the story was MSNBC it would have done Time-Life no good, as they didn't run any ads there. As I said, right place, right time.

Here is one other example of how this can play out.

When I was in the mail order business I received a pre-publication (it contained no ads) first issue of "Penthouse" magazine Since they were promising sales of 250,000 I decided to take a chance and placed a small ad, as their advertising rates were very low.

That issue sold just over 1M copies. Since their second issue had already been "put to bed" they couldn't change their rates, at least not yet. That second issue sold 1.5M copies. So, for a combined circulation of 2.5M we had paid for ads based on rates equating to 250,000 per issue (it was the equivalent of "buy two and get four free"). These were the two most successful ads we ever ran – yes, a windfall.

There are also many occasions you can create your own windfall by knowing where and when to do so.

1) Most people play golf as a form of relaxation (although that's hard to believe when they are throwing a club, after a bad shot). However, if you are good at picking up "vibes," you can often use those hours for your business benefit.

When I lived in Connecticut I went to play golf on a Saturday morning. One of the people in our foursome introduced himself as an executive with IBM. Over the course of the next four hours he talked a good deal about his employer, as did I. When we finished, and were relaxing over a beer (why do people, including me, use the word "over" in a situation such as this?), I asked if he would introduce us to someone at IBM who might be able to make use of our agency's services. He said that he would be happy to. A week later we met with that individual and, shortly thereafter, they were a client.

The next time we played he brought a friend along. This gentleman was a high ranking executive with UPS, something he only mentioned in passing. I sensed that he had no interest in talking about work so I didn't – for the next nine months. At that point he casually mentioned how pleased he was by the fact that I had done no "courting" in the interim. As our conversation progressed he offered (without me having to ask) to hand deliver a letter to their Director of Marketing, with a personal endorsement of me – and my employer. A week later we met with that individual and two months later we were able to add their name to our client roster.

There is another way you can be the "creator" of a windfall. While the Gulf War story, talked about a few paragraphs ago, may have sounded unique, that's not exactly true. In fact there are times where you can maintain almost total control, in advance of an actual occurrence. The CNN story had a lot of luck involved. This one doesn't.

If I were the Red Cross I would provide a series of thirty-second and one-minute appeal messages to the Weather Channel, and tell them not to run them until notified.

Every time there is a weather related disaster, especially hurricanes (which begin being reported about well before their arrival), the Weather Channel's audience grows ten-fold, but the advertisers only have to pay the rate-card dollar amounts, which are very low. People who are interested enough in a weather story, to cause them to change channels, are much more likely to make donations to assist the people they are watching.

I have written to three Red Cross executives, regarding this suggestion but the only responses I received were requests for donations (meaning that no one read my letters, even though they were addressed to specific individuals). This was incredibly dumb of them since they knew nothing about me, including the possibility that I might be prepared to make a major contribution/bequest to their organization.

After this happened, for the third time, I switched my "disaster relief" donations to the Salvation Army. The Red Cross lost a repeated donor, simply by failing to be responsive.

Position Yourself to Succeed

1) About six months after taking the job of running the Crisis Center, here in Arizona, I had the occasion to play in a charity golf tournament, sponsored by a consortium of Rotary Clubs. I convinced my Board (and it wasn't easy) that it would be worth it for them to authorize my $150 entry fee. My argument was that I might make some good contacts with an organization known for their philanthropy.

Good contacts indeed. I was paired with their District Vice President who expressed a strong interest in what we were trying to accomplish. Over the next year I got to give more than 40 speeches in front of local clubs. At the end of that year, we received a check for $125,000 from Rotary, the amount needed to construct one of the eight houses on the "Kids Campus" we were planning to build.

2) A year after arriving in the Valley of the Sun, I volunteered to assist at the largest spectator-attended golf tournament on the PGA Tour. This event is put on by The Thunderbirds, an amazing group of about 100 executives who, along with about 4,000 volunteers, raise $5M for charities, year after year – even during recessions.

Their average annual attendance is more than 500,000, including at least 150,000 fans on the Saturday of the event. After three years I took over as the head of the division I had been working at. A year after that, the fundraising group that put on the tournament, gave us $125,000 – to build another one of our houses. While I can't prove that there was any connection here I am almost sure there was. I say this because, when I went to present our "Eight-House Plan," before I could open my mouth the Chair of their Donations Committee said, "Philip, before we get started I want you to know how much we appreciate all your volunteer work."

Check Them Out - Then Be Creative

In our "Kids Campus" venture we were partnering with Habitat for Humanity. I asked their Executive Director if he could arrange a meeting with Home Depot, one of their major sponsors. He said that he would be happy to but cautioned me that they were able to donate no more than $50,000, to a local non-profit, in any given year.

Before my meeting I did some homework. Among the things I learned was that their fiscal year began on Feb. 1st. After explaining our project, to their four regional Vice Presidents, I asked for the following – a donation of $25,000 on January 31st, a donation of $50,000 any time during the following 12 months, and then a donation of $50,000 on Feb. 1st the following year (yes, it was $125,000, but spread out over three of their fiscal years – actually 367 days). Although I am an optimist by nature, when they said, "We'll get back to you," that optimism waned a bit.

One of them called a week later and said they liked our creative solution and they would be making three contributions, of $50,000 each ($25,000 more than we had asked for), in the form of debit cards, which were as good as cash to us, given all the building materials we were going to need – and this cost them less than the $125,000 in cash I had asked for, as they would be donating "marked-up" products in lieu of currency. Just to make sure the process would work smoothly, I took the first of what would eventually be 15 $10,000 cards to their local store. All I bought was a screwdriver so you can imagine the look on their cashier's face

when she swiped my item ($2.59) and then the card
- which showed an opening balance of $10,000. She
had to get a supervisor to confirm that this was on the
up-and-up.

NUGGET

**Location, timing and it never hurts to spend some time on
a golf course. And, as I have said several times, a bit of
research, coupled with a creative approach, can go a
long way.**

Eight-Point Type Is Not OK – Neither is Intentionally Misleading the Public

I rarely turn down business, but that doesn't mean that it
hasn't happened.

Earlier this year, in my mail, I received an offer that made
me think of other times something similar had happened.
It was from an insurance company, offering rates that
were spectacularly low. Next to their chart was a small
#1, indicating a footnote. When I went to check it out
I discovered, written in almost-impossible-to-read eight-
point type, that these rates were only good in the state
of South Dakota.

Not only would I never buy a product from a company
such as this, I would never take them on as a client,
unless they agreed to change the type size in the
footnote portions of their direct mail pieces and no
longer do promotions that equated to "bait and
switch."

As you can probably tell by now, I believe in pushing all
four corners of the envelope – but not when it comes to
intentionally misleading the customer.

For those of you who read the papers with any frequency, you surely have seen full-page ads offering anything from Amish fireplaces to fireproof vaults. Every one of the vendor's "products" provides something "free," as long as you pay for something else in the offering. Their ads tell you that you only have 48 hours in which to order (although the same ad will run week after week). And one of them is giving away a "stack" of $2 bills. When you read that eight-point type you discover that their definition of "stack" is two bills. Finally, have you noticed what they don't tell you?

They never provide the name of the company, the address of their company or the phone number of their company, probably because they don't want customers knocking on their door, telling them that they are charlatans. As far as I'm concerned, if they are not willing to tell me who and where they are, I'm not willing to send them my money.

Actually, in this case just cited, I did place an order – after being assured that if I was dissatisfied I could return it, and that they would pay the shipping charges, in both directions (I recorded those assurances).

The product was a portable cooling unit, guaranteed to cut down the portion of my electric bill that related to air conditioning.

I obtained some pretty sophisticated measuring equipment and discovered that, after several tests, under different types of conditions, the product raised the ambient temperature by two degrees.

Of course I sent it back after, once again, being reminded of the gullibility of the general public. Most people, in a situation like this, either think that the problem is their fault, or that it's too much of a hassle to return it. How do I know this is true? Because the company ran the ad for this product, week after week, starting in the late spring.

My favorite (I'm being more than a bit sarcastic here) was when one of their ads said that they had allocated a special part of their inventory (try not to smile when I tell you that the number they gave was 6,486), for Arizona. The two caveats were that you only had 48 hours in which to order (although, once again, the ad kept being run) and that it was only available in select zip codes. They then proceeded to list every zip code in the state, with the exception of one in the northeast corner of the state – a part of the Navajo reservation, where there is no electricity.

One "unique" aspect to their ads was the fact that they never seemed to sell any product because every time they reran this "promotion" they stated that they had allocated exactly 6,486 units for Arizona. So, as I just said, either they had not sold a single one, or they were lying. I'll let you decide (I'm guessing that the reason this number ever changed was because they were too cheap to have the type in the ad reset).

Why can they keep getting away with this? Because they state that any unhappy customer can get a full refund. I can give you a pretty good idea how this can work.

About 25 years ago someone I knew kept running ad that said "Five brand new towels for $1 + $.35 for postage and handling – Satisfaction guaranteed (which did not include the return of the p & h charge). What they sent out, much to the negative surprise of their customers, were five handi-wipes that could have been purchased in any supermarket for $.50. They sold slightly more than 1M sets and received 175 of them back, requesting a refund. Why so few? Think about it. Someone wanting to send it back would have had to purchase a mailing envelope of sufficient size, then go to the Post Office and pay the mailing charges – all to get $1 back. Would you have bothered? Of course not – and they knew that.

The Power of One

If you believe that one person cannot make a difference, consider these two examples.

A couple of years ago Phoenix radio had a drive-time "shock jock" commentator whose nicest comment was referring to Michelle Obama as a "miserable wretched excuse for a woman." I contacted the station several times, but to no avail. So, for a couple of weeks, I forced myself to listen to his show so that I could make a list of his sponsors.

I started writing to them (always including the quote you just read) and, by the end of the month, more than 50 % of them had pulled their ads. Before the end of the next month that show went off the air. The announcement said that it was a "mutual decision." What do you think?

About a year ago my local paper's gossip column started becoming more and more salacious. Their stories were about nothing other than celebrity divorces and crime. And the headlines were such that no responsible parent would let a child read them.

I began an e-mail campaign directed at the reporter, the Entertainment Editor, the Editor and the Publisher – and I asked friends of mine to do the same. After a couple of months of barraging them with complaints, from no more than five people, the language all of a sudden became both civil and relevant. Did we affect this change? You can decide for yourself but I should point out that two of my "small circle of friends" identified themselves as shareholders in their corporate parent.

Planting a Seed

As promised a previous chapter, here is how to "protect" your customer names, which may be your most valuable asset (see previous reference regarding the Sharper Image).

Any list of names you rent out should be "seeded." For example, if I were renting out 5,000 of my names to Company W included in those names would be mine, with a middle initial of G (my real middle initial is M).

What should happen is that I should get one mailing from Company W, and it should be the one I approved (renters can't change the contents of a mailing once you've signed off on it). If I get more than one mailing from Company W they have copied the list, which is illegal, unless a defined number of uses had been agreed upon and then it has to be an exact figure – it's usually two (you have the right to approve the second mailing if it's any different from the first one). And, if I get a mailing from another company, where the label reads Philip G. Barnett, I know they have sold my list, which is also illegal.

One other tip about mailings. If you are the one doing them, add several names (of people you know and who will report back to you) to any list you're using (again including your own). These should be people as close as your own house and as far away as the other side of the country. Ask the recipients to inform you the date a particular envelope arrived. What you want to do is document results for as many different types of mailings as possible (i.e. first class, third class, etc.) This information can prove to be very useful insofar as future planning.

Furthermore, if you are mailing packages have at least two sent to you and another pair to someone living on the other side of the country. One should go via the Post Office and other using UPS. Aside from the length of time it takes the items to arrive, you want to make sure that the packaging material you use is substantial enough to insure that its contents do not arrive damaged.

Mail it ASAP? Not So Fast

One of the fascinating things about having Donald Trump as a client involved decision making. The statement you hear from most of the people you do work for is, "OK. Now give us some time to think about it." With Donald, if that thought process took more than 10 seconds, it probably meant he had skipped his morning cup of coffee.

Donald purchased the Eastern Airlines Shuttle in 1989. After retrofitting all the planes he wanted to have a launch party celebrating his newest acquisition. He didn't have to be told that, if he announced that there would be shrimp, the media would turn out in force, which they did.

The Trump Shuttle made Donald part of "OnePass," the frequent flyer program that was currently in place, in partnership with Continental Airlines. To make sure everyone knew what was going on, he told us to prepare a mailing that would go to the 800,000 "One Pass" cardholders (note: in fact checking this I have learned that, at any one time, this program has been called

"ONEPASS," "OnePass" or "One Pass.") And this was not to be just any mailing; it was going to be a "Donald" mailing.

The envelopes and letterhead were gold embossed. The paper was "wedding invitation" quality. Postage stamps were used in lieu of metering and a machine, similar to the one in the White House, was used to make Donald's signature appear real.

Donald wanted the mailing, announcing the "beginning of a new age in aviation," to go out the day before the first flight. We were able to talk him out of this, after pointing out that, through no fault of his own, that first flight could be delayed, or even cancelled. Were that to happen the press would jump all over Donald, accusing him of "premature celebration."

It took a bit longer to convince him not to do the mailing on the day service began. The last shuttles didn't depart until 9 PM, so there would still be a lot of time for something to go wrong.

The result was a letter that began, "As of yesterday the world of aviation will never be the same" - when writing for Donald I always looked at the assignment the same way I would if it were the script for the voiceover talking about a soon-to-be-released action movie.

I suppose there are those who will say that we were being far too cautious. And, the way things turned out, they would have been right. However, as anyone in this type of business knows, had we thrown caution to the wind, it would have been inviting the fates to intervene, to the point that the inaugural flight would have had a flat tire, just as it was pulling away from the gate – and the airline's AAA coverage wasn't due to go into effect until the following day.

Test, Test & Test Again – But Don't Bother If You Won't Use the Results (or, Playing With the House's Money Remix)

One of the great things about a discipline like direct response advertising is that it allows you to test with incredibly accurate results. You can test everything from a list of names, to a product, a price, etc. If you use enough names to make the results statistically reliable, the amount of information you can obtain is worth more than just "a lot."

However, if you're not going to act, based on the results you get, what's the point?

Here's an example.

A gentleman I know (another "Mr. Jones") had a product he wished to sell (a package of motivational videos, designed to assist teachers). His initial potential audience was clearly defined – 140,000 school principals.

We did a very clever test mailing to 7,000 randomly select names from the full list. It was a 6" X 9" color postcard with some "teaser" copy. The purpose was to direct the recipient to his web site where they could get complete information, watch and listen to samples and place an order. The "package," of seven DVDs, sold for $90 and, for the purpose of the test, a minimum order of $720 (eight packages) was required – remember, we were communicating with principles, not teachers, which made it more likely that the purchaser would want multiple sets.

My client was very nervous, as was I. He had put up $5,000 of his money (against his family's advice) which included $1,500 to me. That was much less than I might normally charge, but I didn't think he could deal with the figure I would have mentioned, had the circumstances been different. What we did agree on was that if the test was successful, and a rollout was done, I would receive a percentage of the net revenue. This had the potential of me receiving a good deal more money than I would have made, had this been a strictly fee-based relationship (the same as what happened with ABC Automotive, described earlier).

The test results bordered on being spectacular. The 7,000-piece mailing, which cost $3,500, resulted in 5,200 "hits" on the web site (some may have been duplicates) and 41 orders. The 328 sets ordered, which cost $3,000 to produce and ship, brought in revenues of $29,520.

Let me repeat that - $5,000 in costs (which included my $1500 fee) and $29,520 revenues. What an ideal situation. And, there were still 133,000 names to contact.

Now, as is the case with many people new to business, advice arrived from many places and Mr. Jones certainly got a lot of it. As a result, instead of enjoying his success he found himself with a handful of questions. The good news was that they were almost all legitimate and they could easily be answered.

My client had a concern that the $720 minimum order was too high and was that the $90 per package was too low (although the test did not necessarily support this opinion). What I suggested to Mr. Jones was that he do another series of mailings that included the following offers:

- Mail to the original 7,000 names (minus the 41 who had ordered). Explain that you have realized that many school budgets are very tight so you have reduced the minimum order to either two or three packages ($180 - $270).

- Mail the exact same postcard to a new 7,000 names. This will allow you to confirm the initial results.

- Send another 7,000 names a postcard that directs them to a web site where the minimum order is lower.

- Send another 7,000 names a postcard directing them to a web site where the unit price is higher.

It would cost about $14,000 to do these mailings so, as the saying goes, Mr. Jones would be playing with the house's money. And, the results from these four mailings would paint a very accurate picture as to how to approach the remaining 112,000 names.

So, what did Mr. Jones choose to do? Absolutely nothing. Other things crowded his agenda and he didn't have the time. I begged, I pleaded and I cajoled but I got nowhere. He decided to play a version of "take the money and run" because, deep down, he didn't believe that the test results could be replicated (They didn't have to be. If the response was only half of what it was for the test he would do very well indeed).

Nonetheless he decided to "quit while ahead," as his profits were half of his annual salary. The adage says, "No risk/no reward" but in this case it was much better since there would be no real risk (he would no longer be spending any of his own money) and the potential reward was huge.

However, this was a person without an entrepreneurial bone in his body. He decided that he didn't want to go further because he had already risked his own money once and did not want to do so again. I tried explaining to him that he should not treat anything beyond his original investment (even double that amount) as his own money, at least not yet - but to no avail.

I wish I had an answer here. I know people who would trade in their first-born child for results like this. The initial test suggested that net profits on a full mailing would be $400,000 and there would be no risk. The roll-out could always be done in a way that Mr. Jones would only spending profits, never his own money – but it never happened.

Oh yes, I got screwed and learned another lesson. Mr. Jones and I had agreed upon what I was to receive from the roll-out, but there was no wording requiring that a roll-out occur. There are several people named "Jones" in this book. This is the only one I continue to refuse to speak to.

NUGGET

During the time I spent overseas I had the opportunity to meet a German businessman (he described American beer as "water with a head" and proceeded to introduce me to "the good stuff." Good indeed – after two steins I had trouble walking).

He told me about a negotiation he had with a gentleman, in Japan. They were just about to sign a joint-venture agreement, worth about $100M USD, when his Japanese counterpart said, "Is it really necessary for us to sign this? We both trust each other so a handshake should be good enough."

His immediate response was, "I totally trust you. The person I don't trust is the one who has had too much to drink tonight and, as a result, might crash into your car. I would then be forced to tell your partners, people I've never met, to trust me, that this is what you would have wanted them to do" (he got his signed contract).

Testing Price Points

When you are ready to bring a product or service to market, one of the first things you must decide is your selling price.

If it is a situation where you will be competing with something that is already out there, you will have some guidance. However, if there is nothing like what you will be selling, there will have to be some educated guess work.

Here is some general advice.

For the sake of this example I will use a base figure of $1000 (your competitor's price). If your product has a few more bells and whistles, you should test two price points.

Offer your "stripped down" version for $900 and the "deluxe" one for $1200. This will create an appeal to those who are dollar conscious and a different one to people and/or businesses who want the latest-and-greatest.

How many buyers will go for the "up-sell?" I have no idea – and neither do you. So how do you make your determination? You're about to find out.

Your goal should be to learn is how many purchasers will be willing to pay the higher price.

There is an overwhelming body of evidence that shows there is some point where the person with the checkbook or credit card will say to themselves, "As long as I'm prepared to spend $900 I probably should buy the upgraded version if its price is "X." Once again, neither of us know what "X" equaled, so it's time to do some testing.

Pick three similar markets. In the first one set your prices at $900 and $1100, in the second one those figures should be $900 and $1200, with the third one being $900 and $1300. Once your sales figures are in (covering a period of at least six months), it's time to do some calculating.

I'm sure that, while the deluxe version of your product will cost more to produce, the additional costs will be more than covered by your additional revenue.

When you feel comfortable that you have discovered the most profitable selling price, do one more test.

Let's say that $1200 is the figure you come up with. Make that your "baseline," a price that should be maintained until it's proven otherwise as far as profitability. With this in mind I would test $1200 vs. $1400. If the latter generates higher profits (which doesn't necessarily mean more units sold), that becomes your new baseline.

(Note: There is one factor that has not been included so far, but should be part of your decision making process. Specifically this is what's going on in the market, regarding your competitor's pricing and the selling prices offered by other new entries to the category).

How Much Are You Worth?

The same process holds true if you are going to provide a service. In this case it's easier to see what's "out there."

Look at what happens if you are a consultant. If the average fee is now $100 per hour, and you can provide essentially the same service, your initial fees should be $80 an hour and $120. The higher rate might, for example, cover a "complimentary" two-hour introductory presentation. And, you might also consider adding a $130 possibility which would add a two-hour session, at no charge, where you would present your findings and recommendations.

Whatever it is you decide here, you should go through the same testing process, Remember, you don't know and I don't know, but your customer/client will fill in the blanks.

Once, when I told a prospective client that my consulting fee was $300 per hour (less than most attorneys charge these days), he asked me how could I possibly justify a fee that high. My response was to tell him that, for all intents and purposes, he would be paying me less than the minimum wage – by a lot.

I went on to explain that I had more than 20,000 hours of experience in the arena we were talking about. Included was a litany of programs that worked and those that didn't – and why. Being overly conservative I would take only 100 of those hours and deem them totally appropriate to the situation at hand. It may have taken me 100 hours to compile my "book of knowledge" but I could teach/apply it within one hour, once I accumulated a wealth of background information (for which I didn't charge).

So, I would be paid $300 for 100 hours worth of what I know. This works out to $3 per hour – as I said, well below the minimum wage.

You've Got to be Kidding Me

Here's one more story, presented to minimize the fact that this book is out of balance (which it still is) when it comes to my successes compared to failures.

Earlier I wrote about the strangest man I have ever known. To substantiate that opinion, here's the story of how we first met.

345

I contacted "Mr. Strange" because I had received a duplicate mailing from his restaurant/club and I wanted to offer to have his mailing list "cleaned" for him. He seemed interested and suggested that we meet for lunch. While we were dining he mentioned an idea of his. He wanted to produce a CD called "Theme Songs from the Soaps." Before he finished explaining himself I fell in love with the idea. I have never watched a soap opera in my life but I knew how to reach almost every person who never missed an episode.

He asked me to put together a very brief plan (his attention plan was shorter than my son's, when he was a teenager with ADD) defining what I would do as his advertising agency, with me receiving 15% of the billings.

I went back to see him the next day, knowing that if I waited any longer he might forget our conversation. This was one time that, while I heard and understood what he said, I didn't do what he asked (if necessary I knew that I could produce what he requested in less than two hours.

What I did show him was a plan, under which we would become partners. I would handle everything from soup to nuts, except for the design of the CD's "cover" (he was a very talented artist).

It took him less than five minutes for Geordie to agree with my proposal. His first (and only) question was, "How much will it take to get started?" I told him that, in order to cover the first two ads, office space, a designer for the ads and a salary for me, I would need $80,000. He said, "OK, let me find my checkbook." It took him about a half an hour to do so, at which point I had a check for $80,000 in my hand. I told you he was strange. He had known me for less than two hours before he gave me this money.

The first two full-page ads, in "Soap Opera Digest" and "Soap Opera Magazine," were smashing successes.

At that point I recommended that we try a two-minute television commercial, to run during various soap opera episodes. The nice part about this was that we could purchase inexpensive local spots, to test out the concept.

He loved this plan and, within three weeks we had the spot produced and edited (I found an ex New Yorker who understood the meaning of the word "urgent"). We selected five markets and booked the time. But then disaster struck.

The day before the commercials were going to run I got a call from Barry Goldwater, Jr. (Geordie's "advisor") who told me to cancel the airings. It seems that my partner did not have the ASCAP rights for any of the 16 songs.

When I got over my disappointment, I suggested that we hire an attorney to get those rights, and pay the songwriters a royalty on each CD sold (actually we wouldn't have had a choice when it came to doing that). My partner's reaction? "Let's forget about the whole thing. I'm bored with this project."

Did I tell you he was very strange? Yes, I know I did but, in this case, it's worth repeating. Counting the cost of the TV ad production he had laid out well over $100,000. I made one attempt him to change his mind (getting the song licenses would cost no more than $10,000 and we had 2000 CDs in my office) but to no avail.

I did define this as a failure, and from a marketing standpoint I guess it was. Then again, I got paid $30,000 for three months work so I guess that, on the economic side of the ledger (my ledger), I did quite well.

I have been asked, more than once, why I didn't put up the $10,000 myself, given how successful it appeared the program was going to be. In this case I plead guilty to taking the money and running because I was, at the time, broke and I decided that one check in my bank account was worth more than 2000 CDs in the closet.

No matter how many suggestions I make in this book, please remember that there are times when "special circumstances" overrule making a decision that, while correct, is not realistically appropriate.

NUGGET

I know that I stated that one should never wait until every "i" is dotted, and every "t" is crossed. Otherwise, you can never move forward. However, there are always a few capital "I's" to be dotted, and T's" to be crossed, and, if you don't take care of those, you may end up getting sued.

(Note: To be technically correct, a capital "I" doesn't get dotted and a capital "T" does not get "crossed").

ME? GULLIBLE?

I admit that it never dawned on me to ask about the ASCAP approvals in advance although I was well aware how dangerous assumptions can be. I relate this to an incident that seems to happen almost annually in NYC.

Out in front of a very upscale restaurant there is a tripod that says "Acme Valet Parking." Over the course of 30 minutes a half dozen drivers will avail themselves of this service. The least expensive car they usually see is a Lexus or three-year-old Mercedes. When the owners of these vehicles walk outside, having finished dining, there is no sign and their cars have disappeared.

I'll tell you this. As "street smart" as I think I am, I doubt I would ever have thought about checking with the restaurant to see if they provided valet parking services.

But I'm not alone. There was a new, and very expensive, French restaurant a block from where I lived. When I read this story I walked over there and observed for about a half hour. Not a single person hesitated a second before giving their keys to the kid standing next to the valet parking (a legitimate service) sign (and it couldn't have been that they were returning customers, as the establishment had only been open for two days). For those of you think I may have been aiding and abetting a series of criminal acts, before making my observations I had confirmed that the valet service was legit.

It really is amazing how easy it is to prove any one of us to be gullible.

For some strange reason (I'm beginning to think that all my reasons are strange) this reminds me of a "not-the-same" yet similar incident from about 10 years ago. It took place in Dallas. I have no idea if it's truth or folk lore, but it really makes no difference.

One morning, when the husband came out of his house, ready to go to work, he found an envelope under his windshield. It said, "I'm sorry I put a dent in your back fender. If I report one more incident to my insurance company my rates are going to skyrocket. When I did this I didn't have any cash with me, but I did have my four season tickets to Sunday's Dallas Cowboys game. I'm going to be out of town this weekend and was going to give them to a co-worker, but I'd rather you use them, as my way of apologizing."

The husband was thrilled (it was a very small dent) and a few days later he, his wife and their two sons, headed off to their first Cowboy's game. When they returned, four hours later, it was to a virtually empty house – almost everything they owned had been stolen.

Hmm, let's see. Who could have known that there would be no one at home that Sunday afternoon?

Don't Do This

Here are two variations of something you never want to say, when you are sitting across from another person, whether that be in an interview or a presentation. The first is "May I borrow a pen?" and the other is "Do you have something I can write on?" While your request will probably get you what you need, I can guarantee it will become one strike held against you. In the back of the other person's mind will be the thought that you did not arrive prepared. What you should do is over-prepare so that if he says, "Do you happen to have an extra pen?" you can respond, "Would you prefer black or blue ink?"

The Word "No" Can Have Three Meanings

When you ask for something, such as a donation, there are four possible results. One is absolutely good, one is absolutely bad while the middle two remain to be seen.

What you want to hear is "Yes." What you don't want to hear is "No, absolutely no."

There are those who think these are the only possibilities (I'm not going to include "maybe" because that is a meaningless word).

If you are one of those people who believes this you are – how should I put this politely – never mind, you are wrong because there are three versions of "no."

The first one has already been mentioned but consider this - it might also mean "No, at least not now." This says that the door has not been slammed in your face. Your response should be, "When would you like me to get back to you?" Whatever the answer is, whether it's in a couple of weeks, in a couple of months, or early next year, put a note in your "tickler" file, wherever that may be – probably on your computer or PDA.

The reason is that something to do six months from now is easily forgotten if not written down in a logical place. And, there is another reason easily defined as "too soon/ too late." I know of two situations where the person someone was "soliciting" had made note of what was said. In the first story the "seller" did not do what was requested – wait until the beginning of the following year to call. When he got to talk with the person he spoke with previously, he heard one of the worst things imaginable. The other voice began by saying, "Didn't I tell you......." Ouch – that's no way to start a relationship.

In the second "event" (I was the person on the wrong side of this exchange) the buyer knew he would need more product, but not for seven months. A month or two prior to then he was going to ask for bids. For some unknown reason I didn't write this down when he told me. When it finally came to mind I called the buyer. What I heard was, "I'm surprised I didn't hear from you earlier. The bidding process ended a week ago." Ouch again. And by the way, if you think that the buyer should have called to remind me, as the saying goes, "You have another think coming."

The other "No" is when nothing happens – no call returned or no letter responded to. In this case, I keep writing or calling – until I am specifically asked or told not to. When I was the Executive Director for a non-profit, I sent 11 letters to one person before I got a check (it was for $100,000). Along with it was a note that said "Enough already – no more letters please." Suffice it to say, aside from an acknowledgement letter (the donor needed that for tax purposes) and a thank-you note, I never "darkened his mailbox door" again.

Not Invited So Please Don't Show Up

While on the subject of raising money, I'm going to provide you with an event that is not a golf tournament, dinner, gala, run or walk. In fact, as you are about to learn, it really isn't an event at all. Rather than describe it I will simply let you read what follows, as the actual mailing explains the thought process, better than anything I could come up with in the form of a summary.

I hope this makes you smile, to the point that you can say, "Hey Joe, you've got to read this."

#10 Envelope

Hillary Clinton, Bill O'Reilly,
Brad Pitt, Barak Obama,
Colin Powell, Tiger Woods

Stamp

and Philip Barnett
1234 56th St.
Scottsdale, AZ 85255

are some of the people we expect will turn us down, and for good reason. After all, it could be worth a lot more than $198,000 to "Just say no."

Letter

Dear Philip,

This year the West Valley Child Crisis Center has decided to push the corner of the envelope a bit when it comes to a fundraising event. After all, there are only so many golf tournaments and charity walks you can participate in.

Instead of the ordinary and mundane, we plan to have a High Tea outside, at the Botanical Gardens, on August 23, 2007 at 3:00 PM, to celebrate the fact that, historically, it's the hottest day of the year.

We know you find this intriguing but it gets even better – wait until you hear the price.

It's only $2,500 per couple, or $1,500 if you can't find a date. Naturally, to recognize the importance of this event, it's black tie and "someone will probably want to buy a new dress."

Just picture yourself, seated out among the cactus, soaked in perspiration, as a WVCCC representative reads the expanded version of our mission statement. The speaker we have in mind is from the south, and speaks a little slowly, so we expect he'll talk for about an hour. And, you'll be delighted to learn that the person introducing him once held the record for the longest congressional filibuster.

This doesn't sound appealing? A bit outside your budget? Allergic to cactus? Your dermatologist told you to get no more than three minutes of sunshine a week? Already have a root canal appointment for that afternoon?

We understand. After all, you're not going to be the first person to come up with some flimsy excuse.

And so, because it appears that this is town filled with wimps, we've come up with an "opt out" fee. It's $100 and it allows you to pass on these festivities. If you have a last minute change of heart (because of a single cloud in the sky and the temperature has dropped below 115 degrees), you will be turned away at the gate – and given a ticket to an air-conditioned movie theatre.

Think of it – for only $100 you will not have to put up with any of this, along with the possibility of ending up in the emergency room with heat stroke.

But, as they say in all those television infomercials, "Wait, there's more."

Your total savings go way beyond the price of admission. Take a look at the attached "Economic Impact" statement to see the real amount of money this can mean to you.

Take the $4,245 (that's what, as you will see, you would have spent, less the $100 you're going to send in), put it in your IRA account, and let it sit there for the next 20 years, earning 8%. (when this was written, several years ago, this was a reasonable rate of return). When all is said and done you'll have$18,752.

BUT THAT IS PEANUTS – compared to what really will happen.

Because you're not going to attend this year we fully expect that you'll wiggle your way out of the 2008 party (same day, same time but different location – outside the new Convention Center). The main course will be bacon and eggs, cooked to perfection – on the sidewalk.

To be really conservative we won't factor inflation into our projections and therefore assume that all costs remain the same. This means that, next year, you will save the same amount, but only get to invest it for 19 years (eventually giving you $17,363). Of course, in point of fact, all your expenses will not remain the same as inflation never stops. It may get very low but it still will occur every year.

However, we will pledge, right now, that the cost of your "thanks, but no thanks" $100 non-appearance fee will never change. Taking inflation into effect, this means that your real savings will probably exceed $400,000.

Let's cut to the chase and agree to the fact that you're never going to show up and that each year you'll get to invest your savings, for one year less than the year before.

What will you end up with? Well, I hope you're sitting down because the figure is:

$198,835 (actually in excess of $400,000)

You are not seeing things – these figures of $198,835 and $400,000 are correct. That's what you will have accumulated by simply sending in the $100 each year, banking your savings and letting good old compound-interest make you rich.

And, if that's not enough, the $100 is tax deductible.

Finally, we implore you not to decide you actually want to attend. No one has done so yet, which means we don't have to rent tables and chairs, find a caterer, hire a band, etc. And we won't have to make sure that there is a team of paramedics in attendance. So, if you simply check the box that says "No, I can't make it but here's my $100" we'd be really, really grateful as it also means that we get to stay inside. So please, help us keep our cool and "Just Say No!"

Cordially,

XXX

P.S. It dawned on us that you probably have some friends who would love to be "uninvited." We've enclosed a form on which you can provide their names and contact information. And, when we send them this "non-invitation" we promise not to mention your name (unless you are crazy enough to ask that we do).

Economic Impact

This is what it might cost you to come to our event (gas not included)

Two tickets to our "Desert Heat Gala"	$2,500
New dress for one of you	$ 600
Tuxedo rental (for the one not buying the dress)	$ 200
Babysitter (kids are out of school)	$ 25
Speeding ticket/Traffic school because you leave too late	$ 150
Replacing diamond stud earring that gets lost	$ 250
Cash bar (water is the cheapest item at $5 per bottle)	$ 100
Silent auction item (you really didn't think there wouldn't be one?)	$ 500
Tips for bartender and valet parking	$ 20
Total	$ 4,345

Return Card

You people must be out of your minds. To sit outside, in the desert, at 3 PM in the middle of August? What are you, nuts?

___ No, I will not be attending your "marshmallow roast" with me as the marshmallow. However, I do appreciate all the money I'll be saving (and making) so I've enclosed my tax-deductible donation of $100.

___ I'm just like the option above but I'd like to give

_____ a lot more $_____

_____ a little less $_____

Contact and credit card information

Referral Forms (for three people)

I'm not the only one who has no intention of showing up. The following individuals are just as sane as I am so I suggest that you "uninvite" them. You _____may_____ may not use my name when doing so.

Contact information

If They Are Smart Be Smarter – Or Maybe Not

The company I worked for, when the "Turn $.20 into $200,000" event took place, was owned by a husband and wife. They split the responsibilities pretty much down the middle, and one of the items on her side of the ledger was "Legal."

Early on in her relationship with their attorney, she learned that he (as is the case with most lawyers), had a timer on his desk. It was started when a conversation began and stopped when it was over. The reason for this was that it allowed clients to be billed in 15 minute increments.

This particular "barrister" offered what he referred to as "courtesy calls" – any discussion that lasted less than five minutes did not generate an invoice.

When she became aware of this policy she got her own timer. As soon as Anthony picked up the call, she started hers. When it reached about four and a half minutes she would say something like, "I'm sorry Tony, I've got an urgent call to take. I'll give you a call tomorrow."

To the best of my knowledge, in the two years I was there, the company never received a bill for legal services.

Now, as clever as this was, it did have me wondering. Would I want someone representing me who fell for this over and over again? I think not, as I want my counsel to be one of the sharpest knives in the draw.

It did remind of a chapter in a novel I read, sometime in the middle of the last century (it was called "The Ninth Wave" written by Eugene Burdick, one of the best-selling authors of his time – "Fail Safe" and "The Ugly American," are among the books he wrote). He describes a high stakes poker game that the book's lead character got to play in. His roommate went along as an observer and, when there was a break in the action, he pulled his buddy aside and said, "Hey, while I was watching I realized that two of the guys are cheating. You should say something." The response he got was, "I figured that out by the fourth or fifth hand. But think about this. They know each others hands, while I now know both of theirs, as well as mine. Advantage me."

NUGGET

Before you point fingers, or make accusations, stop and think for a minute. You might be better off letting others think they have an advantage over you whereas the exact opposite is true.

When I was at the trade show in Germany, the one I mentioned earlier, I hired a young lady to man (can a woman "man" a booth?) the booth with me. I was the only one who was aware that she spoke eight languages. Potential customers would discuss the types of deals they were looking for, with me standing no more than ten feet away from where I was, secure in the knowledge that I could not understand a word they were saying. Technically they were correct but my "secret weapon" provided me all the details I needed, before negotiations began.

No Holds Barred - Unless They Last Longer Than Two Minutes

(Note: If I don't get this to the printers soon the book may never get published. I say this because, as I've been doing my editing and re-editing, something happens that requires its own chapter, as is the case here).

I just placed a phone call and, when I asked to speak to a specific person, I was put on hold. I got to listen to three minutes of very nice classical music, followed by five minutes of silence. I decided to try again. The person who answered the phone (the same individual) apologized for the fact that we were disconnected, a fact she was aware of but I was not. Once she realized what had happened she should have called me back immediately. She didn't. She made a mistake.

Unless extraordinary circumstances are involved, no one should ever be left on hold for more than one minute. This rule excludes industries such as banks and insurance companies, since they wouldn't recognize phone etiquette if the rules were delivered to them on a silver platter (more about that in a minute).

After that one minute you should either be taken to that person's voice mail or a "living soul" should come back on the line and ask if you would like to leave a message.

And the people answering the phones should know the status of every person in their company – specifically if the person is in the office and, if they are not, when they are expected.

The extreme case of how something should not be handled occurred five minutes ago. I had called (for the 4th time in the past week) a person I had been working with previously. The first two times I was told that a message would be forwarded for her. The 3rd time I called her direct dial number (which I had been given during my 2nd call) and left a message in her voice mailbox.

When I got through today, to try to find out why she hadn't gotten back to me, I was told that she was on maternity leave and had been so for the past two weeks.

This situation was so horrendous I don't even have to explain why as it is, I'm sure, self-evident.

Now, back to those businesses that have "we provide no customer service" departments.

What I don't understand is why, on their web site, they don't include their telephone drop-down menu, so I would know which sequence of buttons to push – immediately. I have had experiences, just like many of you I'm sure, when I've had to listen to five such menus, only to discover that I probably should have pushed a button on the first of those, but couldn't figure out how to go backwards. And, to make matters worse, at no point was there an option to speak to a real, live individual.

I'm pretty sure that this is intentional. Since no one calls customer service to tell them how great the company is they want you to give up (throw in the towel, or disconnect the call yourself). These guys have figured out that, at worst, they might lose a few customers, but that would be more than compensated for by the fact that they wouldn't have to hire the number of people it would take to handle the job properly (which might explain why their profits are so high, and why they can pay top executives, eight-figure salaries, even when they are doing a terrible job?).

But, it is not all bad news. My local utility company has a system that should be the customer service standard. When I get their voice mail they give me the choice of waiting on hold, or being called back, with an assurance that I will not lose my place in line. If I decide on this option they have me punch in my phone number, at which point they tell me when to expect a call (i.e. 20 minutes). I done this at least half a dozen times and they have never called later than they promised (once again, under promise and over deliver – that "20 minutes" was never more than 15).

The Dollars and Sense of It

Take a clue from the cable TV folks, or the cell phone companies. It's what the payments over X number of months are that tell the real story.

Let's say you have a "typical" product – when you sell it, one third of what you receive should cover your cost of goods and labor, one third is gross profit and one third is everything else, including advertising, marketing, and overhead - rent, insurance, utilities, etc. Furthermore, your records, or the industry averages, say that your customer will stay with you for three years.

You sell something for $100 a month, or per use. You "bank" $33, you spend $33 on the product itself (including materials, labor, FICA taxes, benefits, etc.)

and the other $33 gets allocated to the other areas, mentioned in the previous paragraph.

Your annual gross profit is $396. So, how much will you be willing to spend to acquire a new customer? If you say anything less than $300 you are being far too conservative. If you spend $300, your gross profit, in year one, will be $96 and in years two and three it will be $396. Your three year total will be $888.

Get Up and Go - Or Sit Down and Wait

There are two businesses that are competitive with each other, in many ways. Both of them have a piece of software that is essentially the same. Both of them know that the product is only 50% of what it should be (although the public will not be aware of this fact)

Company ABC puts the product up for sale (Product 1.0). Knowing that they have a long way to go 100% of their net revenue goes the research needed for the first upgrade, necessary to release version 2.0.The following year it's 60% of what they hoped for, but it now only requires 80% of their net revenue to create 3.0.

You can see where this is going. By the 6th year they are 98% percent there (Product 6.0) but they then stopped trying. They know that that last 2% would require an inordinate amount of money and time, with no assurance that it would accomplish anything. Meanwhile company XYZ waits until they reach that 98% figure.

So, let's sum this up (Note: the product sells for $100 and costs $20 to manufacture). At first glance the numbers that follow may look complicated but at second glance I believe you will find them to be anything but.)

	ABC Inc.	XYZ Inc.
1st yr sales (100 units)	$10,000	-0-
1st year exp. research	$10,000	$10,000
1st year cost of goods	$ 2,000	n/a
1st year net	- $ 2,000	- $10,000
2nd yr sales (200 units)	$20,000	-0-
2nd year exp. research	$ 8,000	$ 8,000
2nd year cost of goods	$ 4,000	n/a
2nd year net	$ 8,000	- $ 8,000
3rd yr sales (300 units)	$30,000	-0-
3rd year exp. research	$ 6,000	$ 6,000
3rd year cost of goods)	$ 6,000	n/a
3rd year net	$ 18,000	- $ 6,000
4th yr sales (400 units)	$ 40,000	-0-
4th year exp. research	$ 4,000	- $ 4,000
4th year cost of goods	$ 8,000	n/a
4th year net	$ 28,000	- $ 4,000
5th yr sales (500 units)	$ 50,000	-0-
5th year exp, research	$ 2,000	- $ 2,000
5th year cost of goods	$10,000	n/a
5th year net	$ 38,000	- $, 2,000
6th year sales	$ 60,000	$60,000
6th yr research	-0-	-0-
6th year cost of goods	$ 12,000	$12,000
6th year net	$ 48,000	$48,000

Summary

Sales	$210,000	$48,000
Research	$ 30,000	$30,000
Cost of goods	$ 40,000	$12,000
Net after six years	$140,000	$ 6,000

And finally:

Since I know that you've already read my book (after paying for it, I hope – it's no fair if you give it to someone else after you've finished – what's known as intellectual "double dipping," I have two other favors to ask of you. The second one appears at or near the very end of this book (please believe me when I tell you that this book really does end).

Here is the first one:

REAL LIFE 101, 102, etc. (or, in today's vernacular, 1.0, 2.0, etc.)

While I would love to think is that this would be a trickle down process (coming from the government), all of us know that, since the government has run out of money, there will be nothing to trickle down from above.

So, my first favor is directed at anyone who is teacher or principal, a member of the PTA, a parent or grandparent of a school age child, a couple who are thinking about having a child or children and finally, anyone with a half a brain. Hmm. It seems as if I've pretty much covered everyone, unless you happen to be an individual who does not qualify under any of the above criteria, in which case you are probably qualified to run for Congress.

As you may be aware, most colleges say that their role is to teach you the theories that relate to the subject matter. In my four years at an "institute of higher learning," the only class I had that dealt with practical knowledge, was "Accounting/Statistics." Prior to that I learned nothing regarding "how" to do things – not in high school, not in junior high school/middle school and certainly not in elementary school. Oh, wait a second – I forgot about my shop class.

The result is that, when students leave the womb known as school, they are equipped to do almost nothing, except keep going to school or teach what they've learned, which has the students going around in "this stuff that won't do me much good" circles.

This is not intended to cover those who go on to graduate school, where more practical aspects of one's future come into play (i.e. nursing, law, medicine, etc.). That being said, I know very few graduate students who can explain all the clauses in a mortgage or insurance policy, or who know how to see if they are being overcharged by their electric company.

I believe that, somewhere among all that theory, students should learn about the following. And these are only a sampling, as I'm sure there are dozens more.

- Time management

- Practical numbers – how to balance a checkbook, simple and compounded interest, credit card charges and interest rates.

- How to read and understand a utility bill, a phone bill, a cable bill, a cell phone bill, a PDA bill and any bill related to your computer

- How to read and understand a mortgage application and monthly statement.

- How to read and understand insurance policies – health, automobile, life, liability and homeowner's.

- How to change the oil in your car.

- How to repair a toilet that keeps running.

- How to file a complaint.

- How to cook something that requires three ingredients, where none of them are water

- What constitutes sexual harassment.

- What constitutes bullying.

- What are the laws regarding driver's licenses and the purchasing of alcoholic beverages and firearms.

- What to do in the case of various types of emergencies (i.e. when to call 911).

- What phone numbers and web site addresses you should know by heart.

- What are the laws regarding privacy and how to protect yours.

- What are the laws regarding slander and liable.

- The basic tenets of etiquette.

- What do to if approached by strangers.

- What to do in case of an accident – home, car, school and store.

- Where is your closest hospital emergency room. How do you get there.

- How to shut off the water in your house.

- How to use a fire extinguisher.

- How to properly wash and dry clothes, dishes and a car.

- The proper way to brush your teeth and trim nails.

- What to expect at the dentist's office.

- What kind of inoculations should you have.

- Nutrition – how to read labels – for calories, ingredients, and RDAs.

- Educated consumerism – i.e. comparing prices per ounce.

- STDs

- Knowing how babies are made and what to do if you don't want one (with abstinence being one of the options).

- Why certain professions are better than you think – i.e. my plumber, who works for himself, makes over $100,000 a year, and so will his son, who will be taking over the business in two years. By the way, neither of them went to college.

- etc., etc., etc.

As you can see many of these are age appropriate, and related to having a need to know. However, with each passing year, things such as those listed above become less and less exclusive. For example, when I was in the 6th grade it would never have dawned on my parents to show me how a fire extinguisher worked (I'm not sure if we even had one). Today I cannot imagine not teaching a child this skill.

And think of the benefits to the parents. If, on a Sunday morning, your toilet suddenly keeps running, instead of calling a plumber, who will charge you $75, take your child (or let them drive/pedal) to Home Depot, pick up the necessary parts for less than $5, and let them fix it for you. With the $70 you've saved you can get some really good sushi that night.

SUMMARY

I usually begin the summary portion of presentations by saying, in the words of Dr. Seuss, "Here is what I would do if I ran your zoo."

- **I would never, ever, have a customer I didn't know a good deal about; including what it was that made them a customer in the first place. To a lesser degree, this also hold true for inquiries.**

- **I would always say thank-you, for a first order or contribution, and I would do it in writing – hand written, hand addressed and with a stamp on the envelope. Depending on the nature of your business you might have to set certain thresholds (i.e. $100 contributors), regarding future orders/ donations but it should always be done when a "relationship" is first established.**

- **I would strive to be different – a bit larger, a little smaller, a smidge brighter or a tad earlier. The worst you can do is – well, there actually is no worst thing involved here. Even if you don't get the job or piece of business my bet is that you will** be appreciated and thought of the next time an opportunity comes up.

- I would understand the importance of the first impression. If it results in some type of order, I am aware that the second impression may well be more important."

- I would constantly check to make sure that "they" understand what "you" have said or written and that "you" do the same.

I always close my marketing seminars with the same story. It is designed to make people laugh, but also to think a little bit as it addresses the fact that, all too often, we only look for the major breakthrough or big picture. An alternative approach is to observe the small, obvious pieces. The very well-know adage says "You can't see the forest for the trees" meaning that you often get buried in minutia to the point that you never get to see that view from above. I respectfully disagree, at least in most cases, to the point that the adage should be "You can't see the trees for the forest" – that you spend so much time focusing on the umbrella, that you fail to recognize that without the spokes, that umbrella would collapse.

Those of you, who do jigsaw puzzles, will understand that's how solutions come about. You may know what the final product will look like, but are aware that it must be put together, piece by piece. "Trickle down economics" may work as a distribution system, created and managed by governments. However, businesses do not work that way, at least not until they are very large. Their buildings must rest on solid foundations. Otherwise there will be nothing capable of supporting the roof, from where the "trickling" comes. If that foundation is not solid, that water running down from the highest part of the structure, will quickly erode the base.

It seems that Sherlock Holmes and Dr. Watson were tracking a criminal across the badlands of England. It got to be late and they decided to camp out for the evening.

After being asleep for a couple of hours, Sherlock Holmes woke up and nudged Dr. Watson who was lying next to him. "Dr. Watson" he said, "Look up and tell me what you see"

Watson struggled to get his eyes open and finally said "Well Holmes, I see a lot of stars."

"What does that tell you Dr. Watson?" asked Holmes.

"Well," he replied "if you're talking about astronomy, I'd say that there are thousands of planets and hundreds of galaxies. If you're talking about astrology, it appears as if Leo in on the cusp of Capricorn. If you're referring to meteorology, it looks as if tomorrow is going to be a beautiful day and, if you're talking about theology, I would say that God is all-powerful and we are small and insignificant. What does it tell you Holmes?"

Sherlock Holmes stared at him, paused for a moment and said, through clenched teeth, "Watson, you idiot. Somebody stole our tent."

Ladies and gentlemen, boys and girls and children of all ages - don't spend an inordinate amount of time worrying about dealing with universe size problems. Take care of where you "live" (your store, agency, etc.), especially in seeing to it that those who visit either remain or come back often, and that you treat them with respect. If you do this the "big" problems will take care of themselves and pretty soon you'll need a larger tent.

NUGGET - The final one.

Think back on some of the stories you've read and how many of them related to interpretation, context and perspective. Just recall Sherlock Holmes, J. Edgar Hoover, my really angry customer and "LUNCH."

Remember this. Just because one person is talking and the other one is hearing, doesn't guarantee that there is any communicating going on.

Those who know me well are aware that the words "finally" or "final" almost never mean what they suggest. I have used that word as many as six times, in one document. One of the reasons I do this is to avoid what I consider to be the "will-they-find-the-P.S" syndrome.

I once e-mailed a question to a friend and, when he didn't answer it, I called to see if there was a reason why. When I was told that the answer had been provided, as a P.S., I realized that when I'm reading a letter on line I rarely scroll down, once I've seen who "signed" it.

I use to send letters with enough P.S.'s to merit their own page. However, when I discovered that what I had missed was the most important part of my friend's response, I went to multiple uses of the word "finally." In the newspaper business this would be called, "Above the fold". In this case it is everything above your "electronic signature."

NUGGET

(I wasn't completely honest when I said that the previous nugget was the final one – but I did warn you this might happen. In fact, as it turns out, it does not even hold the penultimate title, since this one does).

In a recent interview, 85-year-old Tony Bennett related that he practices his scales every day. When asked why he said, "On the first day I don't do it I'll know. On the second day the musicians will know and, by the third day, it will be the audience that knows.

Consider how this might apply to you, perhaps as an employee of an agency or business that provides products/services to businesses/individuals. On the first day you will know that you've slacked off. On the second day it will be your co-workers and on the 3rd day your clients/customers who will become aware.

What I do, in order to always feel as if I am in the loop, is something that always makes me feel as if I am in the loop.

I maintain a document (now on my computer) for every project I'm working on, and every active client. Before I go to sleep I make sure that there is one entry on every one of those pages. Even if I spend an entire day working with Client Q, I make sure that clients L, M, and N get a little piece of my mind. This way, when one of them gets my undivided attention, a week or two later, I don't come to their table empty-handed.

MY FINAL (I SWEAR) NUGGET–
"THE ENDLESS SUMMER"

Some of you may recognize this as the name of a documentary, released in 1966. It was the story of two "surfer dudes," in search of the "perfect wave." They traveled to every surfing paradise, as well as some places where "no man had gone before." But, no matter how spectacular the waves they found, they were convinced there was a better one somewhere else, so they ended their quest feeling unfulfilled (how sad – what they were doing should have made them happy).

I relate this to the phrase "dotting all the "i's" and crossing all the "t's." Quite simply, if you insist that this must be done, nothing will ever happen. Those who seek perfection will end up doing nothing but that – "seeking." The perfect example is this book. It has been through a couple of rewrites and several editing sessions. However, when I got to the point I found myself saying "Oops, I really wanted to include the story about the guy who got swallowed by a really big fish" I realized that if I didn't turn off my "editing ignition," I would be saying "Oops" for months, if not years on end.

Absorption

What have we (actually this should say "you" since I've already learned this stuff, often the hard way) learned here? A number of worthwhile things I hope. These should include the facts that "All good things come to those who wait" is almost always a fallacy, as is "Patience is a virtue." As Woody Allen once noted, "80% of succeeding is just showing up" and you can't do that if you are waiting or being overly patient. **So, put your foot in the water and walk in knee deep, waist deep, belly button deep and finally shoulder deep. Then turn around and wave to all those people on the shore – the ones waiting for the "perfect wave."**

THEY SAID IT – I DIDN'T (Except For a Few Times)

These may be called adages or clichés. I call them words to live by. If none of them are foreign to you then you probably did not need to read the book – which is why I decided not to include them in the introduction.

I am not using quotation marks and attributions because in many cases I am paraphrasing and I don't always know who the original author was. The ones with an asterisk are "originals," at least until some proves otherwise. In the first one only the second half of the sentence came from my fertile mind, as is the case with the one that begins with the words "The journey of 1000 miles.....and the one that starts with the words "The cows will come home ...."

Pay special attention (memorizing them wouldn't hurt) to the first six – the ones I've already inundated you with. The rest appear in no particular order of importance.

You never get a second chance to make a *first* impression and you never get a second chance to make a *second* impression. *

In the land of the blind the one-eyed man is king.

What did I say/write vs. what did they hear/read.

Your best customer is your customer (lifetime value).

Under promise then over deliver/ Create a level of expectation, then exceed it.

ANSWER THE QUESTION

If you don't know where you are going, any train will get you there.

If you don't understand the problem it is highly likely that you are part of it.

An ounce of practice is worth a ton of preaching.

You have been given two ears and one mouth – and they should be used in that proportion (insofar as I am concerned, do as I say, not as I do).

'Tis better to have loved and lost than never to have loved as all.

Always be pre-emptive. An error doesn't become a mistake until you refuse to correct it.

The cows will come home before you find every "i" that needs to be dotted and every "t" that needs to be crossed. 98% is good enough as that last 2% will break your heart – and keep you unpublished, or late with an assignment. *

To thine own self be true.

Jack of all trades, master of none is a very bad idea – people want to hire specialists – people who are really, really good at one thing.

Luck is the residue of design – solid planning puts you in a position to be "lucky."

Instant success often comes after 15 years of hard work.

Light travels faster than sound.

Consider the source – don't waste time or emotions on meaningless people.

Before you seek revenge, dig two graves (don't bite your nose to spite your face).

The most important thing about having power is knowing when not to use it.

No risk, no reward.

A goal is a dream with a deadline.

Fear is often an acronym for "False Evidence Appearing Real"

The journey of 1,000 miles begins with but a single step (but, if it's in the wrong direction you might end up 2,000 miles away from your desired destination). *

It is amazing what you can accomplish if you do not care who gets the credit.

You shouldn't try to erect a building until you're sure the foundation is solid. *

PPPPP – Prior Planning Prevents Poor Performance.

Once you obtained permission, plagiarism is the highest form of flattery.

All people are equal, but some are more equal than others

It is much easier to return from a destination than it was to get there in the first place. *

80% of success comes from just showing up.

Don't waste any time standing in front of the mirror of unreasonable expectations. *

The worst hour of your life lasts only 60 minutes, if you choose to have a short memory. The best hour of your life can last forever, if you allow it to. Remember, your memory should be like a bunch of safety deposit boxes, and you are the only one with the keys. *

Perspective - To an ant colony a drop of dew is a flood.

The greatest justice in life is that your looks and vision go simultaneously.

Humility – A wealthy British gentleman was taking his son to visit London, for the first time. When they got seated on the train the youngster asked, "Father, why do we have to sit in 3rd class seats?" His father responded, "Because there is no 4th class."

The best reason to reach for the stars is because, if you miss, you just may get a large piece of the moon.

Always strive for "discernable differentiation" (don't be a clone).

Disinterested third-party intervention can often be the best way of getting your point across.

Who I Am, Where I've been & what I've done (What Makes Me Tick & Tock)

"If you ask me for the time I will tell you how to build a clock."

Even though I plead guilty to this observation, in the case of this book it is "guilty—with several explanations."

Before I tell you anything about me, which may end up being more than you wanted to know, I'm going to provide another of my multiple mea culpas, ones that have reared their heads more than once, as you wended your way through my words.

No matter how hard I tried I could never come up with a sequencing pattern, in so far as the order the chapters should go in. I even went so far as to print out each chapter separately. I then put all of the papers on my living room floor and started walking around, shifting chapters as I did so. Unfortunately, about five minutes after I started wandering all over myself, I kicked an open bottle of wine (red). Since I knew that what I wrote was still on my computer, I opted to try to rescue the carpet. By the time I got done pouring club soda on almost everything within sight, half of the pages were unreadable and my computer had run out of toner.

I took this as a sign and finally gave up (something that you probably know to be evident). I can assure you that by the time you got to take a look at the forest (the whole book) all the trees (the chapters) should have made total sense What I suggest you do is go back and dog-ear the pages where you find the strength of my wisdom and insights to be so overwhelming that you know you'll want to read that chapter again.

(Note: A good friend, who did some proofreading for me, called and said, "Philip if the sentence you wrote about your wisdom and insights is representative of the rest of the book, I'm not going to purchase a copy." I assured him that I was just teasing, and that this sentence would be deleted before a single copy of the book was printed. Obviously I lied because had I been telling the truth you wouldn't have just read this paragraph).

Since this is the first time we are meeting I believe that introductions are in order. Obviously I get to go first – since I don't know who you are, at least not yet. I hope that changes when you decide to use my contact information on the back cover.

And this holds true, even if you only want to point out that I don't know what I'm talking about, that I'm outspoken, opinionated to a fault, stubborn, obnoxious, a typical ex New Yorker and an egomaniacal/egocentric/egomaniac.

I will tell you that I have already been accused of being all of these, and several others, unsuitable for family reading. I begrudgingly agree with everything except the first one as I do know what I'm talking about. Of course your reply may well be that, by the virtue of making this statement, I am providing absolute proof that I an egomaniacal – egocentric – egomaniac.

As mentioned earlier, if this has not already come to mind, I'm sure you would like to remind me that, if I keep stop patting myself on my back so often, I will eventually dislocate my shoulder.

OK, now that we've gotten past defining the personality of the author, let me give you a very brief extract of my resume (this is like having you check the wall in your doctor's office, to make sure there is a diploma from a medical school).

I grew up in Brooklyn, NY and will always have a bit of concrete running through my veins (and arteries). I graduated from Hobart College, in Geneva, NY. I have a Bachelor of Arts degree, with a split major in political science and economics. My overall GPA was 3.2. While I was pretty pleased with this it didn't overly impress my parents. I was reminded of this, earlier in the year, when I heard an exchange of dialogue on the TV show "Glee." Michael Chang (the best dancer in the cast) told his girlfriend that he was going to have to give up all extra-curricular activities because his father was very upset with his chemistry grade. When she asked what it was he said "A-." Her response was, "Uh oh, an Asian F." I don't think that Jewish parents are that unrealistic but I do think that my B+ GPA was seen as nothing more than a C.

I would like to tell you that it was this high because I appreciated the importance of education (which I do). Actually the driving force was that, if you were on the Dean's List (3.0 GPA), you were allowed unlimited cuts in the following semester. Since I was working very hard on getting a Master's ranking in bridge, this extra time proved to be very helpful.

The fact is that every "report card" I have ever received included some variation of the phrase "Could do better." I have no argument with that. I was fortunate to be able to do some solid "skating" as a result of having a very high IQ (north of 160) and relishing most tests, instead of fearing them. My SAT scores were 800 in math (twice) and 765 followed by778 in English (my shoulder is beginning to hurt).

I'm not sure if this is still done today but way back in the last century everyone took the SATs twice, in both our junior and senior years. My guidance counselor needed some guidance since she never told me that colleges would accept the scores obtained in my third year of high school so it was not necessary that I take the tests again. Perhaps the most unique thing about this is that my four closest friends had higher averages on their pair of scores than I did – and each one of them got report cards (which did not reflect SAT scores) that said, "Could do better," the same observation that was made on mine.

There obviously were some students who knew about the "no need to take them a second time" rule. I learned of this when a scandal broke out (not at my school) when some kids "sold" their services and took the exams for others, getting paid the princely sum of $100. While this may not sound like a lot, it was 1959 and I can assure you that no one my age had ever seen this amount of money, at one time (back then it cost $.25 to see a double-feature at the local movie theatre, where popcorn came in only one size, and set you back only $.10).

My one wish about my high school years is that I had a whole bunch of teachers like Mrs. Venit. She told me, and my four best friends, that we were not going to get away with coasting through her class. She went on to add that if the entire class turned in the exact same essay, the rest of her students would probably get a B. Conversely, our grades, for identical work, would either be a D or an F (whatever happened to the letter "E"?). It was the hardest I ever worked in one semester but it was also the time that I learned the most. She not only knew that I could do better she was going to take it upon herself to see that I did. And did I did.

My biggest claim to fame in high school was that, in a basketball game, I "held" Connie Hawkins to 28 points (he was the leading scorer in the country at that time, averaging just under 44 points-per-game).

A few years ago I was at a fundraiser held here in Phoenix. I mentioned this "feat" of mine to a group of people (in this case I wasn't boasting because someone else started a conversation related to the most unusual thing we could think of, from our teenage years). What I didn't realize was that Connie was standing a few feet away (he had played for the Phoenix Suns and now worked in their Community Relations department). Connie didn't say anything but did smile slightly.

Unfortunately (for me) some very rude person in the group asked me how much of the game Connie played. Very sheepishly I mumbled, "The first half."

Although good athletes abounded (I was not one of them) as it turned out, in this time frame, the most successful (ultimately) people from my school, and several of the ones that surrounded us, were Neil Diamond, Barbra Streisand, Woody Allen, Carol King, Neil Sedaka, Carole King and Simon & Garfunkle. I actually played against Neil (S) in a playground league – but only once. At the time he was studying to be a concert pianist and his parents were afraid he might injure a finger or two.

During in my last semester in college I received a score of 722 on my LSAT (Law Boards). To show you how meaningless things like this can be, I attended Columbia Law School for six weeks, before dropping out. It seems that there was no test that measured desire or passion for the matter at hand. Reaching the decision to leave was relatively easy. Figuring out how to tell my parents was an entirely different story, as it took me two days of rehearsing what I was going to say to them.

This was the first of many times that I was glad I was a New York Times junkie. As a result I was aware of the fact that, in the very near future, there was probably going to be a large build-up of U.S. forces in Viet Nam. Since my draft classification was now 1A, but I fervently objected to the upcoming war (and didn't want to head for Canada), I enlisted in the National Guard. At that time they were so desperate for people that they were offering a $50 bonus if you got a friend to join with you. Six months later it was costing $5,000 (under the table) to get into a unit.

My experience in the military is not worthy of more than a sentence or two. When my six years were over I was the only person in my outfit who was not asked to re-up. In fact, I was told that if I tried, my application would be rejected. It seems that I kept using a word the Army hates – that word was "Why?"

I am convinced that my first job was the best one I have ever had, have and will have. I was the Assistant Director of Advertising and Public Relations, for Radio City Music Hall (RCMH), in charge of the publicity for the Rockettes. If that job had paid anything resembling a decent salary, I might never have left.

What made it almost ideal? There are a myriad of reasons and here's but one.

382

When I started at RCMH I was the eighth of eight executives. The #7 position was held by my boss. In other words, I was as low on the totem pole as one could get.

In my third week of work I received a call from Jim Fairchild, the President of the theatre (I was shocked to learn that he even knew my name). Jim, who was British by birth, had a very close friend (they grew in England together), who visited NYC periodically. Quite often he stopped by unannounced, as was the case that day.

Mr. Fairchild said, "Philip, a friend has just come by to see if I might be free for lunch. The fact is I'm not, as all of us (meaning the seven people above me in the food chain) are involved in a very critical meeting. So I'd like you to do me a favor. Please go down to the Executive Entrance (which was on the 50th St side of the theatre.), introduce yourself, and take him to the Rainbow Room (the very well known restaurant atop what was then the RCA Building – the NBC Building today, better know as "30 Rock") We have a corporate account there, so you can sign for the meal."

When I agreed to do so (I don't think that "no" was an option), I realized that I didn't know his friend's name. So, before hanging up I asked, "Who is it that I will be meeting?" He replied, "Archibald Leach."

For a reason I still can't fathom, I knew that person's other name, which you are about to find out because there, standing in the special downstairs lobby, stood Cary Grant.

Earlier in the book I mentioned that there was a time where, contrary to the way I appear now, I found myself intimidated. Well, make this time #2.

I managed to introduce myself and explain why I would be his dining partner. What happened next rivaled the words that had been spoken to me, six years earlier, when my "first love" poignantly (if you will recall) said, "Thanks, but no thanks." Except this time there was no sadness attached to the equation.

In order to get from RCMH to the RCA Building, all we had to do was cross a one-way side street – a distance of 50 feet, at most. It was a beautiful day, in mid-June, and the lunch crowd was out in full force.

Almost before we stepped off the curb there were people coming at us from every direction. Mr. Grant paused, looked over his left shoulder, then over his right shoulder, and said to me, "Philip, I am very impressed. It appears you have quite a following here in New York."

I'm sure you can now appreciate why I loved this job.

Since then I owned two different small businesses (the poster company and the bike rental shop), worked for two advertising/marketing agencies, two manufacturing businesses and have consulted for IBM, UPS, TWA (when there was a TWA), the Mayo Clinic and a number of businesses whose name you wouldn't recognize. I have also served as a Peer Grant Reviewer (six times) for the U.S. Department of Education. Cumulatively we awarded just under $600M.

I have just concluded a 14-year career in the non-profit arena. This included stints as the Executive Director for three organizations. My peers hated it when I described myself as being a "salesman" but, after all, that's what you're doing when you are trying to raise money – it's just that our "products" were quite a bit different than any other. During my time in this "business" I was able to raise something north of $15M.

I was married for 17 years (to a TWA flight attendant) and have now been divorced for 23. I am a single dad with a story I just might turn into a movie script. Justin is my ex-wife's sister's child. She overdosed six weeks after giving birth and no one stepped up as the father. While we had not planned to have kids, adopting seemed like the natural thing to do. Even though he was a blood relative of my ex, I got custody – simply because I asked and my request was not contested.

Justin was 12, burdened with ADHD at the time of the divorce, and 16 when we moved to Arizona. Our relationship has been a bit of a roller coaster ride, but, even though it began as two steps back for every one forward, it got to two steps in the right direction with one the other way. Now, neither one of us ever has to look back over our shoulders because, aside from an occasional bump here and there, all is good.

He just married an absolutely wonderful girl, although the way I learned of this was, to understate things, a bit unusual.

Justin was working in the sales department for a company in Colorado. Included in his territory were several Eastern states, including Pennsylvania.

Up until that point he had only a few meaningful, serious relationships and I was not aware of anything that suggested a change in that pattern – at least not until June in 2011.

He called me from Allentown, PA to tell me that he had met a really nice girl but that both of them agreed that they didn't want it to be a "couple." Four days later his call was to tell me that they decided otherwise. Then, three days after that, while sitting in the airport, waiting to return to the Rocky Mountains, he let me know that he and Diana were getting married in September.

It was two weeks into July when they both got on the phone and revealed the fact that they had actually gotten wed that past December (no shotguns were necessary). Since they both had vowed their undying love they decided to take advantage of the tax benefits involved. However, they were going to have an "official" ceremony in September (it was a very nice affair).

(Note: You may not be aware of this. One of the most popular days for giving birth has always been Dec. 31st, when labor is often induced. As long as there are no health issues involved, this can save one thousands of dollars in taxes, as you get an additional deduction, no matter what day of the year a child is born. I remember reading a story, years ago, about a woman who gave birth to triplets on the last day of the year. This saved the family more than $5,000. Conversely there is always the case of a child being born five seconds after midnight. While this may gain recognition as the first baby born in that year, they can wave goodbye to those savings).

If my advice had been asked for I probably would have suggested that they slow down a bit. Whether or not they would have listened to me is irrelevant given what has taken place. And besides, Justin lucked out. As much as I love him, if he introduces Diana as his "better half," I think he might well be correct.

Introduction to the Expanded Introduction

I'm going to introduce this introduction (prequel) with a comment and a few apologies. Since both this and the chapter that follows were originally intended to be at the front of the book, there are some words that relate to the future (i.e. "as you will learn") as opposed to the past (i.e. "as you have just learned").

- There are few things in my life that I've enjoyed as much as writing this book.

Those who know me well will attest to the fact that for me, writing is almost an addiction, so this was like being on an ongoing high – and it's not illegal (drugs), harmful to my health (smoking) or fattening (chocolate). On the flip side of the coin is the fact that editing, rewriting, re-sequencing (several times) and then editing again, has been almost painful at times – to the point that I considered taking drugs (but I didn't), smoking (but I didn't) and chocolate (I can say that I didn't as long as you don't count the Girl Scouts' "Thin Mints". C'mon, give me a break – they really are thin).

(Note: I'm going to tell you a story about "Thin Mints." At first I thought that my purpose would be to "amuse" you but quickly realized that it's a great example of superb salesmanship – performed by a 10-year old girl.

My next door neighbor had four children – three boys and Annie, who was a Girl Scout.

One day Annie knocked on my door to see if I wanted to buy some cookies. I knew my wife (at that time) loved "Thin Mints," as did my brother-in-law, who was "temporarily" living with us (he came for a two-week visit and stayed for five years – that's not a complaint by the way, as it assured that we always had a reliable baby sitter). With that in mind I gave Annie an order for 18 boxes, figuring that these would last the three of us at least a month.

A few weeks later I saw Annie coming up my driveway, pulling a wagon that was overflowing with boxes. I met her half way and said, "I guess we're the first stop on your delivery route." She replied, "No, these are all for you.

"But Annie," I said, "I only order 18 boxes and it looks like there are a lot more than that in your wagon."

That's when Annie explained. "You're right, but these are not all yours. Mrs. Barnett ordered 18 boxes and so did Turner (my brother-in-law)."

It seems that Annie had been "casing" our house to make sure that, when she came over to make her sales pitch, only one of us was there. I don't know what she is doing now, but I hope she runs for office one day. This country could use a lot more elected officials who know how to effectively accomplish what they set out to do.

And ours was not the only house where she used this "technique." When all the dust had settled (maybe "cookie crumbs" would be more accurate) she was the #1 cookie peddler in our entire county.

There is one footnote here. Earlier I mentioned that I thought that the 18 boxes I had ordered would have fed the three of us for a month. That turned out to be a rather naïve assumption since the 54 boxes were gone before the end of 30 days. Of course, when you consider that this was less than one box per person, per day, it doesn't sound quite as bad).

There will be times I will appear to be sexist. That is as far from the truth as imaginable. What it does point out is that I must have missed a couple of grammar classes. Sometimes I will say "him," when I mean "him and her". Other times I will bail out by using the word "their" instead if "his and hers." What I won't do is spend too much time thinking about which version is correct.

I have an aversion to semi-colons and an addiction to commas and parenthetical phrases. A friend once pointed out that I had opened a parenthesis on page one of a letter and didn't close it until the middle of page three. She went on to tell me that she has come to the conclusion that the best and easiest way to read any of my mini-thesis is to take a pair of scissors, cut out the parenthetical phrases, and then connect the two parts of the actual sentence.

I will spend far too much time trying to determine whether or not to use an apostrophe. For example, as you will learn later on, I was the President of NAUPA, the college equivalent of the PTA at Northern Arizona University (NAU) for three years. During my entire term in office, I was never sure if the "P" stood for "Parents," "Parent's" or "Parents'." I think was correct most of the time but, when I wasn't I'm sure you still understood what I meant.

Aside from my DVR (now I control my television set, not the other way around), the two greatest inventions in my lifetime are the microwave oven and Spell Check. Why Spell Check? When I was in the 6th grade we were given a 100-word test, to determine who would represent our class in the school's Spelling Bee. They were pretty difficult words so, when I tell you that I had a score of 79, you might think, "Not bad." Well, you should immediately rethink your reaction – I got 79 wrong.

Prequel a/k/a Introduction (Expanded)

What you are about to read represents personal experiences. A close friend, who read an earlier draft, said to me that the letter "I" appeared too many times, to the point that he thought this might be some kind of an ego trip. He's probably partially correct. After all, don't most people like the thought of having their name on the cover a book? This must be true as I've never heard anyone state, "I never have had anything interesting or worthwhile happen to me, and I have no opinions about anything."

As to my overuse of the letter that falls between H and J, I am aware that 'There is no I in team," but this is not a team effort. I use the "I word" so often for credibility. Almost everything you are about to read – both the good and the bad – involved me, in some way, shape or form. Should there be 3rd party stories they come from someone I could trust, as I know how easily things can get lost in translation.

To put this in numerical terms, 85% of this book is 100% accurate, as these are personal experiences. 10% are things I have been told by people I have faith in and the other 5% is either totally fictitious (but provided to make a specific point) or analogous to the fact that every time you tell someone about the fish you caught, its size keeps getting bigger.

There will be many times when I you will read the phrase, "What did I say/write vs. what did they hear/read."

Now, it may be that you will misinterpret something I have written, although I'm going to try very hard to keep that from happening. However, you don't have to worry that all I am is a conduit, passing along things other people told me. As I just stated, in almost every case, what follows are experiences that I have my experienced. Some have been pulled out of my memory vault but, for the most part, they have been transcribed from notes which were, more often than not, written on paper napkins (food seemed to jostle my memory), Post-it notes, and even on the back of utility bills.

This book is not a fairy tale. You will never read "Once upon a time" (with one exception, that you've already read), and there is no way for me to predict "happily ever after" although, if you take what I'm saying to heart, that may well be the result.

For those of you old enough to understand this reference, what you will read represents the Reader's Digest Condensed version of me. To look at this from a slightly different perspective, you can consider this book to be the equivalent of roughly 3,500 "tweets." To learn more, all you have to do is ask, but be sure to allow for at least a half an hour to peruse my response.

Dedications

Aside from Michelle, Jackie, Violet and Mary (for reasons you already know) there are too many others to mention – the scenarios and examples I have provided involved anywhere from one to five hundred people. That being said I'm going to totally ignore what I just wrote by "naming some names."

I want to give thanks to my good friend Tom Ambrose. He did not write this book but he was the driving force in so far as encouraging me to move my words from my computer to actual printed pages. The comment that clinched things was, "I don't want to embarrass you by having my second book published before your first one."

Tom is humble. I am not. This is a good thing because, if I were, we would sit across from each other saying nothing more than, "Aw shucks. It was nothing special that I did." Likewise, if Tom lacked the humility that I seem to have lost, somewhere along the way, our weekly lunches would probably consist of each us trying to convince the other that they "had to" order something specific on the menu – and so what if one of us was allergic to it.

And I owe a special debt to Kristen Young, my "Social Media Muse." Before she started "clueing me in" what I knew about Facebook, LinkedIn, Twitter, Classmates, blogs and YouTube could have been summed up on a page that remained blank (does that qualify for an A+, for neatness?). Now, although it was far from "all of a sudden," I can use these tools to help sell my book.

Kristen also did most of my graphic designing. I can explain how good she is in two sentences (very rare for me). Every time she gave me some options to choose from I was almost stymied. It really is difficult to pick something when everything is excellent.

If you are ever in need of someone with enough artistic and technology talent to fill an entire room, you can contact Kristen at www.10leaf.com.

This "Tom/Kristen Duet" should actually be a trio that reads "Tom, Kristen and Go Daddy." (www.godaddy.com).

I have done the homework for you. When it comes to website design and hosting they are the fastest, the least expensive and, of greater importance, the most talented. And you don't have to take my word for it. Just visit www.whatacrock.info and see the magic that they wove for me.

Shame on me as to this next one, although kudos of this kind are not often considered. After all, when thinking about a book what comes to mind are things like printing, graphics, layouts, covers, etc. But there is something that can render all of these meaningless and can give someone a negative impression of what you've done before they even look at the cover, let alone the first page.

What I'm talking about is the packaging you use when you are sending out copies directly. If it arrives torn, or otherwise damaged, you are getting off on the wrong foot.

(NOTE: Before shipping a package to anyone else, send it to yourself and, if possible, to a friend who lives on the other side of the country. This will tell you if your packaging material is up to the task).

Once again I will keep you from having to search by providing the only resource you will ever need. The name of the company is "ULINE" and you can easily find them via Google.

Every time I've called them they answered the phone before the first ring was completed so, obviously, I've never been put on hold. When I identified some items I thought might work (four of them), they were sent to me, at no charge – not even for the shipping – and they arrived the next day. None of these turned out to be large enough so the process was duplicated – again, no charge for anything and in my grateful hands the next day. The perfect package was then sitting in front of me. I knew we would find it eventually as they stock more than 22,000 items, in six different warehouses, all around the country.

On the day before I'm writing this, at 4 PM, I ordered 100 bubble-pack envelopes from ULINE. They arrived today at 12:30 PM.

I really hope I sell a million books. Of course my checkbook would be grateful but I'd love to be able to place orders of that size with them. I know of no better example of the Golden Rule – "Do unto others as you would have others do unto you."

Next, but certainly not, least is Ron Thomas, the person responsible for the wonderful graphic that appears on the cover of this book. One of the things that makes Ron so special is that all I had to do was give him a brief description of what I thought I wanted the design to be. Three days later I got back a rendering of exactly what I wanted the design to be.

And finally there is Jerry Weinsheink and his company, Top Banana Promotions, here Scottsdale, Arizona. Any of you who have ever had to order a product before will appreciate what a pleasure it is to work with Jerry. When I explained to him what I wanted, a few golf shirts and sweatshirts, with the book's name and logo on them, he quoted me some prices. After I indicated that those were too high for me (I did not require any top-of-the-line merchandise), he asked me how much I wanted to spend. I provided a figure and got to hear those magical words "we can do the job for that amount."

Oops. I have neglected to mention the most important entity of all – my publisher.

If you are thinking about writing a book, think again. Are you willing to make the kind of commitment it takes? Actually the writing is the easiest part – it's the editing that can wear you down.

However, if you decide to move forward that move should be to go to www.createspace.com.

Once again, I'm going to save you a lot of time and energy. Don't bother with anyone else. I've checked out

at least a dozen of their competitors and they are, hands down (and even hands up) the best.

Before describing why I speak so highly of them, let me mention two things I know you'll find appealing.

- I've never gotten to hear the end of any song that plays, when I'm put on hold. That's because my longest wait cannot have been more than 20 seconds.

- They must have read my admonition – "Under promise the over deliver." They always err on the safe side. However, the longest anything took to accomplish, when I had been told five business days, was three. And, in one case I had what I was looking for in two hours.

Now, as to the "what makes them so good" (as if the two things I just wrote about aren't enough).

- They are fully staffed, with incredibly talented, and infinitely patient, individuals. I was assigned a team of ten people and, no matter who I spoke with, they were totally up to speed on my project. They take such detailed notes that they could bring in a new employee in the morning and he or she would be a "veteran," able to competently work with me, before lunch.

- This is not "their first time at the rodeo." I can almost guarantee you that you can't come up with a question they haven't heard before. When you think about it, in and of itself, that's no big deal. What is, however, is the fact that they answer all of them. Actually, I should really even take this one step further. Their answers are almost always correct and, on the rare occasion that they don't know the correct response they will never pretend to. What you will hear instead is" Can you hold on for a minute while I ask somebody else?" The next time I have to wait for an entire minute will be the first time.

- They are never patronizing nor do they ever pander. There are times I'm sure I asked the exact same question at least a half dozen times. On none of those occasions did I hear something like, "I thought we already discussed that." And, if I say something to the effect of "this is what I think we should do," they never hesitate to tell me that it's a great idea if they know it's not a great idea. If they stopped right there they would be far better than most. However they always take the next step. My suggestion usually indicates something I am trying to accomplish, something they picked up on immediately. When I get back from them are things to consider that will allow me to reach my goal but done in a way far, far better than I could have even imagined.

Someone once asked me if I could name the most important day in my life. It turns out that the answer was much easier than I first thought although, technically, I wasn't around and wouldn't be – for several years.

It was the day my mother met my father. Without that happening there would be no me. That represented "in the beginning," but it's more than that.

My Dad, a nationally renowned surgeon, who earned his way through medical school by giving classical music piano lessons, was the ultimate Renaissance man. He was a "scratch" golfer, an art collector and he showed me that I could love baseball and books, football and the fine arts and, of greatest importance, that there was no such thing as being "too smart."

My Mom was the one who made sure that I stayed within the white lines and that the greater the trust I warranted, the more the distance between those two lines would widen – although there were a few, less than memorable times, when they almost touched. She was named "NYC Charity Woman of the Year" (twice). She once said that if I ever told anyone that I was "too busy," I had better be already be doing two things at once.

Between them I think I inherited some pretty good genes. Coupled with a wonderful childhood this allowed me to step into the real world, both competent and curious.

In retrospect, there is one special group of people that also deserve to be recognized – and they are all the people who have taught me. Some have been teachers and others, in one form or another, mentors. I know you will find this difficult to believe but some of the really important stuff I've learned revolves around the words "respect" and "humility."

The first of these really does not come into play, vis a vis what you've just finished reading (i.e. I persist in trying to open car doors for dates, even in the face of the fact that most of them are walking down the street before I get around to their side of the car – their explanation is always the same – "I didn't think people did that any more"). Actually that example is more a case of good manners (what used to be called "chivalry"). Nonetheless I have been, am and always will be, respectful to anyone who earns and/or deserves it – and even some that don't.

As far as humility is concerned I think you're just going to have to take my word for this, as I have not provided a great deal of evidence to support that contention. One of the nice things about being the author is that I can say, "My game, my rules." Could the game have been a lot shorter? Of course. But if it was I wouldn't have had nearly as much fun as I've derived by it being this long. Besides, this way I never will feel that I have to justify the price you paid. This book can eat "Who Moved My Cheese?" for lunch, as long as there is some sourdough bread, couple of slices of ham, some spicy mustard and a chilled bottle of "Thunderbird" wine (I prefer the Tuesday vintage).

Author's Plea

This is another chapter that was originally going to be at the front of the book. However it dawned on me that, as was said to Tom Cruise in "Top Gun,", "my ego was writing checks that my body can't cash" in that I was assuming that everyone is going to actually get through to the last page.

I have now stepped away from that mirror of unreasonable expectations, and accept the fact that there may be a couple of you who will be quoted as saying, "To tell you the truth, I actually could (and did) put it down. Since I never got to the end please tell me, did Rhett Butler ever give a damn?"

To be brutally honest (is there such a thing as being placidly honest?) I have just joined Facebook, LinkedIn, Classmates and I think I understand how to "tweet." There are two major reasons I have resisted the "Social Media" (especially Twitter) until now.

I still remain uncomfortable with Twitter as the thought of being restricted to 140 characters is something I have trouble getting a grip on (the previous sentence alone has 113 characters in it and if I were to include this comment I would be up to 195). In this regard the New York Times was kind enough to print my letter pointing out the fact that, if Abraham Lincoln had attempted to use Twitter, to deliver his Gettysburg Address, here is what it have looked like.

Four score and seven years ago our fathers brought forth on this continent, a new nation, conceived in Liberty, and dedicated to the proposition that all men are created eq

(Note: If commas count as characters he'd have had to chop off the e and the q).

The other reason relates to one of the explanations I once gave when asked why I never tried cocaine – I was afraid I would like it too much.

I am aware that I have a psychological makeup that welcomes addictions. While I was eventually able to stop smoking, doing the same with writing would be asking too much of myself. Of course nobody would be forcing me to respond to another person commenting about one of my many opinions.

Theoretically true but practically wrong because I wouldn't be able to help myself. Putting more opportunities on my plate might cause me to OD, and the consequences would not be pretty. I would probably end up arguing with the editor of a high school paper about why they wouldn't print my letter regarding marginal tax rates.

The point I'm trying to make here is this - I am still not at all that comfortable using all the social media genres to contact people to tell them about this book as I am a true technology Neanderthal. But I'm guessing that most of you are – via your Facebook page, a blog, a tweet or a text.

So, please, please, please tell your friends about "WHO MOVED MY CHEESE?" **WHAT A CROCK!** And let them know that they can purchase a copy of their own by going to www.whatacrock.info and clicking on "Order Now"

And I hope that not finishing the book will not deter anyone from informing your friends, relatives, neighbors, co-workers and people you pass on the street. After all, there are so many things you can still say. For example:

- **"Just because I didn't like it doesn't mean you won't."**

- **"After reading just a few chapters I discovered that I'm more insightful than the author, so I had no need to finish it. However, you should probably read the whole thing."**

It just came to mind that my request is probably ridiculous since if someone did not finish the book it is highly unlikely they got this far. However, since there is that "phone call one in ten-million possibility," I decided to not delete it.

And, of course, if you end up loving the book, liking it a lot, liking it or even not being offended by it, you could write things such as:

"Put away the sliced bread. 'WHO MOVED MY CHEESE?' **WHAT A CROCK! is better. But make sure you read it before slathering on the peanut butter and jelly."**

"WHO MOVED MY CHEESE?" **WHAT A CROCK! won't make you smart, but it will make you smarter. It won't make you funny, but it will make you funnier. And it won't make the author rich, but it will make him richer."**

Just think, you can be one of the leaders of my uncompensated sales team. And, if you are really good at your job, and I sell lots of books, I will thank you in my next one, which is already in the process of being written. The working title is **"READ THIS BOOK IF IT TOOK YOU MORE THAN ONE MINUTE TO FIND THE CHEESE YOU LOST."**

Thank you so much. Without your support I would be exactly where I am right now – without your support.

Philip Barnett

February 2012

SO REMEMBER – SPREAD THE WORD. PLEASE TELL EVERYONE YOU KNOW TO GO TO WWW.WHATACROCK. INFO THEN CLICK ON "ORDER NOW."

Let's see if we can establish a legitimate chain letter. Please ask your contacts to do the same thing I am asking of you – to alert their contacts. If I remember the multi-level marketing pyramid correctly, it will only take six such sets of actions before the entire world (including Kevin Bacon) will have the "Go out and buy now" message - although, through the magic of technology, you can purchase the book without "going" anywhere.

pbarnett6@cox.net

www.whatacrock.info

www.marketing101.me

As both you and I probably expected, I couldn't resist one more thing – this time it's a quiz.

A Quiz

In a small city, that could be located anywhere, there are four people who each find themselves $100 in debt - the hotel owner, a produce supplier, a farmer, and a prostitute.

One day a very rich man comes to the hotel and says that he'd like their finest suite. He is told that it is $100 a night. He agrees to pay that, as long as he can get his money refunded if he's not satisfied. When the hotelier agrees the man gives him the $100 and explains that he has to go to a meeting but that he'll be back in an hour to look at his rooms.

As soon as he is out the door the hotel owner takes the $100 and goes to see his produce supplier. He hands him the money and tells the recipient that this clears up his debt. The produce supplier agrees and immediately heads off down the road. When he gets to the farm he tells its owner that he's paying up his $100 debt.

The farmer marks his account "paid-in-full" and drives into town to give the money to the local prostitute. She had provided "favors" the night before, with the understanding that she would be paid $100 within a day or two.

As soon as she has her hands on the cash she decides to settle up on her outstanding debt to the hotel where she plied her trade. So off she goes and a few minutes later the hotel owner has her $100 in his hands.

No more than a minute later the rich guest arrives back, He goes upstairs, examines the suite and storms back down to the lobby. "That is totally unsatisfactory" he screams. "I demand my money back."

That $100 hadn't even found its way into the cash register when it was being returned to the indignant client-not-to-be, who left immediately.

So, at this point, all four $100 debts had been settled, no one had to do anything in that one hour, other than pass along money, and each one of these citizens now owed nothing.

Now, aside from the obvious fact that prostitutes rarely extend credit, how does this happen.

I have finally decided to treat this as I did the Rubik's cube. I admitted that I couldn't figure it out, as is the case with this story.

So, I am turning to you, the reader, for assistance. I'm sure that there are those of you who are more logical/smarter than I am (although probably not so borderline arrogant) and that someone will provide me with an explanation.

Oh, What the Heck (or, Let's Start an Argument)

To be faithful to myself I will use the word "best" instead of "favorite."

Best movie – "The Sting"

Best show – "Man of La Mancha"

Best performer – Eric Clapton

Best song(s) – "Sultans of Swing" (Dire Straits), "Diamonds and Rust" (Joan Baez) & "Hallelujah" (by almost anyone)

Best concert – "Concert for George" (in a landslide)

Best album – "Abbey Road"

Best book – "Day of the Jackal" (and "WHO MOVED MY CHEESE?" **WHAT A CROCK!)** – I have just dislocated a should due to excessive back patting)

Best author – David Baldacci (and Philip Barnett – I have now dislocated both shoulders)

Best television series – "St. Elsewhere," "Hill St. Blues," "Homicide – Life on the Streets," The West Wing" (the best of the best), "Friday Night Lights" (the second best), "Rescue Me" and my latest entry, "The Good Wife."

Worst television series – This would require a separate book as there are far too many to name.

Best actor – Dustin Hoffman (who else could have played both "Rainman" and Tootsie?").

Best actress – Meryl Streep (pretty much every movie she's appeared in).

Testimonials II

"Philip has a tendency to display his extreme confidence and intelligence, but he always backs up his boasts with relevant experiences and a razor-sharp mind. Anyone interested in personal and professional development should read his book because he only pats himself on the back when referring to something that worked, and that has done so repeatedly. I have a great deal of respect for this well-traveled and well-accomplished friend and thinker."
Derrick Hall
President & CEO, Arizona Diamondbacks

"This book is filled with at least a hundred practical, actionable, common sense ideas... not cheesy analogies. It will help you not only improve your company's marketing strategies, but your own life plan as well."
Tom Ambrose - Executive Director, Big Brothers Big Sisters of Central Arizona

"Philip and I attended college together. This means that 2012 marks the 50th year of our friendship. I mention this because it means that I've know him since before he began his interesting and unusual journey, temporarily culminating in WHAT A CROCK! After reading his book I've told all my competitors not to waste their money on it. If they all listen to me they will soon be rapidly diminishing images, in my rear view mirror."
Stephen Draizin
Chairman of the Board
RAD Energy Corp.

"I met Philip, quite by accident, on a golf course. Within a couple of months we became good friends and, not shortly after that, the agency he worked for was able to list IBM on their roster of clients. This can be explained in one short sentence. IBM does not "suffer fools gladly."
Calvin LaRoche
Former VP – IBM

"This was like taking an entire semester of nothing but marketing classes. If I had been in school, what I learned in WHAT A CROCK! would have required 15 credits at $150 each, for a total of $3000, instead of $19.95. I'm going to take the difference ($2980.05) and use it for a down payment on a new car."
P.M. Roberts
Lodi, CA

"I have known the author of WHAT A CROCK! for almost 30 years. In fact, for several of those years, he reported to me. There were a couple of things I could always count on – that his thinking would be creative and his approach aggressive. In some ways our agency was almost too big for him, in that we had some very large businesses as clients, so being 'politically correct,' was often a necessity. I can assure you that Philip has never been 'PC,' which explains why he flourished when he went out on

his own. Unless you are someone who keeps your feet planted, on the white line that runs down the middle of the road, this is a book you should read."
Dennis Eastham
Retired - Former CEO, Barry Blau & Partners; CEO, Brann Worldwide; CEO, Protocol Marketing Group.

"For each time I smiled or laughed, I learned something I could implement almost immediately. To give you an idea of how valuable this book is, I will tell you this. I smiled at least a dozen times and I laughed out loud twice."
Evan Altera
Chicago, IL

"It has been said that you can learn more about a person's character in one round of golf than from sitting in 100 meetings with them. What I can tell you, after dozens of 18-hole 'adventures,' is that Philip is the type of person you should want to work with. He is smart – both street smart and book smart and, even when he hits four balls in a row into the water, he never blames the weather, or throws a club."
Rick Neylon
Managing Partner, Neylon Consulting, LLC

"Every time I read a book that might provide me some tools that I think will help my business, I 'dog-ear' the pages I want to go back to. Up until now, my 'dog ear' record was four. That has now been shattered as I now have 23 pages with a fold in the corner. Incidentally, once I finally found my copy of 'Who Moved My Cheese?' I discovered that there were none."
Randall Ballinger
Flagstaff, AZ

"In the twenty plus years I have know Philip I have always been intrigued by his intellectual curiosity and his combative verbosity. This project is representative of many of our conversations."
L. Don Brown
Past Sr. VP – Kraft Foods and Coors Brewing

"I have read at least a dozen self-help books, and attended a handful of "motivational" seminars, the last one about a year ago. If I was given a quiz, where I would have to demonstrate what I learned, I would flunk - probably with an embarrassing grade. I'm pretty sure that won't happen with WHAT A CROCK! since I've already implemented three suggestions I found."
Dean Chitwood
CEO, D & L Communications Systems

"I never knew I could smile and take notes at the same time."
Andrea Heald
Endicott, NY

"WHAT A CROCK!? What a crock."
This was the only negative "review." However, since it came from a person who has been unemployed, for almost two years, I put it on my table, right next to a grain of salt.
Cheese Head
Green Bay, WI

"Read this book. Go to work. Implement a few of the suggestions. Ask for a raise. If you are like me, you might get one even before you request it."
Joanna Greene
Colorado Springs, CO

"I am in charge of the customer service department at a mid-size company, with 20 people on my staff. After finishing WHAT A CROCK! I asked our VP if I could purchase a copy for everyone who reports to me. I could have just passed around my copy, but I wanted everyone to have their own - so they could take it home and read it more than once."
Betsy Allen-Pastore
E. Hartford, CT

"Under normal conditions I would recommend the pages I think you will find especially helpful. In the case of "Who Moved My Cheese?" WHAT A CROCK! it would be easier to tell you which pages to skip."
Alan Sidel
Brooklyn, NY

"I have an order in for six copies. One is going to my son who will be graduating college soon and begin his search for his first real job. Another copy is for my daughter. She has just started the college application process. Three copies will be for my husband, to give to the members of his sales staff (having read the book, this was his idea). He told me that they seemed to be in the doldrums lately and 'Who Moved My Cheese?' WHAT A CROCK! will provide several kicks in their butts. The final copy is meant for me. I hope to launch my first business late in 2012 and I've already learned how to save several thousand dollars in the process of getting started, as well as how to create revenue, almost from day one."
Jennifer A. Brookwood
Santa Barbara, CA

"Within two weeks after I finished this book I tried out one of the suggestions ('You'll Be the Only One There')." I employed it on two different sales calls and, on both occasions, my clients told me that it was the most impressive form of 'relationship cementing' that they had ever experienced."
Edward Fiore
Sales Manager
Philadelphia, PA

Made in the USA
Charleston, SC
03 April 2012

EL GATO ENSOMBRERADO
Dr. Seuss

Traducción de
Georgina Lázaro
y
Teresa Mlawer

RANDOM
HOUSE

Visit us on the Web!
Seussville.com
rhcbooks.com

Educators and librarians, for a variety of teaching tools, visit us at
RHTeachersLibrarians.com

Library of Congress Cataloging-in-Publication Data
Seuss, Dr., author, illustrator.
[Cat in the hat. Spanish]
El gato ensombrerado / por Dr. Seuss ; traducción de Georgina Lázaro y Teresa Mlawer.
— Primera edición.
  pages cm. — (Beginner Books)
Originally published in English by Random House Children's Books in 1957
under the title: The cat in the hat.
Summary: A zany but well-meaning cat brings a cheerful, exotic, and exuberant form of chaos to a household of two young children one rainy day while their mother is out.
ISBN 978-0-553-50979-3 (trade) — ISBN 978-0-553-50980-9 (lib. bdg.) —
ISBN 978-0-553-52421-5 (ebook)
[1. Stories in rhyme. 2. Cats—Fiction. 3. Spanish language materials.]
I. Lázaro León, Georgina, translator. II. Mlawer, Teresa, translator. III. Title.
PZ74.3.S39 2015 [E]—dc23 2014033308

MANUFACTURED IN CHINA
16 15 14 13 12 11 10 9

Todo estaba mojado
y el sol sin alumbrar.
Nos quedamos en casa
sin salir a jugar.

1

Me senté allí con Sara,
los dos viendo llover.
Dije: —¡Cuánto quisiera
tener algo que hacer!

Muy lluvioso y muy frío.
¡Olvida la pelota!
Nos quedamos en casa
viendo caer las gotas.

2

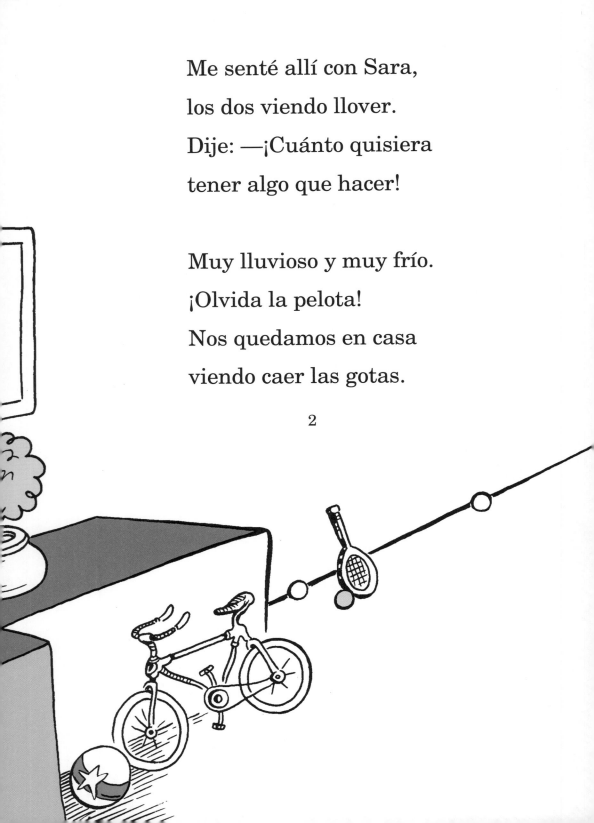

Y todo lo que hicimos

fue

estar

ahí

sentados

mirando la ventana

aburridos y hastiados.

¡Y entonces
se oyó un ruido
que nos hizo brincar!

¡Miramos

y lo vimos justo cuando iba a entrar!

¡Miramos

y lo vimos!

¡El Gato Ensombrerado!

Y él nos miró y nos dijo:

—¿Qué hacen ahí sentados?

—Ya sé que está lloviendo
y que el sol no ha salido.
Vamos a entretenernos
con algo divertido.

—Conozco algunos juegos

que podemos probar.

También sé nuevos trucos

—añadió sin parar—.

Muchos trucos muy buenos

que les voy a enseñar,

y sé que su mamá

no se va a disgustar.

Sara y yo no supimos

entonces qué decir.

Mamá no estaba en casa,

pues tuvo que salir.

—¡No! —dijo nuestro pez—.

Se tendrá que marchar.

Díganle a ese gato

que NO quieren jugar.

No debe estar aquí,

ni muy cerca siquiera.

No debe estar aquí

si su mamá está fuera.

11

—¡Vamos, no teman! —dijo
el Gato Ensombrerado—.
No son malos los trucos
que tengo preparados.
Podemos divertirnos
muchísimo los tres
con un juego que llamo
¡ARRIBA-ARRIBA-EL-PEZ!

12

—¡Bájame! —dijo el pez—.

¡Que no quiero caerme!

¡Bájame! —dijo el pez—.

¡Esto NO me divierte!

13

—No te vas a caer.

No temas —dijo el gato—.

Parado en la pelota

te sostendré bien alto.

¡La taza en el sombrero

y un libro en una mano!

Pero eso no es TODO . . .

—siguió diciendo el gato.

14

—¡Mírenme ahora! —dijo—.

¡Miren aquí primero:

la taza y un pastel

encima del sombrero!

¡Puedo cargar DOS libros!

¡Puedo subir el pez!

¡Y un barquito y un plato!

¡Miren, todo a la vez!

Y brincar en la bola.

Sí, saltar de este modo.

¡Arriba, abajo, arriba!

¡Oh, no!

Eso no es todo . . .

—¡Miren,

mírenme AHORA!

Divertirse a mi modo

es muy entretenido,

mas deben saber cómo.

¡Puedo subir la taza,

puedo cargar los libros,

la leche y el pastel

y el pez en un rastrillo!

¡El barco de juguete,

también un muñequito!

Y, miren, con mi cola

agarro el abanico.

¡Mientras brinco en la bola,

con él me echo fresquito!

Pero eso no es todo.

¡Oh, no!

Eso no es todo . . .

Es lo que dijo el gato . . .

¡Y entonces se cayó!

Se cayó de cabeza

y se hizo un chichón.

¡Sara y yo juntos vimos

TODO lo que cayó!

21

¡Y así en una tetera

el pobre pez cayó!

—No me gusta esto —dijo—.

¡No y no! ¡Claro que no!

Esto no es un buen juego

—dijo cuando salió—.

Ni un poquito me gusta.

No, no. ¡Claro que no!

22

—¡Ay, mira lo que hiciste!

—le dijo el pez al gato—.

¡Mira bien esta casa!

¡Mira por cualquier lado!

¡Dentro, en el pastel,

hundiste aquel barquito!

Revolviste la casa

y doblaste el rastrillo.

Cuando mamá no está

DEBES quedarte fuera.

¡Sal de la casa! —dijo

el pez en la tetera.

25

—Me gusta estar aquí

más que estar solo fuera

—dijo entonces el gato

al pez en la tetera—.

Yo NO me quiero ir.

¡Por eso NO me iré!

Así

    es

      que . . .

¡Ahora voy a mostrarles

un juego que yo sé!

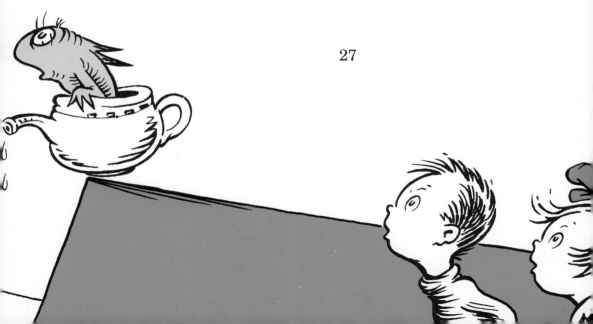

Sin más salió corriendo.

Veloz, como un león,

el Gato Ensombrerado

volvió con un cajón.

Un cajón grande y rojo

con un gancho,

cerrado.

—¡Miren el truco! —dijo

el Gato Ensombrerado.

Se subió sobre él,

saludó y habló luego:

—EL-CAJÓN-DIVERTIDO

es el nombre del juego.

En la caja hay dos cosas

que les voy a mostrar.

—Y en voz muy baja dijo—:

Las dos les gustarán.

—Ahora abriré la caja.

Miren con atención.

Dos cosas que se llaman

Cosa Uno y Cosa Dos.

Las dos Cosas no muerden,

no habrá problema alguno.

¡Y de la caja salieron

Cosa Dos y Cosa Uno!

—¿Qué tal? —las dos dijeron

con una sola voz—.

¿Querrán darles la mano

a Cosa Uno y Cosa Dos?

33

No sabiendo qué hacer

mi hermana Sara y yo,

les dimos nuestra mano

a Cosa Uno y Cosa Dos.

Estrechamos sus manos,

pero el pez dijo: —¡No!

¡Las cosas deben irse

de esta casa! ¡Las dos!

—No se pueden quedar
si su mamá está fuera.
¡Pronto, sáquenlas! —dijo
el pez en la tetera.

35

—No temas, pececito,

las Cosas buenas son

—entonces habló el gato

con toda la razón—.

Son mansas. ¡Oh, tan mansas!

Y vienen a jugar.

En este día lluvioso

nos vienen a alegrar.

—Miren, este es un juego
que les gusta jugar.
Les gustan las cometas
y echarlas a volar.

38

—¡En la casa, no! —dijo
el pez en la tetera—.
¡No, dentro de las casas
no se vuelan cometas!
¡Oh, no, esto no me gusta!
¡Todo se romperá!
¡No me gusta nadita!
¡Todo un lío se hará!

Sara y yo entonces vimos

a Cosas Uno y Dos

corriendo por la casa.

¡Pam! ¡Pum! ¡Pam! ¡Pam! ¡Pum! ¡Pom!

¡Las cometas tiraban

todo a su alrededor!

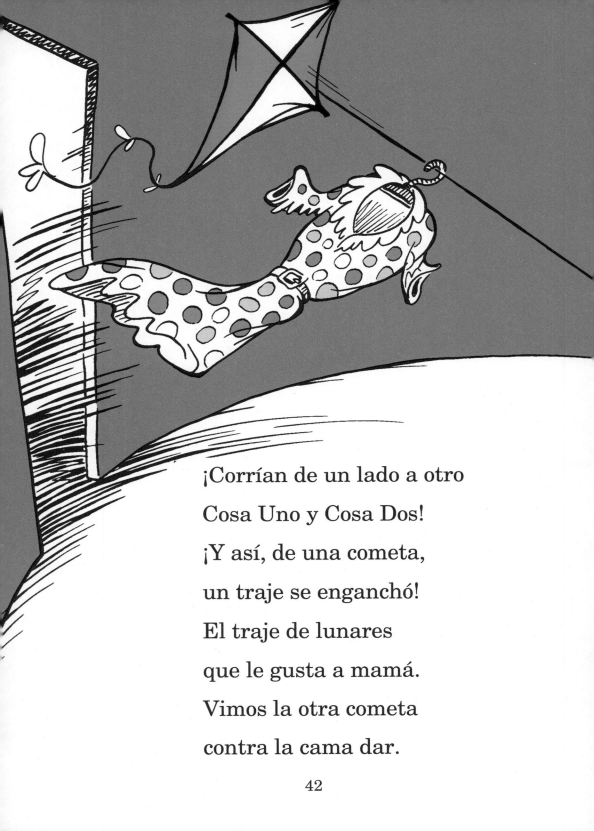

¡Corrían de un lado a otro
Cosa Uno y Cosa Dos!
¡Y así, de una cometa,
un traje se enganchó!
El traje de lunares
que le gusta a mamá.
Vimos la otra cometa
contra la cama dar.

42

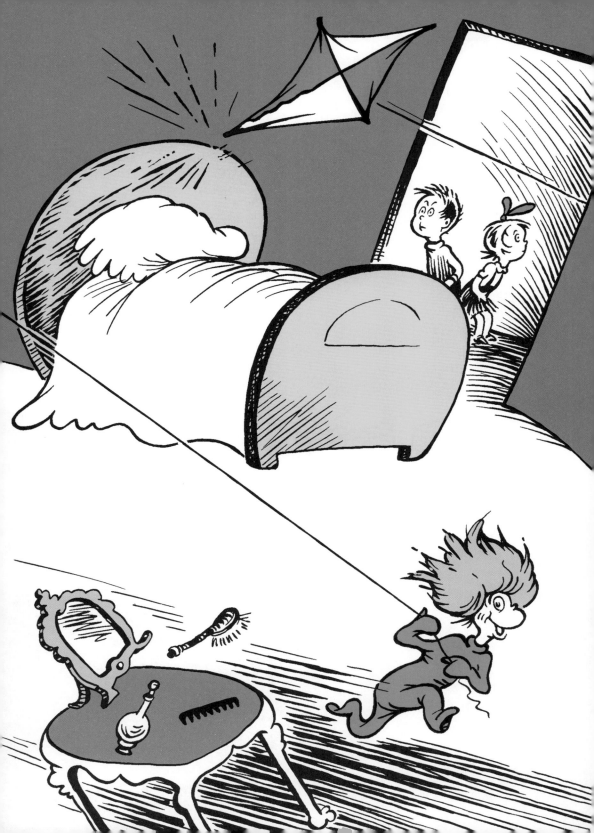

Y siguieron corriendo,

dando saltos, patadas,

grandes brincos y golpes

y muy malas jugadas.

Yo dije: —NO me gusta

de la forma en que juegan.

¿Qué diría mamá

si en la casa estuviera?

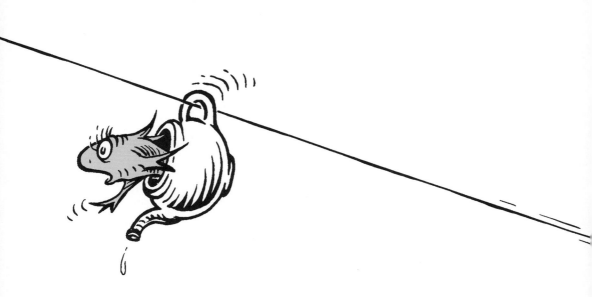

Temblando dijo el pez:

—¡Ay, VEAN lo que pasa!

¡Ahí viene su mamá

de regreso a la casa!

¿Ahora qué dirá?

¿Qué será lo que hará

cuando vea esta casa

revuelta como está?

47

Dijo el pez: —¡Hagan algo!
¡Ya, rápido! ¿Qué esperan?
¡La vi! ¡Vi a su mamá!
¡Su mamá está muy cerca!
Tan pronto como puedan
piensen qué van a hacer.
¡Cosa Uno y Cosa Dos:
a desaparecer!

Lo más pronto que pude
fui en busca de mi red
y sin duda pensé:
«Yo sé que con mi red
pronto a esas dos Cosas
yo mismo atraparé».

50

¡PLOP!, y dejé caer

sin avisar mi red.

¡Y así a las dos Cosas

de una vez atrapé!

Entonces le hablé al gato:

—Harás lo que te diga.

Agarra esas dos Cosas.

¡Sácalas enseguida!

—¿No les gustó mi juego?
¡Lo siento! —dijo el gato—.
Oh, vaya.

¡Qué mal rato!

¡Qué mal rato!

¡Qué mal rato!

Y encerró a las dos Cosas
en el rojo cajón.
Y se fue de la casa
con semblante tristón.

—¡Qué bien! —exclamó el pez—.
El gato ya se ha ido.
Mas al llegar mamá
verá lo que ha ocurrido:
¡Un reguero tan grande
y tan grande y tan hondo,
que va a ser imposible
que recojamos todo!

55

¡Y ENTONCES!

¿Quién estaba de vuelta?

Claro, el gato, que dijo:

—¡Yo lo recojo todo!

¡No teman a este lío!

Yo guardo mis juguetes.

Así es que . . .

ahora les mostraré

otro truco que sé.

57

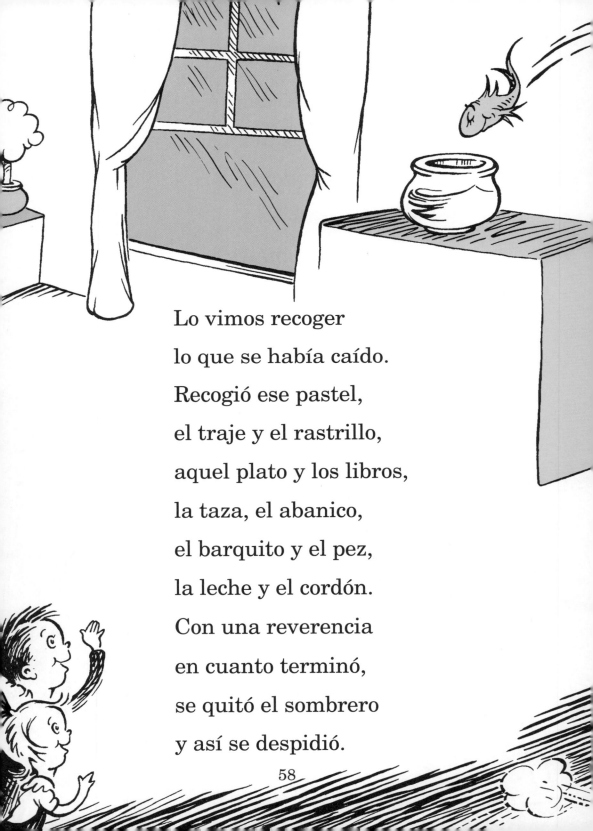

Lo vimos recoger

lo que se había caído.

Recogió ese pastel,

el traje y el rastrillo,

aquel plato y los libros,

la taza, el abanico,

el barquito y el pez,

la leche y el cordón.

Con una reverencia

en cuanto terminó,

se quitó el sombrero

y así se despidió.

Cuando llegó mamá
nos preguntó a los dos:
—¿Se divirtieron mucho?
Cuéntenme qué pasó.

No supimos decirle
ni mi hermana ni yo.
¿Deberíamos contarle
todo lo que ocurrió?

Y, ahora, dime,

¿qué harías

si te pasa algo así?

¿Qué harías si TU mamá

te preguntara a TI?